Royal Fireworks   Language Arts   by Michael Clay Thompson

THE MAGIC LENS

Volume 1

TEACHER EDITION

REVISED & EXPANDED

by

Michael Clay Thompson

Royal Fireworks Press
Unionville, New York

For my dad, Harry Thompson

Royal Fireworks Press
First Ave, PO Box 399
Unionville NY 10988
845 726 4444
Fax 845 726 3824
Email: mail@rfwp.com
Website: rfwp.com

ISBN 13: 978-0-8802-212-8

Printed and bound in the United States of America by American
citizens using recycled, acid-free paper, vegetable-based inks, and
environmentally-friendly cover coatings at the
Royal Fireworks Printing Company of Unionville, New York.

Foreword

I should declare my bias now because I do not come to bury grammar; I come to praise it. This will be, to many, evidence of my naiveté, since teaching traditional grammar has become controversial pedagogy or, at best, questionable judgment. Don't I realize that social realities obviate the teaching of traditional grammar, and that I am wasting valuable classroom time clinging to a pedantic subject my students will neither master, nor apply, nor retain?

Well, no, I don't. From a utilitarian point of view, I think grammar is an intellectual pocketknife; it is small, easily purchased, and so useful that one would not dream of being without it. And not only do I not think that grammar is unteachable, I think that it is one of the most teachable subjects, since its concepts are so few and well defined.

Grammar is so lovely that even if it were useless, one would irresistibly explore it, as one explores chess, or architecture, or the spiral geometries of shells. It is a sort of magic aesthetic lens, through which we can view the delicate structures of ideas. As scientists marvel at the silicate skeletal frames that support and form living organisms, through grammar we view the delicate relationships that give form to the phenomena of the mind. If this comparison strikes you as idealistic and metaphorical, please consider it further. These relationships do exist, and they are beautiful.

There is another thought I would like to address here: Some argue that grammar should be descriptive, a method for recording how people do talk, rather than how people should talk. This argument is, I think, predicated on the correct idea that democracy is precious, and that therefore it is politically wrong to define any group's language conventions as good, or any group's language conventions as bad.

While I regard the descriptive hypothesis as noble in its foundation, I do not think this requires me to abandon prescriptive grammar. I think that the idea of good language has merit. All social interactions depend upon the existence of effective conventions that make mutual understanding possible, and that this is especially so for language. When I examine the language conventions that have been accepted as good English, they seem sensible and valuable—they do make communication clearer, more direct, and more efficient. So though I would oppose describing any dialect of English in derogatory terms, I wish everyone could know the conventions of clarity that have descended to us as heirs of our civilization. In other words, I respect the motivations of the descriptive argument, but I respect the quality of the prescriptive principles. I believe we can have both: appreciation for the cultural richness of colloquial dialects and appreciation for the intellectual excellence of conventional good English.

Introduction

The Paradox of Impossible Simplicity

I'm sure that many English teachers have noticed the same paradox I have noticed, the impossible simplicity of grammar. The paradox is that under seemingly perfect pedagogical conditions, good students often find it impossible to absorb the few simple elements of grammar. I first became aware of the paradox of impossible simplicity when I began teaching English to gifted and talented high school students. In my sophomore and junior English classes, I was receiving students of high academic ability, who had used comprehensive grammar texts, who had been taught by talented teachers, who had taken difficult grammar tests and made high scores—and yet, when these students came into my classroom in August, they could not discuss grammar, they could not explain the use of grammar, and they could not even give elementary descriptions of the parts of speech. When I gave my students a diagnostic test to see if they understood the rudiments of the parts of speech, parts of the sentence, phrases, and clauses, they failed the test. "I don't know," they said, "that grammar stuff."

They were right. The grammar instruction had failed; students had no retention, no appreciation, and no application. Even those who could define a sentence fragment or run-on sentence could not write a short essay free of sentence fragments or run-on sentences. Somehow, the students' awareness of grammar was bounded by the grammar "unit." When the unit reached its end, the students felt rid of the subject, and turned away, leaving grammar behind them—in the grammar unit.

$$||<< \text{ unit } >>||$$

Under adverse conditions, such a disappointing result might be expected. But when the students, the teachers, and the texts are all superb, such a failure is a paradox. How can a simple subject be impossible to learn? How can finite simplicity become infinite complexity?

Something was interfering with the learning process, but what?

Students Felt Overwhelmed

After probing, I noticed several things about my students' difficulty with grammar. The first was that many students seemed overwhelmed by grammar. Somehow, they had gotten the odd idea that basic grammar was a vast sea of concepts, too vast to be mastered. As a result, the students felt not only that they *had not* learned grammar, but that they *could not* learn grammar. (They *had* studied grammar for years without success, and this failure had become their expectation.) This pessimism was one problem I would have to solve before my students would recover the optimism they would need to study grammar. The problem, however, was still to find the *cause* of this hopelessness; why would gifted students, who thought the advanced abstract concepts of physics and biology were easy, think that a few dozen ideas of elementary grammar were impossible to learn?

Pointless?

The second thing I noticed was that the students had no sense of the practical or intellectual *value* of grammar. They no longer wished to learn grammar. They had passed through ten or eleven years of academic life and had been successful without understanding grammar. They seemed to think that grammar was a pedantic absurdity, a teacher-made tempest, insignificant outside of the teapot of the classroom.

So the students didn't care to study grammar, and the students didn't think they could master grammar—these two recognitions seemed valuable but superficial. They seemed to be only symptoms of some underlying mistake. I felt that by addressing only the confidence and appreciation problems, I would be treating the symptoms without correcting the problem. The real problem seemed hidden, disrupting the learning process, even when the students, the teachers, and the texts were all excellent.

The Real Problem

Eventually, I realized why my students didn't understand grammar: they had never really studied it after all! They had repeatedly studied fragments of grammar, but only fragments. The pieces of concepts remained isolated in the students' minds. They remembered a few scattered things about parts of speech, a few scattered things about parts of the sentence, and a few scattered things about sentences. But they had never studied or discussed *grammar*, though most of them could provide a memorized definition of a noun. They did not know how the levels of grammar interrelated, and they had never gotten a view of grammar as a whole. They were like archaeologists, trying to envision a great city from a few dusty potsherds and row of broken pillars. They were confused.

3

A Cogent Disaster

Here is what had happened: motivated students and dedicated teachers had used a logical, seemingly effective but actually self-defeating process in their study of grammar. It was optimistically analytical and linear. It moved from basic elements to advanced elements over the course of an academic year. The process was some variation of the following: The students study parts of speech for the first nine weeks, doing parts of speech exercises, and concluding with a parts of speech test. Then they abandon parts of speech to study parts of the sentence for the second nine weeks, doing parts of the sentence exercises, and concluding with a parts of the sentence test. In the second semester they move on to phrases—only incidentally mentioning parts of speech or parts of the sentence, and concluding with a test on phrases. Finally, they discuss clauses and sentence types, mentioning previous concepts only when necessary, and concluding with a major test on clauses and sentence types. At this point, the teacher wishes that it had been possible to review all of the grammar, to show how the four levels of grammar relate to each other, and to give the students a comprehensive, organic overview of grammar, stressing its joys and applications, but of course there isn't time. It is May 26th, and you can't do everything.

But you can't use what you don't learn until May.

If we represent each month of the school year with a letter, the self-defeating grammar calendar might look like this, with units logically extended through every term:

parts of speech	parts of sentence	phrases	clauses								
A	S	O	N	D	J	F	M	A	M	J	

Each level of grammar is sequentially forgotten, and by May, the confused students are trying to remember exactly what an adverb takes the place of, what pronoun can be a predicate, how do you know if this (?) a sentence, which pronouns modify verbs, whether every participial phrase has a gerund, and who the heck needs this grammar stuff!

The flaw in this process is that in an entire academic year, each of the levels of grammar is studied once, and the whole of it, never. The villain is not the student, the teacher, or the text; it is this well-intentioned, protracted linear sequence, without overview or application. Again, there isn't time for application if it takes you until May to get to clauses!

What if, instead of prolonging the final presentation of grammar until spring, we compacted the instruction into the first weeks of school, and spent the year doing increasingly deep applications of grammar? What if our calendar looked more like this:

parts of speech
parts of sentence
  phrases
  clauses   **APPLICATION:** novels, poems, plays, student essays, research papers

A S O N D J F M A M J

A Compacted, Spiral Method

The compacted, spiral review method in *The Magic Lens* replaces the year-long, segmented, linear units described above. The analogy for the process in *The Magic Lens* is not the moving point on a segmented straight line, deserting each location as it proceeds to another, but the helix looping cumulatively and repeatedly over the same terrain as it circles through time.

We won't wait until May to learn phrases; rather, we will learn all the concepts in a compacted form at the first of the year, and then emphasize continuous four-level application as the primary form of practice. As the school year proceeds, we will not be accumulating material; we will be accumulating comprehension.

~~accumulating material~~

accumulating **comprehension**

The Magic Lens begins with comprehensive lectures on the four levels of traditional grammar, followed by cumulative reviews, applications, and appreciations of grammar. This is accomplished by analyzing, as the primary grammatical phenomenon, the **four levels** of the sentence, such as this one from Dr. Seuss:

	I	do	not	like	green	eggs	and	ham.
Parts of Speech:	pron.	v.	adv.	v.	adj.	n.	conj.	n.
Parts of Sentence:	subject	--------predicate---------					compound --------direct object--------	
Phrases:	no prepositional, appositive, or verbal phrases							
Clauses:	one independent clause, simple declarative sentence							

Sentences are the focus of inquiry because each sentence is a paradigm of grammar, a grammar microcosm, containing all the questions one must ask to understand grammar. A student who understands the grammar of a single sentence—its parts of speech, its parts of the sentence, its phrases and clauses, and the interrelations of these levels—is well on the way to a practical and appreciative mastery of grammar—especially if this happens in September!

In studying the complete grammar of one sentence, the student receives a thumbnail synthesis of what previously seemed an endless list of grammar concepts, and has an opportunity to realize something that often comes as a shock: grammar is not a difficult subject to learn! Basic grammar is only a *four-level microsubject*, a set of logical and interesting ideas—most of which the student already knows. In fact, sixty or so terms are all a student really needs to understand in order to grasp the elements of basic grammar. Once the student realizes that grammar has such small dimensions, he or she often decides that it is worth studying after all.

Using This Program in the Classroom

I use this compacted four-level grammar program in all of my English classes, which, in addition to grammar, contain literature, vocabulary, poetry, and writing. It is not, in other words, necessary to devote an entire course to the teaching of grammar. In fact, this four-level analysis must be applied to writing and reading if it is to have meaning. A grammar program that ends with a grammar test is self-defeating and pointless.

Not a Unit: A Launch

I doubt that I spend any more time on grammar than the average English teacher does, if I spend as much. The difference is not in the amount of time spent; it lies in the way the time is spent. Instead of taking all year to work my way to clauses, I present all of grammar in the first weeks of school, and then spiral back through all of grammar at intervals. Each time, I review all of the previously studied concepts in class discussion, and each time, I follow that discussion with the four-level analysis of sentences. After the first set of discussions, I introduce no new material; the program is a series of comprehensive applications.

There is no grammar unit; by compacting the grammar, I am immediately able to apply grammar to everything we do in English. When the students turn in their very first typed research papers, I am able to use all of grammar in my discussion of their work. I can use grammar all year long, use it as it was meant to be used—as the language of language.

Motivating

At the beginning of the year, I explaining to the students *why* they need grammar, why they have possibly had trouble mastering it in the past, and why that will not happen again. I tell them that this is the year they are going to learn grammar. I show them that it is really learnable, that it is not a cosmos of concepts, but only a four-level micro-subject of sixty or so terms. I explain that we are going to review all of grammar at the beginning of the year, and then review all of it over and over, until they finally understand it, and can use it.

Introductory Lectures and Note-taking

In the first weeks of school, I present the four levels of grammar with lively lectures, sharing my own enthusiasm for grammar as openly as possible. The content of these introductory lectures is, so far as I am able to put it on paper, presented later in this text. Even if students have the *Magic Lens* student book, I have the students take notes on these lectures, just as though it were a college lecture class.

I recommend making old-fashioned note-taking one (but only one) part of any course: it is good practice for college, it teaches students how to listen, it teaches them to evaluate and organize ideas, and it gives them a different learning style process because they are not only hearing and reading ideas, they are writing them, too. I think that having the students themselves write down the ideas is invaluable.

We begin each class by having several students volunteer to read their notes from the previous day; this gives us a chance to review yesterday's main ideas, to correct possible misinterpretations, and to begin today's lecture with focus. It also develops student pride in note-taking.

A personal view of note-taking: I believe that a notebook should be a book, a book of notes—a sort of intellectual diary. I encourage students to take grammar notes in neat sentences and paragraphs, dating each lecture, and being selective about what to write down. I discourage them from writing down only quick outlines, or fragments that will make no sense in two months. I encourage students to use notebooks to collect ideas, not just test definitions, and I ask, "Who wrote down something yesterday that was not just a test definition but was an interesting idea? May we hear what you wrote down?" Having the students write down anything they think is interesting, fun, or enlightening—no matter who said it or what it is about—teaches them to care about ideas as ideas, and to care about their notebooks as collections of ideas.

notebook • a book of *notes*

After hearing notes from yesterday, I begin the lecture with a focusing statement that locates today's lecture in a larger context. I might say, for example: That we're studying grammar, that it's a way of thinking about language, that last week we studied the eight parts of speech, that we are now studying the parts of the sentence, that yesterday we studied the subject and predicate, and that today we will discuss the direct object. And off we go.

It takes a week or more to review the parts of speech, and usually a few days each to discuss the parts of the sentence, the phrases, and the clauses. So, depending on the background my new students have, I might spend two or three weeks in these introductory lectures. The students keep and use these September notes for the remainder of the year, because these lecture notes help them review every time we study a new collection of sentences.

a wonderful question

Why?

Questions

I always encourage questions, explaining that questions show courage and interest, that there is no such thing as a bad question, and that I would be very happy to explain anything over again, no matter how many times I have explained it in the past. I say, "Complete the following sentence: 'One thing that I still don't understand is _____.'"

Student questions are vital to the process. If they will not ask, you can not succeed. Two positive techniques that I use to teach students to ask questions, in addition to the repeated encouragement, are one: to give positive responses, such as "Good question," and "I'm glad you asked that," and two: to thank students for their questions after I answer them. I smile, say, "Thanks for your question," and pick the next hand up.

Careful cultivation of student questions pays rich dividends in teaching grammar, as it does in all teaching. Using these and other techniques, you should be able to create a safe and exciting atmosphere in which students can ask all of the things they really want to know.

There are two things that will destroy this atmosphere: negative peer response and negative teacher response. If other students laugh at or criticize questions, or if the teacher laughs at, or criticizes questions, then all is lost. Questions will cease. It is fatal to the instructional process to say, "If you had been listening . . ." or "Don't you understand that?" or any other negative statement. I believe so strongly that dialogue and questioning is vital to the learning process that I always promise my students that I will never get angry with them for asking a question. I even tell them that they are only human, that they will inevitably get distracted sometimes, and that I would far rather have them raise their hands and ask a question than be confused, even if the reason they don't understand is that they haven't paid attention.

And consider, it is more than possible that the student got distracted in the first place because the lecture was flat for a time, and if one student fell out, others probably did, too. It's best if the students always ask their questions, and if their questions are always welcomed. For pedagogical purposes, there can be no such category as the bad question, though it might sometimes be appropriate to say, "I'd like to go over that again with you later; see me after class, and we'll set up a good time." Usually, however, it is best to answer the question immediately.

After these introductory lectures and a GoBack game to strengthen their definitions, the process changes dramatically. We move into the grammar loops, and also begin applying grammar to all of the other language arts activities we do. Instead of studying concepts, we study sentences and apply concepts, and instead of me explaining concepts and taking questions, I write sentences on the board and ask questions. In fact, the sentence analysis process is a sort of catechism, a cycle of questions that is repeated and that begins over again every time we analyze a new sentence.

Socratic Teaching

This catechism process is Socratic, both in the surface sense that I conduct it entirely through questions, and also in the deeper sense that it often leads us to points of genuine perplexity, where we are all scratching our heads, trying to understand the grammar of a sentence that has come up. We should never be surprised that the real world, including the world of language, is profound.

The Catechism

The process goes something like this: I write a sentence—at the beginning of the year I use the sentences that will actually be on the grammar test—on the board. Let us say that the sentence I write on the board is:

The Andromedans attacked savagely, and we fell back.

The Andromedans attacked savagely, and we fell back.

Teacher: Here we go. This is one of the sentences on your grammar test, so let's go through it together. We will do a four-level analysis, and you take notes to study for the test. Feel free to ask questions. Today, just call out your answers to my questions. Ready?

Students: Yes.

Teacher: What's grammar?

Students: A way of thinking about language.

Teacher: How many levels are there in traditional grammar?

Students: Four.

Teacher: What is the first level?

Students: Parts of speech.

Teacher: What are the parts of speech?

Students: The eight kinds of words in our language.

Teacher: Thanks. Let's do the parts of speech of all of the words in this sentence. What part of speech is *The*?

Students: An adjective.

Teacher: What kind of adjective?

Students: A definite article.

Teacher: What does *The* modify?

Students: *Andromedans*.

Teacher: What part of speech is *Andromedans*?

Students: A noun.

Teacher: What kind?

Students: A proper, plural noun.

Teacher: What part of speech is *attacked*?

Students: A verb.

Teacher: Action or linking?

Students: Action.

Teacher: Transitive or intransitive or neither?

Students: Intransitive.

Teacher: Why is it intransitive?

Students: It's an action verb without a direct object.

Teacher: What tense is it?

Students: Past tense.

Teacher: Is it active voice or passive voice?

Students: Active voice.

Teacher: How do you know *attacked* is active voice?

Student: Because the verb is voiced so that the subject is acting.

Teacher: Good. What part of speech is *savagely*?

Students: An adverb.

Teacher: What does it modify?

Students: *Attacked*.

Teacher: Prove to me that *savagely* doesn't modify *Andromedans*.

Students: Adverbs don't modify nouns.

Teacher: What modifies nouns?

Students: Adjectives.

Teacher: What part of speech is *and*?

Students: A conjunction.

Teacher: What kind of conjunction?

Students: Coordinating.

Teacher: List the coordinating conjunctions.

Students: And, but, or, nor, for, so, yet.

Teacher: What two things does *and* coordinate in this sentence?

Students: Two independent clauses.

Teacher: Good. We'll look at that more closely in a minute. What part of speech is *we*?

Students: A pronoun

Teacher: An object or subject pronoun?

Students: A subject pronoun.

Teacher: Why is it a subject pronoun?

Students: It's the subject of a predicate.

Teacher: What person and number is *we*?

Students: First person, plural.

Teacher: What is *we*'s antecedent?

Students: *Andromedans*.

Teacher: We are the Andromedans?

Students: No.

Teacher: Then what does *we* replace?

Students: You can't tell from this sentence.

Teacher: Right. The antecedent is unknown. What part of speech is *fell*?

Students: A verb.

Teacher: Is *fell* action or linking?

Students: Action.

Teacher: Transitive or intransitive?

Students: Intransitive.

Teacher: What tense is *fell*?

Students: Past tense.

Teacher: Active voice or passive voice?

Students: Active.

Teacher: Good. What part of speech is *back*?

Students: A preposition.

Teacher: What is the object of that preposition?

Students: Oh. It's not a preposition, it's an adverb.

Teacher: If it's an adverb, what does it modify?

Students: .

Teacher: Prove to me that it's not an adjective.

10

Students: Adjectives don't modify verbs.

Teacher: What do adjectives modify?

Students: Nouns and pronouns.

Teacher: Good. That finishes the parts of speech. Are there any questions about the parts of speech in this sentence before we look at the second level of grammar? . . . OK, what is the second level of grammar?

Students: Parts of the sentence.

Teacher: What is a sentence?

Students: A thought.

Teacher: No.

Students: Yes.

Teacher: Prove it.

Student: In a sentence, you say something about something, and that is what a thought is.

Teacher: OK, then what are the two important parts of each thought?

Students: The complete subject and the complete predicate.

Teacher: What part of this sentence shall we look for first?

Students: A subject.

Teacher: Do you see a subject?

Students: *Andromedans*.

Teacher: What is that subject's predicate?

Students: *Attacked*.

Teacher: Once again, is it action or linking?

Students: Action.

Teacher: Therefore, what are we not looking for?

Students: A subject complement.

Teacher: Why are we not looking for a subject complement?

Students: Subject complements go with linking verbs.

Teacher: Then what are we looking for?

Students: A direct object.

Teacher: Is there a direct object?

Students: No.

Teacher: Isn't *savagely* a direct object?

Students: No, direct objects are nouns or object pronouns.

Teacher: Is there an indirect object?

Students: No.

Teacher: How do you know?

Students: There's no direct object.

Teacher: So what?

Students: The indirect object comes between an action verb and a direct object.

Teacher: Is there another subject or are we through?

Students: *We* is a another subject.

Teacher: What predicate is *We* the subject of?

Students: *Fell*.

Teacher: Is *fell* action or linking?

Students: Action.

Teacher: So what are we not looking for?

Students: A subject complement.

Teacher: What are we looking for?

Students: A direct object.

Teacher: Is there one?

Students: No.

Teacher: How do you know?

Students: Nothing receives the action.

Teacher: Are we through with parts of the sentence?

Students: Yes.

Teacher: Do you have any questions, before we go on to the third level of grammar? . . . What is the third level of grammar?

Students: Phrases.

Teacher: What is a phrase?

Students: A group of words that doesn't have a subject and its predicate, and that is used as a single part of speech.

Teacher: What kinds of phrases will we look for?

Students: Prepositional, appositive, and verbal.

Teacher: Any prepositional phrases in this sentence?

Students: No.

Teacher: Any appositive phrases?

Students: No.

Teacher: What's an appositive phrase?

Students: An interrupting definition.

Teacher: Isn't *we fell back* an appositive phrase?

Students: No, its an independent clause.

Teacher: Are there any verbal phrases?

Students: No.

Teacher: Isn't *attacked* a participle?

Students: No, it's a verb, not an adjective.

Teacher: No gerunds?

Students: No, there are no *-ing* words.

Teacher: Are there any questions about phrases before we go to the fourth level of grammar? I would be happy to go over anything you'd like.

Student: Can a participle end in *-ing*?

Teacher: Good question. Yes, a participle can end in many things, including *-ing*. If I say, "Falling suddenly, Starbuck yelped," the word *Falling* is a participle modifying the noun *Starbuck*. Does that make sense?

Student: Yes.

Teacher: Good. Thanks for your question. Any other questions? . . . What is the fourth level of grammar?

Students: Clauses.

Teacher: What is a clause?

Students: A group of words with a subject and a predicate.

Teacher: What clauses do you see in this sentence?

Students: Two independent clauses.

Teacher: What's the first clause?

Students: *The Andromedans attacked savagely.*

Teacher: What's the second?

Students: *We fell back.*

Teacher: What is the sentence structure?

Students: Compound.

Teacher: How do you know it isn't complex?

Students: There is no dependent clause.

Teacher: What is the punctuation rule for this kind of compound sentence?

Students: I,ccI. (Pronounced, "eye-comma-see-see-eye.")

Teacher: Explain the I,ccI rule.

Student: Put a comma before a coordinating conjunction in a compound sentence.

Teacher: Good, thanks. What is the sentence purpose?

Students: Declarative.

Teacher: Thanks. That was a good analysis. Before we go to the next test sentence, are there any questions?

Students: . . .

Teacher: . . .

Students: . . .

Teacher: Ok, let's look at the next sentence on the test. (Writes the next sentence on the board.) Here we go again! What is grammar?

Students: A way of thinking about language.

Teacher: What are the four levels of traditional grammar?

Students: Parts of speech, parts of the sentence, phrases, and clauses.

Teacher: What are the parts of speech?

Students: The eight kinds of words.

Teacher: What part of speech is this first word . . . .

And it begins again, sentence by sentence, using each sentence as a model of grammar. As a teacher, you ask essentially the same questions every time: all of the parts of speech, all of the parts of the sentence, all of the phrases, and all of the clauses. Challenge the students to prove their points; make them explain their decisions; make them identify their nouns, their pronouns, their conjunctions; ask them what is joined by the conjunction, what is modified by the modifier, what is replaced by the pronoun. Ask them why the sentence is punctuated as it is. When they make a mistake, you accept the answer with a straight face, and ask them a following question that allows them to figure out for themselves that they made a mistake. *They* have to solve the problems. And when you have completely analyzed the sentence, you begin all over again: "What is grammar?"

This process takes about five minutes per sentence. Sometimes a call-out method works best, especially at the beginning of the year. Sometimes you can take four volunteers to do the four levels of a sentence, or you can even take a volunteer to do an entire sentence analysis.

After you launch the grammar and begin teaching poetry or literature, you can begin each class period by analyzing the grammar of an interesting sentence from the poetry or literature you are reading. This keeps the grammar alive in the students' minds, and applies grammar in the best way, proving to the students that their study of grammar was worthwhile.

Soon, you will be ready for the next step, which is that instead of you as teacher standing before the room and leading the students through the grammar catechism, you can ask a student to pick a short sentence from the poems or novels you have read and begin tomorrow's class by leading the other students through the grammar questions, imitating the process you have modeled for a month or so. The student should do just what you always do: begin with "What is grammar" and move straight through the sentence, identifying all of the parts of speech, then the parts of the sentence, then the phrases, then the clauses. The student should not provide answers if the other students make a mistake, but should simply ask new grammar questions that lead the other students to the realization that their previous answer was not right. At the end of the discussion, the student will enjoy having the privilege of picking the student who will lead the grammar analysis tomorrow. It is important to pass the leadership from teacher to student in this way because it is the final stage in giving students mastery over the analytical process. They will learn subtleties by selecting sentences and conducting analyses themselves that they would never learn if they remained permanently on the other side of the discussion.

The ability to understand grammar in four levels is the foundation for everything else. Once this foundation is in place, then advanced questions about language become possible. If the students really understand what clauses are, you can discuss how to vary clauses and make them interesting. If the students really understand how sentences are made, you can discuss how mistakes in structure cause mistakes in meaning. If the students have finally learned to talk about language, then you can talk about making language beautiful.

Each section (loop) of *The Magic Lens* contains a number of things to do with grammar, from using grammar to explore punctuation, to using grammar to guess the identities of famous sentences, to using grammar as a way of thinking about language aesthetically. Each loop contains the same components and offers a review of the concepts studied previously. A teacher might use any combination of these components at different times.

Next, let us look at what is included in each of the loops in this text.

The Contents of the Loops

Four-Level Analysis Lecture Notes:

The sentences that appear in the Grammar Review Tests are analyzed at four levels: parts of speech, parts of the sentence, phrases, and clauses. These sentence analysis pages are provided for background; rather than actually lecturing from these notes, the teacher should write the sentence on the board and ask questions that allow the students to discover the four-level grammar of each sentence. This process of four-level analysis has been described in detail above, but it may be beneficial to see what the end result looks like, on a blackboard. In this book, the four-level analysis looks like this:

FOUR-LEVEL ANALYSIS

	This	is	the	desert	where	the	elves	decimated	the	trolls.
Parts of Speech:	pron.	v.	adj.	n.	conj.	adj.	n.	v.	adj.	n.
Parts of Sentence:	subject	predicate		subject complement			subject	predicate		direct object
Phrases:	no prepositional, appositive, or verbal phrases									
Clauses:	one independent clause, one dependent clause, ID complex declarative sentence									

This sentence illustrates the difference between a linking verb with a subject complement and an action verb with a direct object.

On the classroom blackboard, however, the four-level analysis might look like this:

This is the desert where the elves decimated the trolls.

I	pron.	v.	adj.	n.	conj.	adj.	n.	v.	adj.	n.

II	subj.	pred.	subject complement		subject	direct predicate	object

III   no prepositional, appositive, or verbal phrases

IV   one independent clause, one dependent, ID complex declarative sentence

Having analyzed the sentence to this point, with the teacher asking questions and the students solving the levels, the class is now in a position to determine if there is anything in the sentence that is special or creative, and to describe the sentence as a whole, noting its most interesting features.

Binary Diagrams

All diagrams have been redone for this edition of *The Magic Lens*. For years, I have been concerned about the potentially misleading appearance of sentence diagrams as they are traditionally drawn. In a traditional diagram, the horizontal line is always longer than the vertical line; it is the dominating visual element, potentially establishing the false idea that the primary dichotomy in grammar is between the modifiers and the modified:

In fact, the critical dichotomy in grammar is not between the modifiers and the modified, but between the subject and the predicate. It is the *vertical* line in a diagram that must grip our attention, in order to reflect the binary essence of ideas/sentences. After much reflection about how to modify the diagrams, I decided on the simplest approach, a single modification, that lets everyone continue with what they already know about diagramming, but dramatically reorients the appearance. Instead of the traditional diagram with its dominant horizontal,

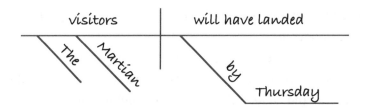

this text will use what we will call **binary diagrams**, which depict the crucial two-part construction of the sentence:

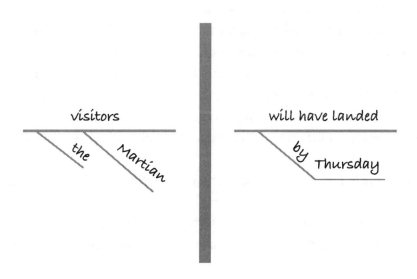

In the **binary diagram**, the image is divided into two clear sides by the enhanced vertical line and the separation of the horizontal, with the subject separate from the predicate; each is a system in itself, and each is in a larger system with the other.

Grammar Review Tests

The Magic Lens contains two 100-question concept comprehension tests based on the Four-Level Analysis sentences at the beginning of each loop. Each test covers five loops. The purpose of the test is to strengthen the students' knowledge of the grammar concepts. These tests incorporate special usage or clause punctuation questions, and students should be forewarned to give special attention to these "extra" concepts.

Copyright: A teacher has the right to copy the tests to pass out to students. Instruct the students not to write or make any marks on the tests themselves; you can collect them and use them again next year. Answers should be recorded only on the bubble sheets.

Grammar Test Keys

Two keys are provided for each grammar test. One is a bubble sheet answer key, and the other is a full-scale key, showing the correct answers in bold face. I have found that using a bubble sheet cut-out overlay, I can grade a class set of grammar or punctuation tests before the students even leave the classroom, allowing them to have instant feedback about their test results. I like to spend the day after the test allowing the students to see their mistakes and to take notes on the specific questions and concepts that caused them problems.

Bubble Sheet Key Instructions: It takes ten minutes to prepare the bubble sheet key, but it saves hours of grading time. Here are instructions for preparing the bubble sheet key:

• Make copies of the bubble sheet and the answer key. Press down firmly when you are making the copy so that no distortion occurs.

• With a pair of scissors, cut up from the bottom of the key along the dotted lines, stopping several inches from the top, at the ends of the lines. These cuts allow you to get a hole punch in to punch out the right answers.

• With a hole punch, punch out the right answers, being careful to center each punch on the plus marks.

• After the right answers are punched out, turn the key over and tape it back together on the back, being careful to tape it cleanly, without wrinkles, and without covering any of the holes.

• Your key is ready.

• On test day tell the students not to fold their bubble sheets, but to turn them in flat.

• As each student turns in his or her bubble sheet, you can lay the answer key down over it, make sure it is aligned properly, and then look through all of the holes. In every hole, you should see that the student has darkened in the circle. If not, put a small slash through the empty circles. Count the slashes as you make them. There are 100 questions on each test, which means that if you put 8 slashes, the student got a 92.

Using this method, you can grade a 100 item test in a few seconds.

• Save your answer key in a safe place for next year.

• The day after the test, pass the tests and answer keys back to the students, and go through the test together saying, raise your hand if you missed number 1...number 2...number 3...etc. For each question, count the hands up and put the number on a blank bubble sheet. Now you know what kinds of questions the students missed most. If only two students missed number 21, but 18 students missed number 32, that tells you to review the content of 32. Since this test goes back over the same content many times, there is a good chance that if 32 was a subject complement question, the students also missed other subject complement questions. Targeted review is now possible.

• Be sure to collect back all tests and bubble sheets from the students.

Ideas

The nature and importance of the ideas employed in these pages is discussed later in the introduction. These ideas are perfect for class discussions, either as a full class or as small groups. Some of the ideas would be suitable as homework problems. No answers or keys are provided for these thinking questions, since the ideas are intended to generate wide-ranging, open-ended inquiry. Use Socratic questioning, allow lots of time for good answers to emerge, and have fun.

Writing Labs

We sometimes teach grammar as though it were quantitative and technical, not suitable for inquiry or investigation. There are, however, many interesting ways of exploring grammar, and the Writing Labs are meant to instill that sense of possibility and to explore the specific questions raised in each Writing Lab. Some of the Writing Labs are suitable for in-class activity, and some would make more appropriate overnight or weekly assignments. Once again, "right" answers are not suggested; open-ended interesting discussions, however, will be generated by these Writing Labs, and it will be important for the teacher to ask the students to support their conclusions with evidence and logic. The Writing Labs are in large print so that a teacher can make a nice overhead transparency from the page.

Quotation Analysis

The Quotation Analysis pages are designed to make students aware of grammar as a vital element in famous ideas of all kinds. Grammar doesn't just live in textbooks; it is part of every sentence. Grammar is part of the world, not just part of school.

Literary Grammar

The Literary Grammar pages present extended passages from literature, and challenge the students to perceive elements of style, as revealed by the grammar of several sentences. These pages are excellent for training students to appreciate writers, and for going deeper into the real nature of choices that shouldn't be just meaningless definitions in the students' minds.

Recipes

In the Recipes pages students are given a grammatical recipe, and must construct a sentence that fits the recipe. It's fun, and the process of generating multiple examples of a single grammatical form is a good way of making the invisible visible. ("Look, this sentence is an example of IT, and this sentence is also an example of IT, and this sentence is also an example of IT . . . .") The Recipes pages are in large print to facilitate making an overhead transparency.

Mystery Sentences

The Mystery Sentences are a popular challenge. They are descriptions of the grammar of famous sentences that the students all know. I read the grammar descriptions aloud or show the description on an overhead projector, and the students have to guess what the sentence is. I have never had a class fail to guess any sentence, although it sometimes takes them time to work out the tough ones. The students always want to do more of these. The Mystery Sentences are also in large print so that teachers can easily make overheads from them.

The Word Within the Word

New to this edition of *The Magic Lens* is a coordinated set of exercises drawn from the vocabulary series, *The Word Within the Word, Volume One*. In most (not all) of these exercises, vocabulary words emphasized in *The Word Within the Word* are in **bold**, and often *italics* are used to call students' attention to grammar. For classes that do not use *The Word Within the Word*, there is no disadvantage; these grammar exercises are from all four levels and operate on a completely stand-alone basis, but students who do use *The Word Within the Word* as their vocabulary program will now see the same words and stems in *The Magic Lens*. In fact, *The Magic Lens* will teach the usage of many of the advanced words from their *Word* lists, since this text asks students to identify the part of speech when they see the word in a sentence. Both programs are mutually reinforcing.

The schedule of the two programs works as follows: *Word Within the Word* Lists 1-10 are used in *The Magic Lens's* introductory grammar lectures. Then *Word Within the Word* Lists 11-20 are used in Loops 1-5, and *Word Within the Word* Lists 21-30 are used in Loops 6-10.

The Magic Lens	The Word Within the Word
Lectures	Lists 1-10
Loops 1-5	Lists 11-20
1	11-12
2	13-14
3	15-16
4	17-18
5	19-20
Loops 6-10	Lists 21-30
6	21-22
7	23-24
8	25-26
9	27-28
10	29-30

This schedule gives teachers of *The Magic Lens* real flexibility. Those who wish can go fast, using an intense, compacted pace that finishes the lectures in just a few weeks, then applying their grammar to other language arts elements as they teach them and working in the subsequent loops as their calendar and *Word Within the Word* schedule suggests. Those who wish to go through the lectures more slowly can devote up to a third of a year to it, until they are in their tenth list of *The Word Within the Word*, and still be coordinated with the vocabulary program.

If a teacher wants to accelerate in either program, no harm is done. The grammar of the *Word Within the Word* pages is accessible, whether or not students have studied the vocabulary.

An Overview of the Year

One way to think about the possibilities for this program, or for coordinating this program with *The Word Within the Word*, is to think of the programs in thirds. Just as *The Word Within the Word* is divided into 30 lessons (with review tests every five lessons that extend the program to 35 weeks), *The Magic Lens* divides beautifully into three parts: the teaching, the first five loops, and the second five loops.

If the teacher schedules the lecture/teaching portion of *The Magic Lens* into the first third of the year (earlier is better), then the students will be equipped for application for the rest of the year. This would correlate with *The Word Within the Word* lists 1-10.

That leaves ten *Magic Lens* loops in two groups of five. These can either be paced out so that each loop is scheduled over a two-week period covering two *Word Within the Word* lists, or else the teacher might like to do two concentrated *Magic Lens* workshops, each of five loops.

In other words: *Magic Lens* loops 1-5 fit into the second third of the year and correlate with *Word Within the Word* lists 11-20, and Loops 6-10 fit into the final third of the year and correlate with *Word Within the Word* lists 21-30.

First Third	Second Third	Third Third
ML Lectures	**ML Loops 1-5**	**ML Loops 6-10**
WWW 1-10	**WWW 11-20**	**WWW 21-30**

This schedule is not so taxing that it can't be included, along with novels, plays, student essays, films, and all of the other language arts activities teachers want to do. Two weeks is more than enough time to do a single loop of Magic Lens; it might take only a day or two, and remember that most of the elements of the loops are optional resources, not requirements.

Punctuation Exercises and Tests

Punctuation is a function of all four levels of grammar: **p as ƒ of G**. When we punctuate, we mark the grammar of sentences: the phrases, the clauses, the parenthetical remarks, the nouns of direct address, the appositives. Someone who doesn't know grammar can not be taught to punctuate.

In this revised edition of *The Magic Lens*, there are short punctuation exercises in each of the ten loops, and also major Punctuation Tests for loops 1-5 and loops 6-10. The extended **P as ƒ of G** tests have been completely redesigned to be copied on fewer sheets of paper.

In all of these, students must know what they are doing. The punctuation exercises are designed to force students to punctuate for the real *reasons*, rather than let them guess at putting a comma somewhere because it sounds nice to do so. This test, in other words, concentrates on the WHY of punctuation.

Experience has shown that the punctuation tests are very challenging, so students should review the **P as ƒ of G** exercises and punctuation rules thoroughly before taking the test.

Punctuation Test Key

There are two keys provided for each punctuation test, a bubble sheet key and a full-scale concept key. The bubble sheet key for this test can be prepared just like the bubble sheet key for the

Grammar Review Test. I recommend reviewing and explaining every answer of every question on the test. If the grades on the first test are low, you may wish to go over it with the students and give them a second chance at it, but it won't be long before your students will be punctuating better and with more real understanding than any students you've ever seen.

GoBack

There *are* things students must memorize. They must know, by heart, the definitions of the major terms of all four levels grammar. At the end of each group of lectures, there are GoBack definitions provided so that the teacher can conduct a GoBack game in class. The purpose of GoBack is to help the students memorize the parts of speech, parts of sentence, phrases, and clauses. Just as in geometry, in grammar it is essential that students know their definitions of grammar "formulas"; if they don't, they won't be able to use it to solve grammar problems.

GoBack must be played with a sense of fun. To play GoBack:

• Call on individual students, one at a time, randomly, so that they don't know who will be called next. From time to time, call on a student who you just called on a minute ago. This will send the message to the entire class that they really have to be paying attention to each question. Even if they just answered one, they are not off duty!

• Ask each student to define a grammar term or to list an important list, such as the subject pronouns.

• Ask these questions in grammar order, beginning with "What is grammar?" and continuing through parts of speech, parts of sentence, phrases, and clauses.

• If a student defines the term correctly, go to another student.

• If a student does not define the term correctly, go back to the beginning: "What is grammar?" Tell the student who missed the definition that you will come back to them shortly with the very same question. The student has that time to check his or her notes, but when you get back to that student with the same question, the student can not read the definition but must look at you while defining.

• When a student misses a definition, be sure to smile and make it OK. This should have a gotcha feeling, more like a move in a game than a failure in a test.

• As the student is getting ready to define the term properly, you go back through all or at least some of the same questions previously answered, but calling on *different* students this time. When you finally get back to the student who missed, you can make some breathless fun of the situation: "OK, Mark, *what is a preposition?*"

• You do this until the class goes from "What is grammar?" all the way through the four levels to the end of clauses, when they first list and then define the four sentence purposes (declarative, imperative, interrogative, exclamatory).

• It might take a few days to finally get this right. The first day you play GoBack, the students might be incredulous. They might not believe that you are serious, that you are going to keep going back until they know all of the definitions. The first day, you might play GoBack for thirty minutes and then let them pick a buddy and study together to get ready for tomorrow's GoBack.

• In this edition of *The Magic Lens*, I've added stages of GoBack definitions, so that if you want to do a mini-GoBack after teaching each level, you can do that. But when you finish all the lectures, be sure to have the final, cumulative GoBack game described above.

GoBack is so valuable in teaching the students the definitions that it is worth considerable time and effort, but a sense of fun is important. Play GoBack at the end of the Parts of Speech lecture series, and also—cumulatively—at the end of the Parts of Sentence, Phrases, and Clauses lectures. At the very end, spend a day or two playing GoBack on all of grammar. It will equip students for success from that time forward.

Alien Grammar

At the end of the grammar lectures, there is another creative opportunity for reviewing grammar, called Alien Grammar. The idea is that our grammar conventions are options: we make a plural by putting an *s* at the ends of most words, but other languages don't. We usually put the verb after the subject and the adjective before the noun, but not all languages do. Alien Grammar lets the students invent a grammar. There is a model provided, but the teacher can assign students to invent their own alien grammars by changing 5-10 rules of English grammar and then writing a passage in the Alien Grammar they have invented. Imagine a language where adjectives end in -*Larry*, adverbs in -*Mo*, and nouns in -*Curly*! This can be a fun homework assignment or small group project. But don't underestimate the depth required; after all, what do students need to know if they are to make up rules that are different from English?

Solecism Theater—Blunder Plays!

After the section of usage rules, there is an activity called Solecism Theater. In ancient Cilicia in the city of Soloi, the citizens spoke a corrupt form of Attic Greek, regarded by the Athenians as crude, foolish, and ungrammatical. This feeling of disdain for the Soloi-cisms spoken in Soloi has given us our word **solecism** (soh-leh-sism), which means a blunder in language, an ungrammatical usage, a misuse of language.

Solecism Theater is a creative play-writing usage project in which students write short, humorous plays that derive their fun from the contradictions and confusions of usage errors. In writing Solecism Plays, students use the usage problems provided in the introductory lectures to this text as a reference. A sample Solecism Play follows this discussion.

Purposes: The purpose of Solecism Theater is 1) to look more deeply at problems of usage and at the possible humorous or disastrous consequences of misusage, 2) to challenge the creative and imaginative abilities in connection with issues of language usage, 3) to have fun thinking of funny situations that errors in language can cause, 4) to enjoy performing in front of the class, and 5) to do some creative writing. Students are encouraged to be witty, to be hams, to relax.

Process: Solecism Theater can be done as an in-class, teacher-assisted activity over several days, allowing students to work either solo or in collaboration (or both), as the teacher prefers. It can also be done as a solo homework project over an extended period of time, allowing students to write and refine their solecism plays in a private creative process. If the plays are written as a solo homework project, then students will later need to team up in class to help each other perform the plays. Solecism Theater would not make a good overnight homework assignment, because of the time-consuming difficulty of the creating and refining process.

Grading: Though credit—even substantial credit—may be given for the completion of the plays, the Solecism Plays are not necessarily graded assignments because they stress fun and creativity and involvement with usage questions, rather than judgment and evaluation. A suggestion:

grade the plays on an all-or-none credit basis, and tell the students that the plays will count so many points on their term averages, contingent only upon satisfactory completion and performance of a play.

Someone Dropped Their Banana:
A Solecism Play
MC Thompson

Fred and Joe enter. Fred looks down, and picks up a banana.

Fred: Look, someone dropped their banana.
Joe: How did you know many people own that banana?
Fred: Hopefully, they don't!
Joe: It makes those people feel *hopeful* to not own the banana?
Fred: Are you trying to aggravate me?
Joe: No, I'm not trying to make you worse; you said it was "their banana," I just want to know who they are, and why they're so hopeful about their banana.
Fred: I ain't never said they were hopeful about no banana.
Joe: Oh, so you admit you said it.
Fred: I ain't never said it.
Joe: Let me get this straight: You said the people don't own a banana hopefully.
Fred: I'll not discuss this farther. I said someone dropped their banana.
Joe: You won't discuss this farther?
Fred: Right.
Joe: Then how close do you want me to stand, so we can talk about it?
Fred: I want you to stand a-ways over there, and leave me alone.
Joe: But you said you didn't want to discuss it farther.
Fred: I ain't gonna discuss it no farther.
Joe: Then why are you sending me farther?
Fred: Your trying to aggravate me, for sure.
Joe: No, I'm just trying to improve you.
Fred: Now, what're you inferring?
Joe: I can't infer anything, you have me confused.
Fred: If you ask me, you are literally a bird.
Joe: I am a mammal.
Fred: I see I can't learn you nothing.
Joe: What do you want to learn about me?
Fred: Your nonsense is making me feel nauseous.
Joe: No, I think you look fine.
Fred: I didn't say nothing about how I look!
Joe: You said you made me sick.
Fred: I didn't never say that.
Joe: That's right, you did.
Fred: See here, even with a lot of dark, rotten places, I'm gonna eat this banana.
Joe: I didn't realize you were sick. What disease do you have?
Fred: I ain't got no disease!
Joe: I'm so sorry to hear it. Where do you have these dark, rotten places, on your stomach? Let me see.
Fred: I never said I had no dark, rotten place, I said there were rotten places on the banana.
Joe: You mean you got a skin disease from a banana?
Fred: This conversation is literally splitting my head.
Joe: Oh, no! Now I understand why you said you were nauseous.

Fred runs away screaming, and Joe sits down, peels the banana, and eats it.

Ideas

A discussion of kinds of thinking
emphasized in *The Magic Lens*

The study of grammar can not succeed if it is pedantic and desiccated, a series of obedient memorizations. Grammar is no less rich or enchanting than literature, history, or painting. To limit grammar to the level of the technical definition is to lose the opportunity for motivating students with the humanity of grammar, with the fascination of the aesthetic thinking that grammar offers, and with the near-visual intricacy of the abstract structures that support thought.

The grammar questions in this book, especially on the Ideas Pages, make use of many thinking and feeling processes, of both sides of the brain. They involve the cognitive, affective, and intuitive domains of inquiry. They are broadly human questions that will involve the students' minds in ways that many of them may never have been involved before, especially when studying grammar.

Dr. Barbara Clark of California State University has argued that intelligence is a whole-brain function, and that learning that involves and excites the whole brain enhances intelligence, while learning that is monotonously limited to one mental activity such as memory will obstruct the development of intelligence. It also seems clear, however, that severely limited thinking processes hamper more than the development of intelligence: severely limited learning processes limit the development of comprehension and care.

Limited processes are limiting processes.

For many students education is a limiting mental experience. Many classes concentrate solely on the process of memory—even to the exclusion of cognition. School often means memorizing what you are told to memorize whether you understand it or not, and whether you understand why or not. It is ironic that educational institutions are sometimes places where questions are not welcome, and where the response to the good question,"Why should I learn this?" is the bad answer, "Because I said to."

Students should be shown that all academic thinking processes—grammar included—have value as ways of comprehending events in their own lives, as ways of defining and creating alternatives, and as ways of choosing among those alternatives.

If we are to teach children to think, it is essential to create a safe environment. The teacher should control the discussion to insure that it does not threaten or embarrass any child. It is best at first to avoid calling on individual students for answers; the concepts are new to the students, so ask the questions to the group as whole, and wait patiently for a good answer.

Wait. One of the grim findings of educational research is the wait-time statistic, which is that teachers typically wait only a few seconds for answers to their questions before answering the questions themselves or calling on another student. In discussing grammar with students, it is important to avoid such a schedule. Investigate grammar in a patient, thinking atmosphere. Ask a question, and wait.

If no student answers in a minute or two (or ten), wait. Let students know that very good answers sometimes take a while to prepare and that you want them to take the time to create good answers.

Waiting for answers lets students know you expect them to think with you and respond to you, and it lets them know that you like them to think and that you have confidence in their ability to create good answers that are worth the wait.

It is worth deep reflection to ask what is communicated by not waiting. The teacher did not wait for me to answer because . . . . Few of the answers would encourage a person who needs academic courage or make him or her feel confident about mastering grammar.

Affective Processes. The processes in *The Magic Lens* are not all actually *thinking* processes at all. In other words, they are not limited to cognitive forms of consciousness, but include ways of being conscious that are not traditionally associated with academic inquiry. Some teachers may even question whether class time should be spent on emotional, aesthetic, or intuitive questions, since these ways of thinking seem more personal and perhaps less educational.

The truth is, paradoxically, that *the affective side of inquiry is essential to cognitive inquiry*, for the affective/intuitive functions are right-brain functions, and profound comprehension must be a whole-brain engagement.

The right brain feeling, sensing, aesthetic, and intuitive operations are not only indispensable to the development of intelligence, they are the secret to the understanding of how knowledge matters. They are the difference between the student who thinks knowledge is irrelevant and the student who does not.

In discussing intellectual processes, therefore, and in using these processes to think about grammar, it is necessary to give a balanced emphasis, to exercise both the left-brain verbal-logical-analytical side and the right-brain affective-aesthetic-intuitive side.

The purpose is to intensely engage the whole brain, and in doing so, to engage the whole person.

Many teachers have already considered the importance of incorporating thinking/feeling process into their classrooms; for others, these ideas may be new. Teachers who are just beginning to consider using a variety of thinking and feeling processes to teach grammar may appreciate a quick review:

Memory. There is nothing low or disreputable about memorization. The ability to *recall* correctly is the excellent foundation upon which high knowledge rests. It is the difference at one level between sanity and insanity and at a higher level between intellectual strength and intellectual weakness. The danger for the bad teacher is to focus exclusively on memory—to equate memorizing with learning. The result of overemphasis on memorizing is superficial knowledge that is a trivial and useless accumulation. The danger for the good teacher is to underestimate the importance of memory in a quest to make higher-level thinking the primary educational experience. The result of underemphasis on memory is thoughtfulness based on dim recollections, inaccuracies, and near-accuracies. *Excellent thinking wants excellent base knowledge for a foundation.*

In teaching grammar, students must *know* the foundation concepts. They should have a firm command of the essential definitions and principles. Only after these are in place are the students in a position to do the really advanced thinking that a knowledge of grammar makes possible. This is why the GoBack exercise is so important to the *Magic Lens* program.

Cognition. Comprehension of what one remembers is a critical: the alternative is confusion. It seems obvious that to be constantly confused would make life all but unlivable—and yet this is what many students experience in the academic world.

Students are constantly faced with demands that they achieve memory over bodies of alien and confusing language; they are chronically disoriented, intellectually. For the teacher of the confused student, it is essential to remember one's own times of confusion, to remember what it was like to be confronted with demands for memory without cognition. This is why "I said so" is a poor answer to the question "Why should I learn this?"

We must remember, first, that, *cognition is the key to memory*; if students can not understand the thoughts they encounter in the classroom, they will not be able to remember them.

Second, cognition is the key to intellectual self-respect; it is too degrading to constantly feel confused by what a teacher is saying, or to feel different because everyone else in the class seems to understand. Third, for obvious reasons, cognition is a key to finding joy in learning.

Finally, teaching cognition is one of the signal differences between bad teaching and good. Unfortunately, many teachers who do teach cognition do not also teach beyond basic cognition; they do not teach advanced thinking skills, and they do not teach to both sides of the brain or to students with different learning styles.

Every English teacher knows students who have memorized definitions of parts of speech and parts of the sentence, but who do not understand those definitions at all. In mastering grammar, shallow memorizing is not only unhelpful, it is destructive because it only teaches students to dislike grammar. The intense study of sentences as models of the grammar system should lead the students from confusion to cognition.

Synthesis. Synthesis is combining. It is bringing previously known things together into a previously unknown unity. It is adding numerous old ideas together to make a new idea. It involves noticing similarities between dissimilar things. It is analogical and metaphorical. Einstein used synthesis when he combined physics and tensor calculus to describe space-time. Artist Pieter Bruegel used synthesis when he used landscape painting, architectural concepts, principles of composition, and other knowledge to paint the tower of Babel in 1563.

Students will often need synthesis to write conclusions in essays and research papers, because synthesis is how one extracts the combined essence from a number of different thoughts.

It is synthesis to understand what mathematics and music have in common, to ask what common causes wars have had, to ask what human traits and behaviors all cultures share. Synthesis is the ability to see unity.

We need synthesis in grammar because we need to discern the similarity between the models we study in class and the sentences we use when we speak and write. Synthesis makes application possible. We also need synthesis in order to understand why adjectives and participles are similar, or why either of those are similar to prepositional phrases, or to adjective clauses. Grammar is replete with similarities of form and function, and it is synthesis that reveals those similarities. A study of grammar that does not emphasize synthesis will miss this richness of similarities.

Divergence. Whereas synthesis is combining many things into one new idea, divergence is generating many new ideas from one thing. It is starting at a single point and producing as many alternatives as possible. It is answering C to the offer of A or B. It is brainstorming. It is searching for a completely different way.

It is divergence to ask how many other ways Dickens could have ended *A Tale of Two Cities*, to ask for many different interpretations of a scene in a novel, to deliberately seek many different perspectives. Astronomers must think divergently to generate new hypotheses for the explanation of deep sky phenomena. Writers, poets, and painters must think divergently to generate creative alternatives.

Perhaps the most familiar way to explore questions divergently is simply to ask what else, how else, who else?

Divergent thinking is part of the creative use of grammar. Such creative questions could include: How else could we structure this idea? How many ways can we modify this subject? How many places in the sentence can we put this modifier?

Analysis. One of the best ways to clarify a confusing problem is to divide the problem into its components and examine them one at a time. Historians analyze the causes of war by separately examining the economic causes, the political causes, and the social causes. In the bodies of essays and research papers, students must use analysis to examine the various aspects of a problem.

People use analysis in conversation to communicate their responses in an organized way. Mathematicians use analysis in order to solve equations in organized ways. Organizations and corporations use analysis to determine how and why failures have occurred. Readers use analysis to understand and appreciate books, by thinking first of the characters, then the plot, then the metaphorical meanings, and so on.

Analysis is like divergence in that each starts with one and ends with many, but analysis is different from divergence in that the many products of divergence are not components. In analysis, the many are the pieces of the one.

Analysis has an important place in the teaching and use of grammar, because grammar is largely an analytical process: we look at a sentence and examine its parts of speech, its parts of the sentence, its phrases, and its clauses. This four-level analytical vision is what allows you to make swift and satisfying decisions about pronouns, about punctuation, about placement of modifiers, and so on. If the students' mastery of grammar never attains this *four-level analysis* stage, in which sentences become *grammatically transparent* to the students, then the students will never apply the grammar they have learned.

Evaluation. There is a misguided bias against evaluation that is sometimes expressed, "Who are you to judge?" Of course, the problem is not whether to judge, but how to judge well. Living imposes the problem of evaluation on every human being, because one is constantly having to choose. Should I participate in this event or not? Should I support this cause or not? Should I spend time with this friend or that friend? Should I read more books by this author? Should I watch more films of this type? Do I like this painting.? Do I like this poem? Is this a good choice of words? Is this a good sentence? Is this a well-organized paragraph? The kinds of choices we are forced to make often plunge us into a subcategory of evaluation, ethics, or moral evaluation.

Sometimes our inexperience with evaluation has serious consequences. There is a deficiency in our ability to help students learn to evaluate literature. As a culture, we have no widely accepted means of intelligently evaluating literature, and as a result, the question, "Is this a good book?" has come to mean "Did you enjoy this book?"

The evaluation process makes use of analysis, divergence, and other thinking processes, but it often applies these processes as lenses through which to view the affective domain. We wind up analyzing what an action does to other people's emotional lives. So evaluation is an effective way to engage both the left and right cerebral hemispheres simultaneously.

Emotion. The right brain is regarded as the site of the affective processes, and the active engagement of these processes is considered essential to the full intellectual comprehension of knowledge. In other words, if the students are to truly understand what they learn, they must be not only logically involved but emotionally involved as well.

They must not only understand the importance of math, they must feel its beauty and excitement. They must be taught how to care. It may seem to be a paradox at first that the difference between the shallow intellect and the deep intellect is emotion, but it is a paradox that vanishes upon the slightest reflection.

Some teachers bristle when the subject of teaching students to care comes up. They feel that they have enough to do without feeling responsible for the motivation of uncaring students. Certainly teachers do have enough to do, and certainly students must accept responsibility for being generally motivated to learn, but it can only be the responsibility of a calculus teacher to explain what is beautiful or exciting about calculus; it can only be the responsibility of the grammar teacher to explain what is exciting and interesting about grammar.

The teacher must accept the responsibility for teaching both the *intellectual content* and the *emotional content* of the subject, because only the teacher is in a position to do so. If the teacher rejects this responsibility, there is no one left in the community who has the expertise to accept it. Parents do not know the subject matter deeply enough, and certainly students should not be expected to discover the emotional content of difficult subjects for themselves, for these are the deepest aspects of knowledge. The teacher has studied the subject for years, but the student has only studied the subject for days or weeks; it is the teacher who must reveal the mysteries to the student.

An English teacher is often faced with the problem of teaching students who have previously learned to hate grammar. This prior aversion must be overcome if there is to be success, so it is essential to focus on the appreciation of language through grammar, on the delights of the insights attainable, on the satisfactions derived through the nice decisions grammar makes possible. Sharing one's own love of language, its subtleties, clarities, and nuances, is one of the most rewarding experiences possible for an English teacher.

Intuition. The intuition is the blue—the blue out of which things come. It is the I-know-not-where. Intuition gives its flashes to the consciousness spontaneously; it cannot be scheduled. It is a source of sudden insights, inexplicable images, beams of inspiration, and surprise solutions. The intuition is the right brain's silent way of enjoying itself. It has a love of connections so tenuous that the connections often seem irrational, but it often supplies the brilliance and originality that distinguish great thoughts from good ones.

We often quit thinking about problems and turn away our attention in order to let solutions incubate; in doing so, we are trusting our intuitive processes to do what they somehow do, and we are asking our left brain rationalism to give up and let the other side have a go. The result is often astonishing, for it is the intuitive content that provides the breakthrough hypothesis with its leap of imagination, or that provides the great poem with its shocking originality, or that provides the great painting with its unexpected vision. Intuition is the Archimedes factor.

It is important to teach students to trust the intuitive side, to teach them not to let the rational side reflexively reject intuitive responses. Students must be taught to cultivate the creative thinkings and feelings and perceivings and imagings that the intuitive side gives to our personalities. Our intuitive sensitivities are powerfully involved in our abilities to love what we learn.

In teaching students about language, we are working in one of the richest fields for intuitive expression; grammar can serve as a way to give meaning and form to such expressions, to make them truly communicable.

Aesthetics. Our artistic and sensory involvement of the world is our aesthetic side. Our aesthetic feelings move us to study sunsets and walk in forests, to listen to water and sing songs, to paint colors, arrange forms, change houses, design buildings, and sculpt sculpture.

Aesthetics is the poetics of poetry, the structure of story, the elegance of equations, the pencil renderings of the architect. Aesthetics is the reason you make some people answer random questions just so you can hear them talk. It is the art of clothes and interiors. It is the passion behind the restoration of crumbling Renaissance paintings.

Our aesthetic responses are always alive, either in the way we receive what we find or in the way we make what we imagine. We can respond aesthetically to things in the world, or we can respond aesthetically to images that we have only found in our imaginations (Leonardo despaired of making the *Mona Lisa* as perfect as what he saw within).

Grammar is, in very large part, an aesthetic process. Much of what we do in applying grammar is to make aesthetic decisions about whether a sentence is beautiful or ugly, clear or cloudy, sharp or blunt, parallel or crooked. Grammar lifts us out of the inarticulate mire and allows us to talk about such questions intelligently; it gives us whys about words, and criteria for thinking about beauty in words.

The most excited and successful students are those who do not approach knowledge as students; they approach knowledge as human beings. As human beings, we spend much of our lives using language; grammar gives us a lifelong chance to use our language with pleasure and clarity, with insight and purpose.

What we must do—our essential task, no less in grammar than in anything else—is to show students how to learn *from the heart of the mind*.

By degrees I made a discovery of still greater moment. I found that these people possessed a method of communicating their experience and feelings to one another by articulate sounds. I perceived that the words they spoke sometimes, produced pleasure or pain, smiles or sadness, in the minds and countenances of the hearers. This was indeed a godlike science, and I ardently desired to become acquainted with it.

-The monster, in Mary Shelley's *Frankenstein*

Grammar

A way of thinking about language.

A Way of Thinking About Language

Grammar: Like formal logic, grammar is a method of critical thinking. It allows us to build good sentences that are consistent and logically valid. It lets sentences contain truth. It allows us to identify and extirpate ambiguities and internal disagreements from our thought. Grammar reveals to us that each thought is a *paradigm of simplicity*, a two-part structure, made of a subject and a predicate about the subject. The form of a thought is:

Grammar shows us the parts of thoughts' subjects, and the parts of thoughts' predicates. Grammar shows us how to simplify thoughts, how to combine thoughts that are aspects of one another, and how to modify thoughts until they are precise. Grammar shows us how to express the truth, and how to avoid contradicting what we have already said. Grammar is a set of principles and reflections about thoughts, and with these reflections, you can think.

We can express some of these ideas succinctly by saying that **grammar is a way of thinking about language**.

Grammar is
a way
of thinking about language.

Grammar lets us think about language by giving us names for different kinds of words and for the different ways that words represent our thoughts and feelings.

Grammar is a small subject with a few, high-precision concepts, and we will see that most terms in grammar are so beautifully named, they are self-defining.

Without grammar, we can't discuss language problems, compare writing styles, or resolve language dilemmas, and it is also more difficult to sort ideas into clear and distinct groups of words. For these reasons, grammar is fascinating and worthwhile.

$$p \text{ as } f \text{ of } G$$

Punctuation Is a Function of Grammar: Punctuation is the art of marking the four levels of grammar so that written ideas and parts of ideas do not become confusing. In other words, when we punctuate, we *separate the groups of grammar from each other*. Since it is grammar we punctuate, it is impossible to punctuate unless we first see the grammatical structures, such as phrases, dependent clauses, and compound sentences. You cannot punctuate a *nonessential adjective clause* if you don't know it's there.

4

Four Levels of Grammar: We do grammar in **four approaches** or levels. They are the **parts of speech**, **parts of the sentence**, **phrases**, and **clauses**. When we analyze the grammar of a sentence, that is what we do: a four-level analysis.

Grammar: **Four** Levels
1. Parts of speech
2. Parts of the sentence
3. Phrases
4. Clauses

These four levels give us four different views of each sentence. The **parts of speech** level shows us each word, one at a time, asking "What is this word doing?" The **parts of sentence** level shows us the architecture of the idea, asking, "What is being said about what?" The **phrases** level shows us the little groups of words in the sentence, groups that pretend to be a single part of speech, asking "What part of speech is this group of words doing?" And the **clauses** level shows us whether or not more than one idea is drawn into the sentence's design, asking "How many different ideas are connected together in this sentence?" Although we will explain the details of this four-level analysis later, we can demonstrate the simplicity of the four levels by looking at a sentence from poet T.S. Eliot:

These   fragments   I   have shored against my   ruins.

Parts of Speech:	adj.	n.	pron.	v.	v.	prep.	pron.	n.
Parts of Sentence:	---- direct object---		subj.	------pred.-----				
Phrases:						--prepositional phrase--		
Clauses:	---------one independent clause, simple declarative sentence--------							

Level? Before we continue, consider for a moment that the word *level* is a strata metaphor. In looking at the parts of speech, parts of the sentence, phrases, and clauses of a sentence, we are *thinking about the same sentence in four different ways*; we are examining four different phenomena within the sentence. Rather than four levels of depth, our four different views are really more like four different views of the same human body, which looks different in visible light, x-rays, infrared images, and CAT-scans. There is only one sentence; it is we who are looking through it, thinking and then rethinking about it four different times.

3

It's not so much to learn.

A Term Total: If you have ever had the sinking feeling that grammar is an endless subject, you should notice a secret (shhhhh): most grammar books are thick only because they are padded with *hundreds of pages of exercises*. The actual content of grammar is tiny. It is *very* learnable. In fact, sixty or so terms are all you really have to know to be unusually competent in your essential grammar, and there are only about twenty key terms! Here are most of the grammar terms you need, with the key terms in bold:

A Term Total

PARTS OF SPEECH	PARTS OF SENTENCE	PHRASES	CLAUSES
noun	sentence	phrase	**independent**
proper / common	fragment	**prepositional**	**dependent**
singular / plural	**subject**	**appositive**	structure
pronoun	**predicate**	**verbal**	simple
subject / object	simple / complete	gerund	compound
relative	**direct object**	participle	complex
demonstrative	**indirect object**	infinitive	compound-complex
person, 1, 2, 3	**subject complement**		purpose
adjective	predicate nom		declarative
degree	predicate adj		imperative
article			interrogative
definite			exclamatory
indefinite			
verb			
tense			
perfect tenses			
helping verb			
singular / plural			
active / passive voice			
action / linking			
mood			
adverb			
conjunction			
coordinating			
subordinating			
correlative			
preposition			
object of prep			
interjection			

1

parts of speech

---

parts of the sentence

---

phrases

---

clauses

Level One: Eight Parts of Speech

Parts of speech: The parts of speech are the eight kinds of words: **noun**, **pronoun**, **adjective**, **verb**, **adverb**, **preposition**, **conjunction**, and **interjection**. Only eight! It is miraculous to have so simple a system for sorting all the words in our huge language. What if we had been assigned the problem of finding how many kinds of words there are in the English language? Would we have discovered a system this easy? Never! We are lucky that—in addition to the eight parts of speech we already have to learn—we do not also have to learn dozens or even hundreds of other parts of speech, such as (just imagine) adnouns, projectives, interverbs, preverbs, postpositions, conjections, disjunctions, and surnouns. From this viewpoint, the eight-category part of speech system is a masterpiece of intelligent simplicity. It is *elegant* in the sense that scientists describe a simple theory as **elegant**.

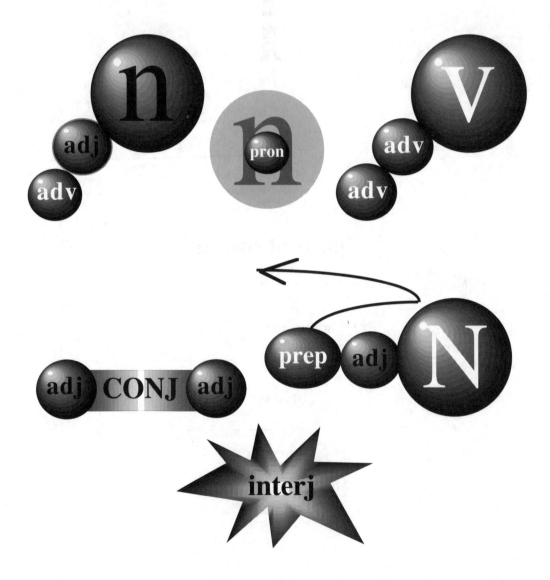

There are only eight kinds of words!

Latin: *nomen*, name.

NOUN

The name of a person, place, or thing.

Noun: (n.) A noun (from Latin *nomen*, name) is the name of a person, place, or thing [*Mozart, Chicago, epidermis, rock, freedom, pulchritude*]. **Proper nouns** (*Mozart*) are capitalized, and **common nouns** (*epidermis*) are not. **Concrete nouns** (*rock*) are names of objects, and **abstract nouns** (*freedom, pulchritude*) are names of ideas. When we call someone by name, the person's name is called the **noun of direct address** (*Livingston*, I presume.). A noun that names a group, such as *flock*, is known as a **collective noun**. Nouns are **singular** (sing.) if they describe individual things, or **plural** (pl.) if they describe multiple things: *boat/boats, flock/flocks, kindness/kindnesses*.

In Walt Whitman's sentence from his great poem *Leaves of Grass*, "O Captain! my captain! rise up and hear the bells," *Captain* is a noun of direct address, and the subject of the verb *rise* is understood to be second person, since the sentence is imperative. In William Shakespeare's *The Taming of the Shrew*, Katherine calls Petruchio "a mad-brain rudesby full of spleen"! Few of us, one imagines, would like to be named by the noun *rudesby*, mad-brained or otherwise.

Nouns from Robert Louis Stevenson's *Treasure Island*: In his 1881 masterpiece, *Treasure Island*, Robert Louis Stevenson used nouns, especially nautical nouns, such as *forecastle, palisade, doldrums, hummock, miscreant, doubloon, buccaneer, capstan, quay, sward, gunwale, lancet, rogue, bowsprit, hawser, slough*, and *truculence*, to give an exotic sense of adventure and romance to his sea tale. Is there a noun from *Treasure Island* that you don't know?

A Classic Noun: *Visage*: The noun *visage*, that indicates the face or the expression on the face, is a true classic noun, that has been in literary use for centuries. Chaucer, for example, used *visage* in his immortal *Canterbury Tales*, written in 1385; he wrote that "This olde man gan loke in his visage," and referred to "Many fair shap and many a fair visage." We even see "Of his visage

39

children were aferd." The changes in spelling over the last five centuries are dramatic. Shakespeare used *visage* in *A Midsummer Night's Dream* to describe how Phoebe doth behold *"Her silver visage in the watery glass."* And in *Romeo and Juliet* we read, "Give me a case to put my visage in" referring to a mask! In modern literature, *visage* continues to have an important role; Joseph Heller, in his 1955 *Catch-22*, described "the sheer force of his solemn, domineering visage," and Robert Penn Warren, in his 1946 *All the King's Men* wrote that "Mr. Patton's granite visage seemed to lean toward me like a monument about to fall."

Four-Level Analysis: Frequently in *The Magic Lens*, you will see a four-level analysis of a sentence from a famous work of literature. Often, most of the analysis will be in gray, letting focus elements be highlighted in black. Even though we haven't studied some of the levels or terms yet, you will still get a brief preview of them. As we learn more, more of the analysis will make sense. In the four-level analysis below, you can see that at the parts of speech level, *Americans* and *summer* are nouns, while at the parts of sentence level each noun plays a different role. *Americans* is the subject of the sentence, and *summer* is a direct object. We'll learn what a direct object is soon.

FOUR-LEVEL ANALYSIS

From Martin Luther King's *Why We Can't Wait:*

	Americans	**awaited**	**a**	**quiet**	**summer.**
Parts of Speech:	**noun**	v.	adj.	adj.	**noun**
Parts of Sentence:	subject	predicate			direct object
Phrases:		no phrases			
Clauses:		one independent clause, a simple declarative sentence			

Here we see both a proper noun and a common noun, a plural noun and a singular noun. The proper plural noun is used as the subject of an action verb, and the singular common noun is used as the direct object.

In the sentences below, the words in **bold** contain important Latin or Greek stems. Which of the words in bold are nouns? For each **bold** word that is a noun, put an *n.* in the blank to the right.

1. The Civil War **antedates** the Korean War by decades. _____

2. The **anti-aircraft** fire shot down the enemy planes. _____

3. The two nations have a **bilateral** agreement. _____

4. The **circumspect** spy is difficult to catch. _____

5. The two together are an interesting **combination.** _____

6. Stubb was **confined** to the ship's hold. _____

7. The lunar lander **descended** through the atmosphere. _____

8. Queequeg's attention was not easily **distracted**. _____

9. She made an **equilateral** triangle with three straws. _____

10. It was an **extraordinary** achievement. _____

11. They were lost in **interstellar** space. _____

12. He received an **intravenous** solution through a tube in his arm. _____

13. The boy was a lonely **introvert** who kept to himself. _____

14. He looked fearfully at the glowing, **malevolent** demon. _____

15. Ishmael had the **misfortune** to forget his wallet. _____

16. The Pequod's voyage is not a **nonprofit** endeavor. _____

17. Flask added a **postscript** at the bottom of the letter. _____

18. Before Romeo left, Juliet had a frightening **premonition**. _____

19. The circle was divided into two equal **semicircles**. _____

20. The lieutenant gave a sharp order to her **subordinate**. _____

In the sentences below, the words in **bold** contain important Latin or Greek stems. Which of the words in bold are nouns? For each **bold** word that is a noun, write *noun* in the blank to the right.

1. The Civil War **antedates** the Korean War by decades. _____

2. The **anti-aircraft** fire shot down the enemy planes. _____

3. The two nations have a **bilateral** agreement. _____

4. The **circumspect** spy is difficult to catch. _____

5. The two together are an interesting **combination.**   noun

6. Stubb was **confined** to the ship's hold. _____

7. The lunar lander **descended** through the atmosphere. _____

8. Queequeg's attention was not easily **distracted**. _____

9. She made an **equilateral** triangle with three straws. _____

10. It was an **extraordinary** achievement. _____

11. They were lost in **interstellar** space. _____

12. He received an **intravenous** solution through a tube in his arm. _____

13. The boy was a lonely **introvert** who kept to himself.   noun

14. He looked fearfully at the glowing, **malevolent** demon. _____

15. Ishmael had the **misfortune** to forget his wallet.   noun

16. The Pequod's voyage is not a **nonprofit** endeavor. _____

17. Flask added a **postscript** at the bottom of the letter.   noun

18. Before Romeo left, Juliet had a frightening **premonition**.   noun

19. The circle was divided into two equal **semicircles**.   noun

20. The lieutenant gave a sharp order to her **subordinate**.   noun

PRONOUN

A word that takes the place of a noun.

Pronoun: (pron.) Pronouns refer. They refer to nouns. A pronoun is a word that we use instead of repeating an **antecedent** (noun); this helps us avoid repeating the antecedent (*ante*: before, *cede*: go) noun over again monotonously. For example, we don't say "Hamlet went to New York where Hamlet went to the opera." How tedious! Instead, we replace the second *Hamlet* with a pronoun: "Hamlet went to New York where *he* went to the opera." By avoiding monotonous repetition of lengthy or compound nouns, *pronouns make language fast*.

PRONOUN

Pronouns may be **masculine gender** (*he, him, his*), **feminine gender** (*she, her, hers*) or **neuter gender** (*it*). Pronouns may also have **person** and **number**:

Subject Pronouns	Singular	Plural
First person:	I	we
Second person:	you	you
Third person:	he, she, it	they

Antecedent: The pronoun's antecedent is the noun the pronoun replaces. The antecedent is named for the fact that it goes (cede) before (ante) its pronoun, and the pronoun refers back to—or replaces—the antecedent. **Hamlet** was he.

There isn't always an antecedent. Though understanding the concept of the antecedent is essential to learning pronouns, it must be said that some pronouns do not operate as antecedent replacers. The indefinite pronouns, for example, do not operate as simple antecedent replacers: **Anyone** who is registered may vote.

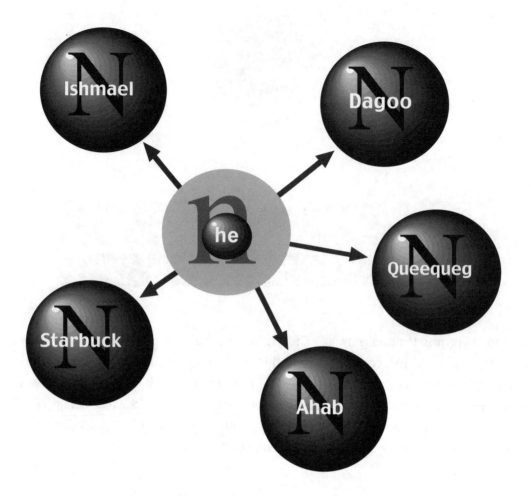

Pronoun non-specificity: Pronouns are NOT specific! They are general. The pronoun *he* refers equally to all male organisms in the world! This ambiguity causes problems when we try to force pronouns—against their universal nature—to stick to a single reference. If you write *he* in a sentence, *he* will attempt to refer to all males mentioned in your paragraph, or even to all males mentioned in your page.

Caution: If you need review on the parts of the sentence (the various kinds of subjects and objects), you may wish to skip ahead to review or preview the parts of the sentence.

It is I, Hamlet the Dane!

Subject pronouns: The subject pronouns are *I, you, he, she, it, we, you,* and *they,* and they are just what their name suggests: we use them to make subjects. They may be used as *subjects* of clauses and as *subject* complements. They are not to be used as objects. Subject pronouns are said to be in the **subject case**. The subject case is also called the **nominative** case. Examples: *It* was *I. She* and *I* went to the cathedral. From Shakespeare: "It is *I*, Hamlet, the Dane!" From Whitman: "I am *he* who aches of amorous love."

Subject Pronouns	Singular	Plural
1st Person	I	we
2nd Person	you	you
3d Person	he, she, it	they

Object pronouns: The object pronouns are *me, you, him, her, it, us, you,* and *them*, and they are pronouns used as objects: they are pronouns that must be used as direct *objects*, indirect *objects*, and *objects* of prepositions. Object pronouns are said to be in the **object case**. It hit *me*. The present was for *him* and *me*. We gave *him* a petunia.

Object Pronouns	Singular	Plural
1st Person	me	us
2nd Person	you	you
3d Person	him, her, it	them

Memorize the subject and object pronouns. Seriously. You *have* to memorize them. Since we use only subject pronouns for all subjects, and we use only object pronouns for all objects, and since it is a blunder to misuse them, you must have the two lists of pronouns memorized (and know the parts of the sentence) if you are ever to master pronoun usage. If you don't memorize the two cases of pronouns, you will say odious and reprehensible things such as, "This epistle is for you and I." You and *me*, please.

He saw he?
Him saw him?
Him saw he?
He saw him.

Thompson's Pronoun rule: A subject is a subject and an object is an object. In other words, use subject pronouns as subjects of clauses and as subject complements; use object pronouns as direct objects, indirect objects, and objects of prepositions. *It* was *he*, but *they* saw *him*. The accolade was for *him* and *me*. (This explanation will make more sense later after we have studied parts of the sentence; at that time, come back and look at this section again, and combine the two discussions together in your mind.)

A **subject**
is a **subject**,
and
an **object**
is an **object**.

In other words, any part of the sentence called a **subject** (subject of clause or subject complement) uses a subject pronoun. Any part of sentence called an **object** (direct object, indirect object, or object of preposition) uses an object pronoun. **A subject is a subject, and an object is an object**. If you know the subject and object pronouns, and you know the parts of the sentence, then pronoun usage is *easy*: just use a subject pronoun for any sentence subject, and use an object pronoun for any sentence object. If you don't know your pronouns and sentence parts, pronoun usage is impossible!

Subject Pronouns (Pronouns for Subjects)	**Object Pronouns** (Pronouns for Objects)
I	me
you	you
he she it	him her it
we	us
you	you
they	them

From Walt Whitman's *Leaves of Grass*:

	I	am	he	who	aches	of	amorous	love.
Parts of Speech:	subj. pron.	v.	subj. pron.	pron.	v.	prep.	adj.	noun
Parts of Sentence:	subject	predicate	subject complement				direct object	
Phrases:						-----prepositional phrase-----		
Clauses:	----independent clause----			--------------------dependent clause--------------------				
	two clause, a complex declarative sentence							

In Whitman's sentence, he uses a subject pronoun, *I*, for the subject of the verb and also for the subject complement (*he*). We will study these parts of sentence later, but for now, just notice that we change pronoun case to match the part of sentence. Whitman also uses the relative pronoun, *who*, to begin his adjective clause.

The song of the subjects, and the song of the objects: Sometimes, we refer to other languages as singsong, and yet, English also has its musical qualities. We do not normally hear the musical qualities of English, because it is so familiar, but when we listen closely, the songs are there. One of the most important is the difference between the sound of subject pronouns and the sound of object pronouns, a sound that lets us keep our ideas clear, even in spontaneous speech. If the subjects of sentences *sound* different, it makes it easy to spot them when words are coming rapidly.

I he she we they

eye-eee-ayay-eye-eee

me him her us them

mmm-urrr-uhh-mmm

Possessive pronouns: A possessive pronoun is a pronoun that shows possession (I realize that this comes as a shock!) and that is used as both a pronoun and as an adjective in order to indicate ownership or possession. Possessive pronouns include: *my, your, his, her, its, our,* and *their*. The possessive case pronouns are *already possessive, and therefore do not need apostrophes*. Diego lost *his* pesos. The dog found *its* doghouse.

My noun!

Its or it's? The word *its* is a possessive pronoun. The word *it's* is a contraction of *it* and *is*. The apostrophe replaces the missing *i*. *It's* too late to lock *its* cage. Do not, not, not use the possessive apostrophe in the possessive pronoun.

it's

Interrogative pronouns: An interrogative pronoun is just what its name suggests: it's a pronoun used to interrogate: *who, whose, whom, which, what. Who* went to the piazza?

Demonstrative pronouns: A demonstrative pronoun is a pronoun used to demonstrate: *this, that, these, those. This* is the dog I wish you to paint. *That* is the opinion of a Philistine.

Demonstrative pronouns as subjects: It is a good idea not to use demonstrative pronouns as subjects, because they have a tendency to be vague or ambiguous. For example, it is better to write, "*This theory of gravitation influenced people,*" than "*This influenced people.*"

Relative pronouns: A relative pronoun is a pronoun that relates an adjective clause to a main clause. The relative pronouns often begin short adjective clauses that interrupt main clauses. The man *who followed you* turned left. The relative pronouns are *who, whose, whom , which, that.*

Who or whom? *Who* is a subject, and *whom* is an object. The composer *who* wrote the *Brandenburg Concerto* was Bach. You asked *whom?*

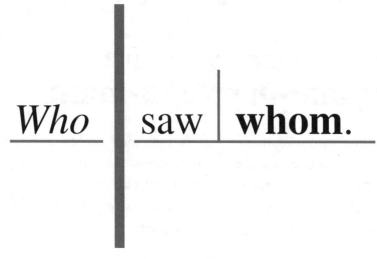

Who | saw | **whom.**

Reflexive pronouns: A reflexive pronoun is a -self or -selves pronoun that reflects back to a word used previously in the sentence. I found *myself* awash on a strange beach.

Indefinite: The indefinite pronouns are general pronouns that do not have definite antecedents: *anyone, anybody, each, all.* Those ending in -one and -body are singular.

Intensive pronouns: An intensive pronoun is a -self or -selves pronoun that is used to intensify the emphasis on a noun or another pronoun. I *myself* agree with that idea.

Types of Pronouns
Subject: *I, you, he, she, it, we, you, they*
Object: *me, you, him, her, it, us, you, them*
Possessive: *my, your, his, her, its, our their*
Interrogative: *who, whose, whom, which, what*
Demonstrative: *this, that, these, those*
Relative: *who, whose, whom, which, that*
Indefinite: *anyone, anybody, each, all,* etc.
Reflexive: *myself, yourself, himself,* etc.
Intensive: *myself, yourself, himself,* etc.

Can we agree?

Pronoun/antecedent agreement in number: A pronoun must agree with its antecedent in number. If the noun is singular, the pronoun must be singular also.

Alexander brought the column to a halt; **he** summoned his mapmaker.
The **soldiers** found Archimedes; **they** did not recognize the crazy old man.
Crick and Watson discovered the double helix; **they** won the Nobel Prize.
If **Hemingway or Fitzgerald** is here, let **him** in.
If **Hemingway and Fitzgerald** are here, let **them** in.
Someone lost **his** copy of *The Iliad*.

Pronoun reference problems: One of the most common problems new writers have with grammar is the **pronoun reference error** (ref). As a result of their universal nature, pronouns are so problem-prone that they almost seem to be malicious, deliberately causing confusion wherever they can. The crux of the problem lies in pronouns not doing what we intend them to do: we intend them to refer to and only to their antecedents. In other words, a pronoun is supposed to stand for a noun. We say *he* instead of saying *Hamlet*, or we say *it* instead of saying *the committee*. As long as it is clear what noun the pronoun replaces, everything is fine. But what if the replacement is not clear? What if we say, *Crick and Watson went to the beach, where he broke his foot*. Well, who broke whose foot?

Everyone is singular! Remember that the *-one* and *-body* indefinite pronouns are all singular, even though they may not seem to be when you first consider them. Some singular pronouns: *someone, somebody, everyone, everybody, each, every*. Someone lost **his** pliers. (Not **their** pliers, someone is not they.)

His, or her, or his or her? In order to avoid the **number disagreement** in a sentence such as *Someone dropped* **their** muffler, we used to select the masculine gender pronoun *his*: *Someone dropped* **his** muffler. We might call this the **macho solution.** While the macho solution correctly avoided the number disagreement, it also created a new problem: it tended to ground our language in a male viewpoint, a bias that modern egalitarian political philosophies correctly deplore. One popular solution to this problem of masculine bias is the **compound gender solution**: *Someone dropped* **his or her** muffler. This solution avoids the number disagreement, and offers political balance, and yet to some ears the compound gender solution sounds awkward. Perhaps the most graceful solution is to use the right gender pronoun when possible (Darius rode his chariot) and otherwise to use an article rather than a pronoun if the gender pronoun is not appropriate. We might call this solution the **article escape**: *Someone dropped* **a** muffler.

Some of the common pronoun reference errors are:

The **missing antecedent**, in which there is no antecedent noun to which the pronoun could possibly refer. (Example: beginning the first paragraph of a term paper with "*He* was born in 1895." He who?)

The **ambiguous reference**, in which there are two or more possible nouns to which the pronoun might refer. (Dickens hastened to meet his editor, but *he* was late. Who was late, Dickens or the editor?)

Some**one** is not they!

The **adolescent they** error (Roy Copperud's term), in which we use *they* or *their* to refer to a singular antecedent (If someone wants a burger, *they* have to buy one). We assume that in describing number disagreement this way, Copperud intended to indicate that number disagreement is a problem that especially bedevils young writers and speakers. The truth is that adults make this mistake too; in fact, John Stuart Mill used the adolescent they in his brilliant essay.

John Stuart Mill's adolescent they:

"If either a public officer or anyone else saw a person attempting to cross a bridge which had been ascertained to be unsafe, and there were no time to warn him of his danger, they might seize him and turn him back."
-On Liberty

This is vague...

The **ghost demonstration** error, in which we use the demonstrative pronoun *this* as a subject of a clause, assuming incorrectly that the reader is sure what *this* refers to. The ghost demonstration error could cause vagueness or ambiguity, or could be based on a missing antecedent. *This* soon resulted in . . . This what?

Solutions to pronoun reference errors: Usually, the best solution is to replace the problem pronouns with nouns. Otherwise, think and rewrite.

FOUR-LEVEL ANALYSIS

From Mary Shelley's *Frankenstein:*

	He	**appeared**	**to despise**	**himself.**
Parts of Speech:	subject pronoun	v.	adv.	reflexive pronoun
Parts of Sentence:	subject	predicate		
Phrases:			--------infinitive phrase-----------	
Clauses:	one independent clause, a simple declarative sentence			

Mary Shelley's used a third person singular masculine gender pronoun as the subject of her idea, and also worked in a nice reflexive pronoun that reflects back upon the subject. Notice that *to despise* is treated as one word; that is how we will treat infinitives (explanation later!)

18

In the sentences below, the words in **bold** contain important Latin or Greek stems. Many of the sentences also contain pronouns, though they are not in **bold**. Underline each pronoun you see, and in the blank at the right, write in the type of pronoun it is: subject, object, demonstrative, etc.

1. It is, or once was, ruled by a **monarchy.** _____

2. The **dullard** was always boring everyone to tears. _____

3. In killing his father, Oedipus was guilty of **patricide**. _____

4. She is an electronic **technician**. _____

5. The **dermatitis** on his skin was painful and unpleasant. _____

6. Balthazar, the scuba diver, collects them—**aquatic** species. _____

7. The deaf moose had injured his **auditory** nerve. _____

8. **Belligerent** nations gain nothing from their many wars. _____

9. The hostile island tribe **captured** them. _____

10. He **incised** the design into the oaken door with a knife. _____

11. **Biomorphic** abstract sculpture resembles these. _____

12. Patton wrote a tedious **autobiography** about his exploits. _____

13. The **porter** will carry your bags to the train. _____

14. Please **inscribe** my yearbook. _____

15. Since Ishmael loved insects, he studied **entomology**. _____

16. The grand jury returned a robbery **indictment** against him. _____

17. A **credulous** person will believe that. _____

18. Fortunately, the **centipede** wears its shoes. _____

19. Ishmael was a **neophyte** in whaling, but he learned quickly. _____

20. He, Ahab, was a lifelong **bibliophile**. _____

In the sentences below, the words in **bold** contain important Latin or Greek stems. Many of the sentences also contain pronouns, though they are not in **bold**. Underline each pronoun you see, and in the blank at the right, write in the type of pronoun it is: subject, object, demonstrative, etc.

1. It is, or once was, ruled by a **monarchy.**   subject

2. The **dullard** was always boring everyone to tears.   indefinite

3. In killing his father, Oedipus was guilty of **patricide.**   possessive

4. She is an electronic **technician.**   subject

5. The **dermatitis** on his skin was painful and unpleasant.   possessive

6. Balthazar, the scuba diver, collects them—**aquatic** species.   object

7. The deaf moose had injured his **auditory** nerve.   possessive

8. **Belligerent** nations gain nothing from their many wars.   possessive

9. The hostile island tribe **captured** them.   object

10. He **incised** the design into the oaken door with a knife.   subject

11. **Biomorphic** abstract sculpture resembles these.   demonstrative

12. Patton wrote a tedious **autobiography** about his exploits.   possessive

13. The **porter** will carry your bags to the train.   possessive

14. Please **inscribe** my yearbook.   possessive

15. Since Ishmael loved insects, he studied **entomology.**   subject

16. The grand jury returned a robbery **indictment** against him.   object

17. A **credulous** person will believe that.   demonstrative

18. Fortunately, the **centipede** wears its shoes.   possessive

19. Ishmael was a **neophyte** in whaling, but he learned quickly.   subject

20. He, Ahab, was a lifelong **bibliophile.**   subject

ADJECTIVE
A word that modifies a noun or pronoun.

Adjective: (adj.) An adjective is a word that modifies a noun or a pronoun: the *red* car. An adjective can be used as a subject complement: The swim was *good*. Why would we wish to modify a noun or pronoun? Instead of modifying nouns with adjectives, why not just use a better noun? Wouldn't it be better to use nouns all the time, and avoid adjectives? Well, even if it were desirable, it would be impossible, because we have only thousands of nouns, but there are billions of things in the universe. We need adjectives to help us describe things for which no exact nouns exist, and to describe all of the things for which we do not know the exact noun. Adjectives also help us to express the subtle differences between very similar things.

Modify? To modify is to change. In what way do adjectives modify nouns? Imagine a **frozen** summit. Think about the frozen summit of the mountain until you can see it in your mind. Now, imagine a **political** summit. Does the second adjective modify (change) the image that you have in your mind?

Adjectives modify
the nouns of the mind.

For example, the adjectives in a novel modify the images we imagine as we read the novel. Some definitions say that an adjective *describes* a noun, but *modify* is better because nouns truly are modified or changed by their adjectives.

Binary: Notice that an adjective is always part of a binary system, like a double star or a planet with one moon. The presence of an adjective implies the presence of a noun or pronoun. Every modifier modifies a modified. If you see *the* in a sentence, look for the noun. A noun can do without an adjective, but an adjective can not exist without a noun or pronoun. If it isn't modifying a noun or pronoun, it *isn't* an adjective. So we can say that an adjective modifies *its* noun, because there is a belonging, a connectedness.

Three degrees of adjectives: Adjectives have a wonderful property: they can change degree. A fire can be hot, hotter, or hottest. Ice can be cold, colder, or coldest. A book can be good, better, or best. These three **degrees** of adjective intensity are known as the **positive** (*good*), **comparative** (*better*), and **superlative** (*best*) degrees. These degrees allow us to make clear comparisons between similar nouns.

good	**better**	***best***
positive	comparative	superlative

Proper adjectives: Proper adjectives are made out of proper nouns. *England* makes *English*. *Rome* makes *Roman*. When we convert the proper noun *Spain* into the proper adjective *Spanish*, we retain the capitalization. In south Florida, Spanish moss hangs from the trees. The reason a school subject such as English or Spanish is capitalized and a subject such as history or mathematics is not is that *English* and *Spanish* are proper adjectives made from the proper names of countries.

$$Spain$$
$$Spanish$$

Articles: The articles are the three adjectives *a*, *an*, and *the*. The **definite article** is *the*, and the **indefinite articles** are *a* and *an*. Notice how logical these names are: we are being **definite** when we ask for *the* book, but we are being **indefinite** when we ask for *a* book. The word *article* comes from the Latin word *artus*, meaning "joint." Where's the joint? Well, imagine if we had no *the*, *a*, or *an*; in rapid speech sounds would blur together, and we might not be able to tell where the nouns were! The articles are little noun-alerts, that sound little bleeps right before nouns, letting us know that what comes next is probably a noun. These little articles break the sentence into nouny segments, like an insect's jointed leg, each segment beginning with a noun alert!

The galleon reached **the** port quickly, without **a** mishap, sailing silently past **the** towering **fort**, with **the** lights of **the** city making **a** glistening **path** over **the** water.

Español: In Spanish, there are masculine and feminine articles! Every noun is either masculine or feminine, and is designated by a masculine definite article, *el*, or a feminine definite article, *la*. So whereas in English we simply say *the* book or *the* window, the books in Spanish we have to change gender between *el libro* and *la ventana*. The articles also change to agree with nouns' singular and plural number:

the book	**el** libro
the books	**los** libros
the window	**la** ventana
the windows	**las** ventanas

Imagine that the English definite article and nouns behaved as the Spanish ones do. What if all English nouns had gender, with the masculine nouns ending in -o and the feminine nouns ending in -a, and we also changed the articles to something like:

the booko
thes bookos
tha windowa
thas windowas

The feeling of Spanish gender-grammar is poetic, as though all things are alive, animate, rather than being inanimate neutral objects. The English definite article *the* expresses part of an anthropocentric world view that regards humankind as primary, other species as practically inanimate, and other phenomena as "inanimate objects." This material view of reality can be detected in the unisex English article.

Good or well? The word *good* is an adjective that may be used to modify nouns or pronouns; the word *well* is usually an adverb that modifies verbs, adjectives, or other adverbs. The *good* athlete runs *well*. We should not say, "I don't feel well," which means that one has no talent for feeling things! We should say, "I don't feel good," which uses the adjective *good* to modify the pronoun *I*.

Adjectives from James M. Barrie's *Peter Pan*: In *Peter Pan*, which he wrote in 1904, James M. Barrie used adjectives such as *rakish, tedious, delectable, unwonted, deft, placid, amiable, elegant, tremulous, debonair, genial, cadaverous, profound, amorous, indomitable, plaintive, fastidious, exquisite, succulent, incisive, impassive, sanguinary, vivid, dodgy, sublime, subtle, malignant, phlegmatic, aloof, somber, nether, adept, inscrutable, bacchanalian,* and *strident* to convey the dreamlike, imaginative images of Never Never Land. Which of these adjectives do you not know? Which ones would best describe Peter?

Adjectives in a sentence from James Hilton's *Lost Horizon*: Look at these adjectives from Hilton's novel *Lost Horizon*. Hilton is using adjectives heavily, modifying his nouns gracefully. What is your favorite adjective/noun combination in this sentence?

> There was something rather **Elizabethan** about him—his **casual** versatility, his **good** looks, that **effervescent** combination of **mental** with **physical** activities.

A Classic Adjective, *Serene*: The adjective *serene* has been an important modifier in English and American literature, giving an important twist to hundreds of nouns. Coming from a Greek word meaning dry, *serene* refers to things that are calm, peaceful, and clear, such as a blue sky. Milton referred to serene angels in *Paradise Lost*, Daniel Defoe described serene weather in *Robinson Crusoe*, and in *Frankenstein*, Mary Shelley's monster observed that "A serene sky and verdant fields filled me with ecstasy." Henry David Thoreau, in *Walden*, noted that his "serenity is rippled but not ruffled." In *Invisible Man*, Ralph Ellison wrote that "he seemed too serene and too far away." In Kenneth Grahame's *The Wind in the Willows*, he describes the moon as "serene and detached in a cloudless sky." Mark Twain once said, "If you see an adjective, kill it." In his classic novel *Tom Sawyer*, however, he described how we "heard the stony-hearted liar reel off his serene statement."

We heard the "stony-hearted liar reel off his serene statement."

From Aldous Huxley's *Brave New World*:

	He	had	a	long	chin	and	big,	rather	prominent	teeth.
Parts of Speech:	pron	v.	**adj.**	**adj.**	n.	conj.	**adj.**	adv.	**adj.**	n.

Parts of Sentence:	subject pred.	---------------------compound direct object-------------------------------

Phrases:	no prepositional, appositive, or verbal phrases

Clauses:	one independent clause, a simple declarative sentence

Huxley's sentence has a cold objectivity that is brought to the sentence by the adjectives. Notice how innocuous the sentence is if we leave out the modifiers: He had a chin and teeth! Adjectives can transform a sentence.

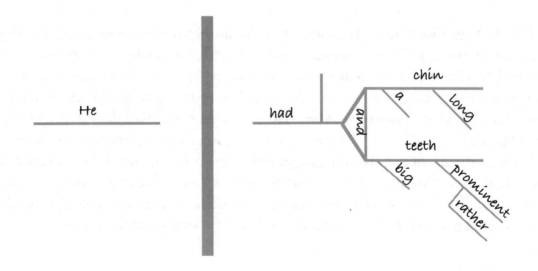

In the sentences below, the words in **bold** contain important Latin or Greek stems. The words in *italics*, including those in both bold and italics, are the subject of this exercise. For each word in italics, write either *noun* or *adjective* in the blank at the right.

1. English contains *many* **homophones** like two and too. _____

2. It was a *specious* argument, but it sounded convincing. _____

3. The *callow* youth was **inducted** into the army. _____

4. The **transfer** was made in the darkness of a *moonless* night. _____

5. The patent is still **pending** on the secret *product*. _____

6. The *two* bacteria were only a **micron** apart. _____

7. The fire **hydrant** stood in *front* of the school. _____

8. An overexposure to *the* sun's **photons** gave her a sunburn. _____

9. The swift god Apollo was a member of the *Greek* **pantheon**. _____

10. He wore a **pentagram** on his sleeve, not an *ordinary* pentagon. _____

11. The strange boy could move distant objects by ***telekinesis***. _____

12. The wild creature had an ***omnivorous*** appetite. _____

13. The surgeon was able to **excise** the *malignant* tissue. _____

14. Johann Sebastian Bach composed ***polyphonic*** music. _____

15. The crash victims suffered ***hypothermia*** on the frozen tundra. _____

16. The amoeba uses its *flowing* **pseudopods** to move. _____

17. The human brain is said to contain over 100 *billion* **neurons**. _____

18. Iron ore is called ***hematite*** because of its red color. _____

19. *Single-celled* animals are known as the **Protozoa**. _____

20. Laws against ***vivisection*** prevent cruelty to animals. _____

In the sentences below, the words in **bold** contain important Latin or Greek stems. The words in *italics*, including those in both bold and italics, are the subject of this exercise. For each word in italics, write either *noun* or *adjective* in the blank at the right.

1. English contains *many* **homophones** like two and too. — adjective

2. It was a ***specious*** argument, but it sounded convincing. — adjective

3. The *callow* youth was **inducted** into the army. — adjective

4. The **transfer** was made in the darkness of a *moonless* night. — adjective

5. The patent is still **pending** on the secret *product*. — noun

6. The *two* bacteria were only a **micron** apart. — adjective

7. The fire **hydrant** stood in *front* of the school. — noun

8. An overexposure to *the* sun's **photons** gave her a sunburn. — adjective

9. The swift god Apollo was a member of the *Greek* **pantheon**. — adjective

10. He wore a **pentagram** on his sleeve, not an *ordinary* pentagon. — adjective

11. The strange boy could move distant objects by ***telekinesis***. — noun

12. The wild creature had an ***omnivorous*** appetite. — adjective

13. The surgeon was able to **excise** the *malignant* tissue. — adjective

14. Johann Sebastian Bach composed *polyphonic* music. — adjective

15. The crash victims suffered ***hypothermia*** on the frozen tundra. — noun

16. The amoeba uses its *flowing* **pseudopods** to move. — adjective

17. The human brain is said to contain over 100 *billion* **neurons**. — adjective

18. Iron ore is called ***hematite*** because of its red color. — noun

19. *Single-celled* animals are known as the **Protozoa**. — adjective

20. Laws against ***vivisection*** prevent cruelty to animals. — noun

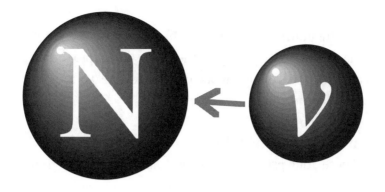

The verb is

about

the noun.

Verb: (v.) A verb is a word that shows action, or being, or links a subject to a subject complement. The verb tells what the noun does or is. If the verb is an action verb, then it might show action on a direct object: *Verdi composed the opera*. Or, an action verb might show simple action not on a direct object: *Verdi composed*. If the verb is linking, then it might link the subject to a subject complement: He *is*. He *is* a poet. Most verbs show actions or make equations.

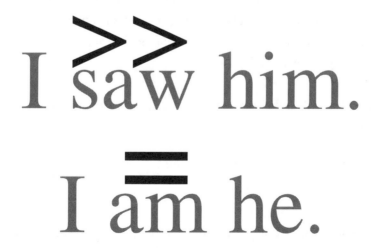

The verb is about the noun. Every sentence has a subject, and the verb (the predicate of the sentence) is about it. The subject will always be a noun or subject pronoun, and the simple predicate is the verb. This means that the verb is about the noun. The verb is saying that the noun did something or that the noun is something.

Four principal parts of the verb: All verb forms are made out of four primary forms that each verb possesses. These four primary forms are called the verb's **principal parts**. The four principal parts are:

the **infinitive**: to do (do), to go (go), to think (think), to dream (dream)

the **present participle**: doing, going, thinking, dreaming, ascending

the **past**: did, went, thought, dreamed

the **past participle**: done, gone, thought, dreamed

Regular verbs: Most verbs make the four principle parts in the same regular way, and therefore, we refer to these ordinary verbs as **regular verbs.** These regular verbs always begin with the infinitive, add **-ing** to make the present participle, and add **-d** or **-ed** to make the past and past participle:

infinitive	present participle	past	past participle
to work	working	worked	worked
to spill	spilling	spilled	spilled

Irregular verbs: Many verbs do not follow this regular pattern. Instead, they have principal parts that are unique and that must therefore be memorized in order to be used correctly:

to shrink, shrinking, shrank, shrunk

to ring, ringing, rang, rung

to break, breaking, broke, broken

to write, writing, wrote, written

Auxiliary or helping verbs: In a **simple tense** the verb stands alone, as a single word, to make the simple predicate. In a **compound tense**, the main verb is supplemented by an **auxiliary** or **helping** verb to construct the tense. The future and prefect tenses are examples of compound tenses that use auxiliary verbs. In the sentence *I will have composed a symphony* the main verb is *composed* and the auxiliary verbs are *will have*.

Transitive verb: (v.t.) A transitive verb is an action verb that acts on a direct object: The harpoon *hit* Moby Dick.

Intransitive verb: (v.i.) An intransitive verb is an action verb that does not act on a direct object: Harpoons *flew*."

Why we call them "transitive": Transitive verbs are action verbs that are called *transitive* because of the **transit** of action or energy that takes place when the subject acts on the object. If I kick the bucket, the energy **trans**fers from me to the bucket I am kicking. The stem *trans* means "across." In an intransitive verb, there is no transfer of energy.

trans
transfer
transAmerican
transcontinental
transit
transitive

Active voice verb: An active voice verb is an action verb that shows the subject acting. Active voice is usually more vigorous than passive voice. "Johnson *discussed* the problem" is active voice.

Passive voice verb: A passive voice verb is an action verb that shows the subject passively being acted upon: The problem *was discussed*. Passive voice can make sentences seem weak, since the subject of the sentence is not doing anything, and passive voice also tends to leave out important information: If I say *The problem was discussed*, we do not know who discussed the problem, but if I say *Johnson and Boswell discussed the problem*, then we have both energy and information. Active voice is vigorous.

Active voice: The meteor **struck** the ship.

Passive voice: The ship **was struck** by the meteor.

Active voice: The Literary Society **presented** Dickens the award.

Passive voice: Dickens **was presented** with an award.

Use of passive voice in scientific writing: Writers of scientific papers often prefer passive voice and past tense in order to describe the results of experiments and scientific investigations. Rather than write, "First, I administered the placebo," a scientist would write, "Placebos were administered to the control group each morning." In science the impersonality we normally avoid in other fields makes sense because it contributes to the inductive, objective, and descriptive tone of scientific inquiry. In writing papers on literary matters and on historical figures, you should avoid passive voice.

Action Verbs can be
Transitive or Intransitive
Active Voice or Passive Voice
(Linking verbs are neither!)

Time makes verbs **tense.**

Verb tense: In *The Great Gatsby*, Scott Fitzgerald wrote, "So we beat on, boats against the current, borne back ceaselessly into the past." True, and we can tell it by the verbs. Verbs show us the poignant temporality of human existence. As living beings, we exist in a moving continuum of time, borne along always, awake or asleep; unable to halt, to slow down, or to return. Time is so central in our experience that we identify it in every sentence we make, and we do it by putting each verb in a time **tense**. In other words, tense gives sentences time. We use six different tenses to indicate time. The six tenses include the three ordinary tenses, and the three perfect tenses:

Six Verb Tenses
1. **Present**
2. **Past**
3. **Future**
4. **Present perfect**
5. **Past perfect**
6. **Future Perfect**

In **conjugating** these six verb tenses, we see that verbs, like pronouns, have person (first, second, or third) and number (singular or plural):

present tense

	singular	**plural**
First person:	I protest	We protest
Second person:	You protest	You protest
Third person:	He, she, it protests	They protest

past tense

	singular	**plural**
First person:	I protested	We protested
Second person:	You protested	You protested
Third person:	He, she, it protested	They protested

future tense

	singular	**plural**
First person:	I will (shall) protest	We will (shall) protest
Second person:	You will protest	You will protest
Third person:	He, she, it will protest	They will protest

present perfect tense

	singular	plural
First person:	I have protested	We have protested
Second person:	You have protested	You have protested
Third person:	He, she, it has protested	They have protested

past perfect tense

	singular	plural
First person:	I had protested	We had protested
Second person:	You had protested	You had protested
Third person:	He, she, it had protested	They had protested

future perfect tense

	singular	plural
First person:	I will (shall) have protested	We will have protested
Second person:	You will have protested	You will have protested
Third person:	He, she, it will have protested	They will have protested

The perfect tenses **have finished**.

Why we call them *perfect* tenses: The three perfect tenses are called *perfect* because the word *perfect* comes from the Latin *perficere*, meaning "to finish." The perfect tenses are the tenses of things that are finished, either finished in the past, finished in the present, or finished in the future. Present perfect indicates action that is finished now. When George MacArthur fulfilled his pledge ("I shall return.") to the people of the Philipines, he said: *I have returned*. Past perfect indicates action that was finished then: *I had returned*. Future perfect indicates action that will be finished in the future: *I shall have returned*.

The word *perficere* further breaks down into the two Latin stems *per* (through) and *fac* (make): the lovely idea is that we are finished with something only when it is perfect, then we are through making it. Notice that the three perfect tenses are the "have" tenses: they all make use of the verb *to have* as a helping verb.

Progressive forms of the six tenses: Every one of the six tenses can also be used in a progressive form, an **-ing variation**, indicating action still in progress. First person singular examples of the six tenses' progressive forms:

Present progressive: I am protesting.

Past progressive: I was protesting.

Future progressive: I shall be protesting.

Present perfect progressive: I have been protesting.

Past perfect progressive: I had been protesting.

Future perfect progressive: I shall have been protesting.

Mood: In addition to the six verb tenses and the progressive forms of those six tenses, verbs have **mood**. There are three moods: the **indicative**, the **imperative**, and the **subjunctive**. The indicative and imperative moods are not difficult; they are the ordinary forms that we already know. The subjunctive mood, however, is different. We use the subjunctive in IF situations, with the verb *were*. We might say that:

the **indicative** is the ordinary mood;
the **imperative** is the command mood, and
the **subjunctive** is the IF mood.

Examples of the three moods:

Indicative: I *am* he.
Imperative. *Be* he.
Subjunctive: If I *were* he…

Español and the soft subjunctive: In English we use the subjunctive mood less frequently than the indicative or imperative moods, but in Spanish the subjunctive is more important. The Spanish subjunctive mood is used to civilize what we say to others, to soften suggestions, to blunt the sharpness of commands, to provide privacy for emotional expressions, and to add gentleness to hopes for things that aren't. It is a way of avoiding the directness of the indicative mood. When expressing a plain statement of fact, the Spanish speaker will indicate the fact with the indicative, but when expressing these more human experiences, the Spanish speaker will shift into the softness of the subjunctive.

| Indicative | I have a book. | *Tengo* un libro |
| Subjunctive | I hope I have a friend. | Espero que *tenga* un amigo. |

Parallel verb tense: The proofreader's mark for parallel construction is //. Parallelism in tense means sticking to the tense you are using, unless there is a reason to change. Keeping verb tenses parallel is good writing technique. I *went* home, *picked* up the apple, *threw* it through the window, and *laughed.* (all past tense) Don't let your tenses wander; control them. Notice how disturbing the unparallel tenses are in the first passage that follows, and how satisfying the parallel (//) tenses are in the second passage:

NOT //

When Charles Dickens **went** to America, he **gives** many speeches, and **feels** that his trip **was** successful. After he **returned** to England, he **begins** to lose the buoyant spirit he **finds** in America, and he **will descend** into melancholy.

//

When Charles Dickens **went** to America, he **gave** many speeches, and **felt** that his trip **was** successful. After he **returned** to England, he **began** to lose the buoyant spirit he **found** in America, and he **descended** into melancholy.

Keep parts of speech parallel in lists and compounds: Parallel construction (//) also means using uniform parts of speech for items in lists and compounds. Keeping lists and compounds grammatically parallel is a good writing technique. Parallel Compound: *John was adjective and adjective* (John was tall and handsome) is better than *John was adjective and a noun* (John was tall and an athlete). Parallel List: *I want noun, noun, and noun* (I want shelter, clothes and food) is better than *I want noun, noun, and infinitive.* (I want shelter, clothes, and to eat).

Verbs in Shakespeare's *Romeo and Juliet*: In the beautiful *Romeo and Juliet*, William Shakespeare used strong verbs to propel the story forward. In *Romeo and Juliet* we see verbs such as *importune, retort, beseech, dissemble, disparage, impute, oppress, descry, prate, feign, confound, conjure, peruse, intercede, denote, doff, wax, presage, impeach, inundate, abate,* and *vex*—a rich collection of vigorous and human verbs that bring life and emotion to the story. Which verb, more than any other in this list, makes you think of Juliet? Are there any verbs here that you don't know?

A Classic Verb: *Condescend*: The verb *condescend* means to stoop down to, to act as though you are superior to someone, and that you have to come down to their low level. *Condescend* was used by Chaucer in 1385, by Milton in 1667, and by Jonathan Swift in 1726. In her 1813 classic *Pride and Prejudice*, Jane Austen wrote, "She had even condescended to advise him to marry as soon as he could." In *Ivanhoe*, written in 1820, Sir Walter Scott's characters are "condescending to avail themselves of the good cheer." In the 1800s, condescend was used by William Thackeray, Emily Bronte, Herman Melville, Charles Dickens, George Eliot, and Thomas Hardy. In his 1901 novel *Kim*, Rudyard Kipling wrote that "she did not condescend to look at them." And in 1911 Frances Hodgson Burnette wrote, in *The Secret Garden*, that "Colin frowned and condescended to look at her."

~~didn't~~ **did not**

~~wasn't~~ **was not**

Avoid contractions in formal writing. Lots of verbs are combined with other parts of speech into contractions. A **contraction** is the combination of two or more parts of speech into one word, such as **don't**, **they're**, and **it's**. There is nothing incorrect about the grammar of a contraction, but the contraction is not in keeping with the serious intellectual tone of a formal essay. Contractions suggest that one is in a hurry and doesn't wish to write out each word. Of course, if there are contractions in a quotation you include in a research paper, then you leave the contraction alone; I am only referring to the use of contractions in sentences you write yourself. Notice that I use contractions in these comments to you. These comments are not a formal essay; they are more like notes from one person to another.

Verbs, a summary: It is critical to focus now on the dichotomy between the action verbs and the linking verbs. We will see that this difference is what determines the other parts of sentence and what determines how to use pronouns.

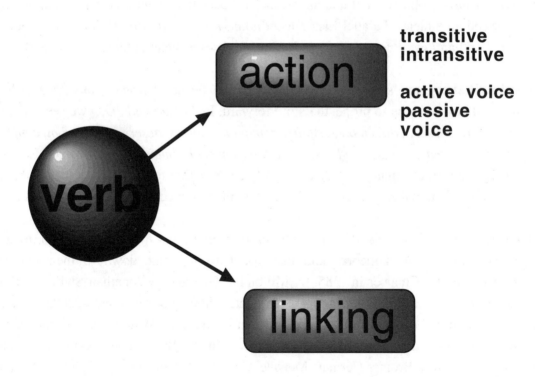

From Oscar Wilde's *The Picture of Dorian Gray:*

	He	**was**	**brilliant,**	**fantastic,**	**irresponsible.**
Parts of Speech:	pron	linking verb	adj.	adj.	adj.
Parts of Sentence:	subject	pred.	----------compound subject complement------------		
Phrases:	no prepositional, appositive, or verbal phrases				
Clauses:	one independent clause, a simple declarative sentence				

This sentence by Oscar Wilde shows the power of a linking verb to make an equation. Here, the linking verb lets three adjectives modify the subject pronoun, *he*. He = brilliant, fantastic, irresponsible.

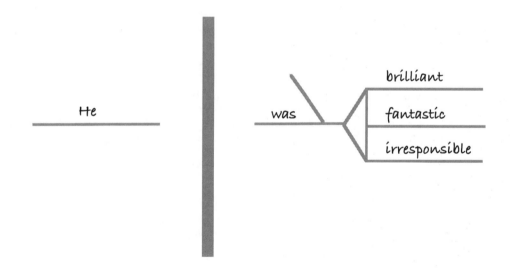

From Edgar Allan Poe's *The Pit and the Pendulum:*

	By	long	suffering	my	nerves	had	been	unstrung.
Parts of Speech:	prep.	adj.	n. (gerund)	pron.	n.	v.	v.	v.
Parts of Sentence:					subject	---predicate (passive voice)---		
Phrases:	no prepositional, appositive, or verbal phrases							
Clauses:	one independent clause, a simple declarative sentence							

Poe's sentence is interesting for its gerund as an object of preposition, and for its good passive voice verb; even though the verb is passive, the sentence still has power, with the eerie verb *unstrung* ringing in the silence of the end of the sentence.

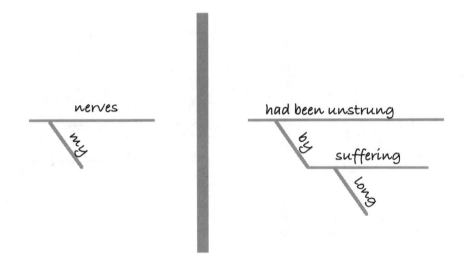

In these sentences, the words in **bold** contain important Latin or Greek stems. Other words are in *italics*. For each word in *italics*, write either *noun*, *adjective*, or *verb* in the blank at the right. If it is a verb, also put *A* for action or *L* for linking.

1.   The crystal dissolved into an ***amorphous*** mass.   _____

2.   The silk ***vestments*** were hanging on pegs.   _____

3.   Pip finally *knew* the name of his generous **benefactor**.   _____

4.   The **ponderous** burden *was* nearly impossible to lift.   _____

5.   His ***corpulent*** body was a result of his love of sweets.   _____

6.   The evil creature *lay* **dormant** for centuries.   _____

7.   There *was* a birthday party for the venerable **patriarch**.   _____

8.   The recently *invented* laser toothbrush is a **novel** idea.   _____

9.   Her ***punctilious*** attention to small details was impressive.   _____

10. Silver *felt* **dejected** when the expedition left without him.   _____

11. The ***devastation*** intensified our need for creation.   _____

12. *Self-motivated* people have an internal **locus** of control.   _____

13. The many-cultured United States *is* a **heterodox** nation.   _____

14. The **amphibians** emerging from the water *had* impermeable skin.   _____

15. Alexander's ***magnanimous*** victory speech was inspiring.   _____

16. The ***euphony*** of Mozart's concerto carried us away.   _____

17. Human beings *have* **endoskeletons**, not exoskeletons.   _____

18. The tremulous dog on the twenty-third floor has ***acrophobia***.   _____

19. The **orthodontist** *straightened* Count Dracula's fangs.   _____

20. The massive **megalith** *towered* over the ancient ruins.   _____

In these sentences, the words in **bold** contain important Latin or Greek stems. Other words are in *italics*. For each word in *italics*, write either *noun*, *adjective*, or *verb* in the blank at the right. If it is a verb, also put *A* for action or *L* for linking.

1.	The crystal dissolved into an ***amorphous*** mass.	adjective
2.	The silk ***vestments*** were hanging on pegs.	noun
3.	Pip finally *knew* the name of his generous **benefactor**.	verb, A
4.	The **ponderous** burden *was* nearly impossible to lift.	verb, L
5.	His ***corpulent*** body was a result of his love of sweets.	adjective
6.	The evil creature *lay* **dormant** for centuries.	verb, A
7.	There *was* a birthday party for the venerable **patriarch**.	verb, L
8.	The recently *invented* laser toothbrush is a **novel** idea.	adjective
9.	Her ***punctilious*** attention to small details was impressive.	adjective
10.	Silver *felt* **dejected** when the expedition left without him.	verb, A
11.	The *devastation* intensified our need for creation.	noun
12.	*Self-motivated* people have an internal **locus** of control.	adjective
13.	The many-cultured United States *is* a **heterodox** nation.	verb, L
14.	The **amphibians** emerging from the water *had* impermeable skin.	verb, A
15.	Alexander's ***magnanimous*** victory speech was inspiring.	adjective
16.	The *euphony* of Mozart's concerto carried us away.	noun
17.	Human beings *have* **endoskeletons**, not exoskeletons.	verb, A
18.	The tremulous dog on the twenty-third floor has ***acrophobia***.	noun
19.	The **orthodontist** *straightened* Count Dracula's fangs.	verb, A
20.	The massive **megalith** *towered* over the ancient ruins.	verb, A

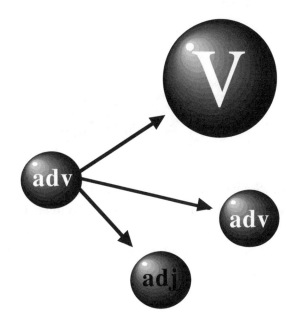

ADVERB

A word that modifies a verb, an adjective, or another adverb.

Adverb: (adv.) An adverb is a word that modifies a verb, adjective, or adverb. Adverbs, please notice, modify three kinds of words that adjectives do not modify. Queequeg swam *slowly*. Ahab is *too* tall. I like you, *too*. He and she swim *well*.

The Crayola Syndrome: Mark Twain wrote, "If you see an adjective, kill it." In using modifiers (adjectives and adverbs), you should ask yourself if you are using too many. Though there are wonderful adjectives and adverbs, there are also many that are tired and unnecessary. It is possible you are using tired modifiers because your vocabulary is weak. Are you saying, "bright yellowy green" when you mean *chartreuse*, or are you writing, "light sky blue" when you mean *azure*? Would you describe something as a "very tall, gigantic statue" because you do not know the word *colossus*? Monitor your use of adjectives and adverbs to make sure you are not using clouds of modifiers to compensate for a weak vocabulary. This should not be taken as an endorsement of pompous or stilted language, which is a different way to use words unpleasantly.

Look at this sentence, found on the Internet:

**"During the first half of the twentieth century
the world greatly changed."**

Remove the useless adverb *greatly*, and you get a strong sentence, ending in two stressed syllables: "During the first half of the twentieth century, the **world changed**."

Very, very, very weak: Sometimes a modifier will backfire, especially when it is overused. One example is the adverb *very*. People use *very* in an effort to intensify adjectives, especially when they sense that the adjective does not express enough intensity. Unfortunately, the adverb *very* often has the effect of weakening the sentence by filling it with empty syllables. Omit the *verys*, and let the adjective stand out strong and clear. Which communicates better: "He was very, very hungry" or "He was hungry"?

The adverb is not your friend.
- Stephen King

Stephen King has written that "The adverb is not your friend." What do you think he meant?

Adverbs in Herman Melville's *Moby Dick*: In his 1851 novel *Moby Dick*, about Captain Ahab and the white whale, Herman Melville used adverbs to modify his verbs, giving an expanded sense of action and event. We see adverbs such as *ere, diabolically, obstreperously, anomalously, irrevocably, jocularly, fain, aesthetically, palpably, vicariously, philologically, profoundly, indolently, circumspectly, peremptorily, obliquely, adroitly, suffusingly, ruefully, treacherously, intemperately, punctiliously, impregnably, vivaciously, sagaciously,* and *ostentatiously*. Do you know all of these adverbs? Which one do you like best?

For each sentence, identify the part of speech of the word in *italics*.

1.   In the spring of 2215, New York was a ***revitalized*** city.   _____

2.   The theory of ***democracy*** was proven very effective.   _____

3.   If there is ***stereophonic*** sound, can there be stereo smell?   _____

4.   Is ***capitalism*** the opposite of Marxism?   _____

5.   The poet was traveling ***incognito*** to avoid recognition.   _____

6.   The economic disasters could not be *readily* **surmounted**.   _____

7.   The senator's **sonorous** voice was *easily* her best weapon.   _____

8.   If the **asteroid** struck *the* earth, it would be a **disaster**.   _____

9.   Her **dynamic** personality made her an *obvious* choice.   _____

10.   Please **synchronize** your chronometers *immediately*.   _____

11.   The *very* hyperactive child suddenly began to **hyperventilate**.   _____

12.   The astronomer was an ***amiable*** individual.   _____

13.   The ***octarchy*** unanimously decided to invade Macedonia.   _____

14.   The dancers' spinning **gyrations** *continued* long into the night.   _____

15.   Their **contradictory** remarks *really* offered a sharp contrast.   _____

16.   Which do you *prefer*, geography or **geophysics**?   _____

17.   Galileo thought that the solar system was ***heliocentric***.   _____

18.   The **thermotropic** plants were *suddenly* killed by the cold front.   _____

19.   Is a *square* a tetragon or just a **tetrahedron**?   _____

20.   The **hydrometer** *accurately* measured the flow of the trout stream.   _____

For each sentence, identify the part of speech of the word in *italics.*

1. In the spring of 2215, New York was a ***revitalized*** city.   adjective

2. The theory of ***democracy*** was proven very effective.   noun

3. If there is ***stereophonic*** sound, can there be stereo smell?   adjective

4. Is ***capitalism*** the opposite of Marxism?   noun

5. The poet was traveling ***incognito*** to avoid recognition.   adverb

6. The economic disasters could not be *readily* **surmounted**.   adverb

7. The senator's **sonorous** voice was *easily* her best weapon.   adverb

8. If the **asteroid** struck *the* earth, it would be a **disaster**.   adjective

9. Her **dynamic** personality made her an *obvious* choice.   adjective

10. Please **synchronize** your chronometers *immediately*.   adverb

11. The *very* hyperactive child suddenly began to **hyperventilate**.   adverb

12. The astronomer was an ***amiable*** individual.   adjective

13. The ***octarchy*** unanimously decided to invade Macedonia.   noun

14. The dancers' spinning **gyrations** *continued* long into the night.   verb

15. Their **contradictory** remarks *really* offered a sharp contrast.   adverb

16. Which do you *prefer*, geography or **geophysics**?   verb

17. Galileo thought that the solar system was ***heliocentric***.   adjective

18. The **thermotropic** plants were *suddenly* killed by the cold front.   adverb

19. Is a *square* a tetragon or just a **tetrahedron**?   noun

20. The **hydrometer** *accurately* measured the flow of the trout stream.   adverb

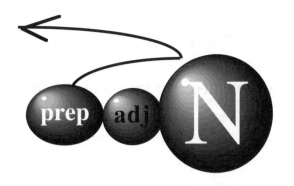

PRE ●●●●●●●●●●●●●●●●●●●●●●●●●●●●●●POST
over the rainbow

PREPOSITION

A word that shows the relationship between its object and another word in the sentence.

Preposition: (prep.) A preposition shows a relationship between its object (the object of the preposition) and another word in the sentence. Prepositions show relationships of time (*before*, *during*, *after*), space (*in*, *on*, *beside*, *around*), and direction (*to*, *from*, *toward*). In other words, prepositions show where two things are located, compared to each other. Prepositions give language its geometry. They are the x,y,z coordinates of the mind. The sphere is *inside* the cube. The beep was *before* the boom. (Or for that matter, the prolegomenon was *before* the epilogue.)

Notice that prepositions are like signs in mathematics, they are small and common, but powerful. To use the wrong preposition is to completely alter the meaning of the idea by changing the relationship between things: would you rather there be a thousand-dollar check *for* you, or a thousand-dollar check *from* you? Like signs in mathematics, prepositions must be used with precision if ideas are to be accurate. Prepositions are called **pre** positions because they come at the beginning of the prepositional phrase; they have the PRE position in the phrase: *in* the boat, *on* the dock, *around* Venus.

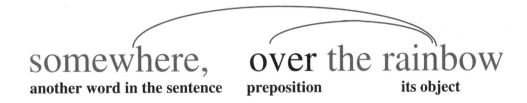

somewhere,   over the rainbow
another word in the sentence   **preposition**   **its object**

From Kenneth Grahame's *The Wind in the Willows*:

The rat only snorted and thrust his hands deep into his pockets.

Parts of Speech:	adj.	n.	adv.	v.	conj.	v.	pron.	n.	adv.	prep.	pron.	n.

Parts of Sentence:		subject		--compound predicate--				direct object				

Phrases: **prepositional phrase**

Clauses: one independent clause, a simple declarative sentence

Kenneth Grahame uses a prepositional phrase *into his pockets* in this descriptive sentence about the rat. The preposition is *into* and the object of the preposition is *pockets*. *Into* relates *pockets* to some other word in the sentence. Since prepositional phrases are like big adjectives or adverbs, what word do you think the prepositional phrase modifies?

Never end a sentence with a preposition? Well, we used to say that. We still deplore such sentences as, "Where are you *at*?" because the meaning of the preposition is incomplete. We want the speaker to finish the idea: Where are you, at home? Where are you, at work? Or we want the speaker to omit the superfluous preposition: "Where are you?" In other cases, however, a concluding preposition does not jar the ear as it once did: "Who is this present for?" is a sentence that would probably not injure the reputation of an educated speaker, even though the stricter "For whom is this present?" is preferred by some. The word *whom* sounds stuffy and inappropriately formal to many people, and it is often avoided with constructions such as, "Who did you go to the theater with?" It is probably still best to follow prepositions with their objects when you can, thus maintaining the logical sequence of the prepositional phrase, as long as it is gracefully possible to do so.

Where are you, at....

There were some things Winston Churchill would not put up *with*: After receiving a Minute issued by a civil servant, objecting to the ending of a sentence with a preposition and the use of a dangling participle in official documents, Winston Churchill returned it with this comment, red-penciled in the margin; what do you think Churchill's point was?

This is the sort of pedantry up with which I will not put.

For each sentence below, identify the part of speech of the word in *italics*.

1. His irrelevant comments were not **germane** *to* the discussion. _____

2. The friendly alien proved to be *well-mannered* and **gregarious**. _____

3. The mariner steered *through* beautiful **ultramarine** waters. _____

4. The anthropologist loved *primates*, most of the time. _____

5. The **pyromaniac** loved starting fires *with* pyrogenic materials. _____

6. The loudmouth's *clamorous* cries could be heard for blocks. _____

7. The candidate received a **plurality** but not a majority *of* votes. _____

8. The job has many *tangible* benefits for a young person. _____

9. The regulations were *too* **stringent** for the footloose, creative artist. _____

10. Did the Emancipation Proclamation *liberate* the slaves? _____

11. There was a jungle *near* the **junction** of the Brazilian highways. _____

12. Would you rather be **excluded** *from* the new group? _____

13. There was a decision to **secede** *from* the Union. _____

14. The Amazon has many **tributaries** flowing *into* it. _____

15. Don't **dignify** his unworthy question *with* an answer. _____

16. Your **lucid** remarks clarified the confusing issue *for* everyone. _____

17. The *eruption* of Vesuvius disrupted our celebration. _____

18. The man *beside* him was certainly no **ingrate**. _____

19. For Cicero, it was a **mediocre** speech, neither *excellent* nor poor. _____

20. The **translucent** material allowed us to see on its *other* side. _____

For each sentence below, identify the part of speech of the word in *italics*.

1.	His irrelevant comments were not **germane** *to* the discussion.	preposition
2.	The friendly alien proved to be *well-mannered* and **gregarious**.	adjective
3.	The mariner steered *through* beautiful **ultramarine** waters.	preposition
4.	The anthropologist loved ***primates***, most of the time.	noun
5.	The **pyromaniac** loved starting fires *with* pyrogenic materials.	preposition
6.	The loudmouth's ***clamorous*** cries could be heard for blocks.	adjective
7.	The candidate received a **plurality** but not a majority *of* votes.	preposition
8.	The job has many ***tangible*** benefits for a young person.	adjective
9.	The regulations were *too* **stringent** for the footloose, creative artist.	adverb
10.	Did the Emancipation Proclamation ***liberate*** the slaves?	verb
11.	There was a jungle *near* the **junction** of the Brazilian highways.	preposition
12.	Would you rather be **excluded** *from* the new group?	preposition
13.	There was a decision to **secede** *from* the Union.	preposition
14.	The Amazon has many **tributaries** flowing *into* it.	preposition
15.	Don't **dignify** his unworthy question *with* an answer.	preposition
16.	Your **lucid** remarks clarified the confusing issue *for* everyone.	preposition
17.	The ***eruption*** of Vesuvius disrupted our celebration.	noun
18.	The man *beside* him was certainly no **ingrate**.	preposition
19.	For Cicero, it was a **mediocre** speech, neither *excellent* nor poor.	adjective
20.	The **translucent** material allowed us to see on it's *other* side.	adjective

CONJUNCTION

**A word that joins two words
or two groups of words.**

Conjunctions conjoin: (conj.) A conjunction is a word that joins (*junct*) two words or two groups of words (such as two phrases or clauses) together (*con*). Hamlet *and* Ophelia were here *or* there, *but* we were *and* were not.

Coordinating conjunctions co-ordinate: Coordinating conjunctions join equals; they are conjunctions that *coordinate* (join two words or groups of words of similar (co) importance). It is essential that you have the coordinating conjunctions memorized, because you need to know them in order to identify and punctuate compound sentences. The coordinating conjunctions are *and*, *but*, *or*, *nor*, *for*, *so*, *yet*.

Subordinating conjunctions subordinate: Subordinating conjunctions join unequals; they are conjunctions that *subordinate*; they join something of lesser importance to something of greater importance. Examples: *if*, *as*, *since*, *when*, *because*, and many others.

I am **and** you are.
I am when you are.

Think of it this way: In engineering we draw designs for joining things together, but we can join them in different ways, and for different purposes. For example, we might use a fixed joint, or we might use a hinge. Either option gives us a joint, but they are not the same. Conjunctions are like this. A coordinating conjunction **co**-orders what it joins, and a subordinating conjunction **sub**-orders what it joins. A good example is the difference between a compound sentence joined by a coordinating conjunction and a complex sentence joined by a subordinating conjunction. In "Dickens had one idea, *and* his wife had another," both ideas are important, but in "Dickens went to America *when* he had the chance," the second idea only helps to support the first. In using conjunctions, it is necessary to use the right one, the one that agrees with the truth of the idea.

Correlative conjunctions: The correlative conjunctions are the multiple-word conjunctions, such as *either/or* and *neither/nor. Either* you *or* I will arrive.

Conjunctive adverbs: Conjunctive adverbs are conjunctions that act both as adverbs and as conjunctions. These include words that are commonly used to begin clauses, such as *however, furthermore, moreover, nevertheless, accordingly,* and *therefore.*

memorize
COORDINATING CONJUNCTIONS
and, but, or, nor, for, so, yet
SUBORDINATING CONJUNCTIONS
if, as, since, when, because, ...

FOUR-LEVEL ANALYSIS

From William Shakespeare's *Macbeth:*

	Fair	is	foul,	and	foul	is	fair.
Parts of Speech:	n.	v.	adj.	**conj.**	n.	v.	adj.
Parts of Sentence:	subject	pred.	subject complement		subject	pred.	subject complement
Phrases:	no prepositional, appositive, or verbal phrases						
Clauses:	----independent clause----				----independent clause----		
	two independent clauses, a compound declarative sentence						

This is an extraordinary sentence, dazzling in its elegance. The trick is that it is a mirrorlike compound, two sets of linking verb equations, with the subjects and subject complements reversing, which causes each to change part of speech!

For each sentence below, identify the part of speech of the word in italics. If it is a conjunction, identify the type.

1. Please **enumerate** *and* explain your reasons.   _____

2. Her character is one of great *personal* **fortitude**.   _____

3. The **osteologist** was called *in* for consultation or referral.   _____

4. **Ornithology** is a science *for* the bird lovers of the world.   _____

5. **Metropolitan** policy required the police to be polite *but* firm.   _____

6. The stubborn old man *refused* to have the blood **transfusion**.   _____

7. He was *not only* egocentric, *but also* an **egomaniac**.   _____

8. The *ancient* poet was **inspired** by the Muse of poetry.   _____

9. Ralph disputed the dialogue, *so* he received a **diatribe**.   _____

10. The **acrimonious** dispute was *disturbing* to everyone.   _____

11. The culprit was **exculpated** *and* escaped punishment.   _____

12. A **pachyderm** *rarely* suffers from dermatitis on its trunk.   _____

13. *When* it opens, will the zoo have a **protozoan** exhibit?   _____

14. The perforations let water **percolate** *and* pass through the membrane.   _____

15. The **pacifists** were not pacified *by* the militaristic speech.   _____

16. *Neither* **demagogues** *nor* pedagogues are to blame.   _____

17. *If* you have **necrophobia**, avoid the necropolis.   _____

18. *Since* you ask, the wealthy **urbanite** had urbane manners.   _____

19. *Because* he had a **pugnacious** attitude, he was repugnant to others.   _____

20. **Ectothermic** species *and* others enjoy the summer warmth.   _____

For each sentence below, identify the part of speech of the word in italics. If it is a conjunction, identify the type.

1. Please **enumerate** *and* explain your reasons.   conj., coordinating

2. Her character is one of great *personal* **fortitude**.   adjective

3. The **osteologist** was called *in* for consultation or referral.   adverb

4. **Ornithology** is a science *for* the bird lovers of the world.   preposition

5. **Metropolitan** policy required the police to be polite *but* firm.   conj. coordinating

6. The stubborn old man *refused* to have the blood **transfusion**.   verb

7. He was *not only* egocentric, *but also* an **egomaniac**.   conj. correlative

8. The *ancient* poet was **inspired** by the Muse of poetry.   adjective

9. Ralph disputed the dialogue, *so* he received a **diatribe**.   conj. coordinating

10. The **acrimonious** dispute was *disturbing* to everyone.   adjective

11. The culprit was **exculpated** *and* escaped punishment.   conj. coordinating

12. A **pachyderm** *rarely* suffers from dermatitis on its trunk.   adverb

13. *When* it opens, will the zoo have a **protozoan** exhibit?   conj. subordinating

14. The perforations let water **percolate** *and* pass through the membrane.   conj. coordinating

15. The **pacifists** were not pacified *by* the militaristic speech.   preposition

16. *Neither* **demagogues** *nor* pedagogues are to blame.   conj. correlative

17. *If* you have **necrophobia**, avoid the necropolis.   conj. subordinating

18. *Since* you ask, the wealthy **urbanite** had urbane manners.   conj. subordinating

19. *Because* he had a **pugnacious** attitude, he was repugnant to others.   conj. subordinating

20. **Ectothermic** species *and* others enjoy the summer warmth.   conj. coordinating

INTERJECTION

A word shows emotion but has no grammatical function.

Interjection: (interj.) An interjection is a word that shows emotion but has no grammatical purpose. In other words, interjections have no grammar tricks; they do not join, or modify, or show relationships, or replace; they just throw (ject) an exclamation into (inter) the sentence. Interjections are the **Batman words**—words that fill the pages of the action comic books. Examples of interjections are *oh*, *ugh*, *oof*, *wow*, *yes*, *no*, *oops*.

All of the other parts of speech participate in relationships with other parts of speech: a noun agrees with its verb, works with its replacement pronoun, or accepts the modification of its adjective; a verb has its subject and accepts the modification of its adverb; a conjunction joins its words or word groups; an adverb modifies another word. Only the interjection stands alone, thrown (ject) splat! into the sentence. It has less functionality than the other parts of speech, and in this sense the interjection has a certain primitive quality. Perhaps the very first word was an interjection: as the saber-tooth tiger bit the Neanderthal's foot, the Neanderthal might well have interjected, "Rahhrgghh!!" In the beautiful poem "Brown Penny," William Butler Yeats used the interjection *ah*: "Ah penny, brown penny, brown penny, / One cannot begin it too soon."

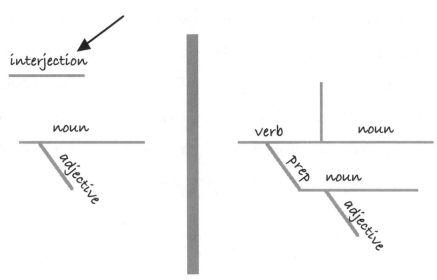

For each sentence, identify the part of speech of the word in italics.

1. *Yes*, his **sedentary** job left him weak and out of shape. _____

2. The *illegible* handwriting said, "Oh, I give up." _____

3. *Wow*, the bitter animosity made him lose his **equanimity**. _____

4. No, the *tortuous* highway was torture to drive. _____

5. Yep, NATO, RADAR, *SCUBA*, and OPEC are **acronyms**. _____

6. Gee, the principles of democracy are *sacrosanct*. _____

7. Why, the werewolf is famous for his *metamorphosis*. _____

8. *Wow*, the **Petrified** Forest is a desert? _____

9. *After* the surgery, it was a **miracle** to look in the mirror. _____

10. After the *manual* labor, she needed a **manicure**. _____

11. *Ugh*! Follow the **directions**, if you want correct answers. _____

12. Golly, the noisy crowd made *vociferous* objections. _____

13. *Dang*, the **demigod** drank from a dainty demitasse cup. _____

14. Fooey, the class reunion left me in a *retrospective* mood. _____

15. The explorer could **sense** the edge of the cliff. *Whew*! _____

16. Yeah, it is time to **solidify** the gains *we* have made. _____

17. *Nope*, primates are known for **binocular** vision. _____

18. Oh, the **curator** of the museum cared for the *Polynesian* artwork. _____

19. *Jeepers*, you like **ultramarine** more than ultraviolet? _____

20. *Well*, what does an **android** resemble? _____

For each sentence, identify the part of speech of the word in italics.

1. *Yes*, his **sedentary** job left him weak and out of shape.   interjection

2. The *illegible* handwriting said, "Oh, I give up."   adjective

3. *Wow*, the bitter animosity made him lose his **equanimity**.   interjection

4. No, the ***tortuous*** highway was torture to drive.   adjective

5. Yep, NATO, RADAR, *SCUBA*, and OPEC are **acronyms**.   noun

6. Gee, the principles of democracy are ***sacrosanct***.   adjective

7. Why, the werewolf is famous for his ***metamorphosis***.   noun

8. *Wow*, the **Petrified** Forest is a desert?   interjection

9. *After* the surgery, it was a **miracle** to look in the mirror.   conjunction

10. After the *manual* labor, she needed a **manicure**.   adjective

11. *Ugh*! Follow the **directions**, if you want correct answers.   interjection

12. Golly, the noisy crowd made ***vociferous*** objections.   adjective

13. *Dang*, the **demigod** drank from a dainty demitasse cup.   adjective

14. Fooey, the class reunion left me in a ***retrospective*** mood.   adjective

15. The explorer could **sense** the edge of the cliff. *Whew*!   interjection

16. Yeah, it is time to **solidify** the gains *we* have made.   pronoun

17. *Nope*, primates are known for **binocular** vision.   interjection

18. Oh, the **curator** of the museum cared for the *Polynesian* artwork.   adjective

19. *Jeepers*, you like **ultramarine** more than ultraviolet?   interjection

20. *Well*, what does an **android** resemble?   interjection

Parts of Speech: an easy system:

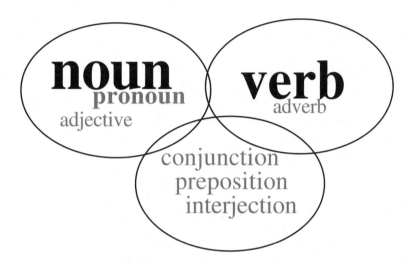

    The Parts of Speech, A Fond Reprise: In other words (be alert, 'cause I'm going to go fast), **nouns** *name* things; **pronouns** make language *fast*; **verbs** make *events and equations;* **adjectives and adverbs** adjust nouns and verbs; **prepositions** show physics and 3-Dness, **conjunctions** connect; and **interjections** insert emotional excitement.

GoBack definitions
Level I
Parts of Speech

It is essential to memorize the major definitions in grammar. GoBack is a memorization game; the teacher asks students definitions, and when someone misses one, you have to go back to the beginning! For purposes of consistency when playing GoBack, you can use these definitions for some of the major terms in the **parts of speech**.

Grammar: a way of thinking about language

The **four levels** of traditional grammar: parts of speech, parts of sentence, phrases, clauses

Parts of speech: the eight kinds of words in English

Noun: the name of a person, place, or thing

Pronoun: a word that takes the place of a noun.

Subject pronouns: pronouns used for subjects of verbs and subject complements

List the subject pronouns: I, you, he, she, it, we, you, they

Object pronouns: pronouns used as direct or indirect objects, and objects of prepositions

List the object pronouns: me, you, him, her, it, us, you, them

Adjective: a word that modifies a noun or pronoun

Article: the three adjectives, *a, an,* and *the*

Definite article: the adjective *the*

Indefinite articles: the adjectives *a* and *an*

Three degrees of adjectives: positive, comparative, superlative

Verb: a word that shows action, being, or links a subject to its subject complement

Conjunction: a word that joins two words or two groups of words

List all the coordinating conjunctions: and, but, or, nor, for, so, yet

List a few subordinating conjunctions: if, as, since, when, because...

The correlative conjunctions: either or, neither nor, not only but also

Preposition: shows the relationship between its object and another word in the sentence

Interjection: shows emotion but has no grammatical function

2

parts of speech

parts of the sentence

phrases

clauses

Sentences do not occur in nature.

SENTENCE

**A group of words that contains
a subject and its predicate,
and makes a complete thought.**

Etymology of *sentence*: The word *sentence* comes from the Latin *sententia*, meaning "way of thinking," or "opinion." That is appropriate because the sentence is the structure with which we think about and communicate opinions and ideas.

Sentence: A sentence is a two-part thought: it is a group of words that contains a **predicate** about a **subject**, and that makes a complete thought. In other words, a sentence is an idea. "Ishmael watched" is a sentence, but "If Ishmael watched" is not a sentence because we are still waiting for the thought to be completed. If Ishmael watched, then what?

Parts of the Sentence: When we study the parts of the sentence, we are studying the structure of thought itself. Sentences do not occur in nature; they are thought, expressed. Hidden in the sentence is thought's secret pattern, and understanding this pattern gives us insight into the nature of clarity. In fact, understanding how sentences are thoughts can give us insight into several different levels of clarity, including clarity of sentence, clarity of paragraph, and clarity of thesis. What is this secret pattern? It is an elegant one: *in order to say anything clearly, we must say two things*. First, we must say what we are talking about, and second, we must say what we are saying about it. Each thought must have these two things.

2

Sentence as paradigm of the mind: This structure of the sentence shows us a mirror image of our own mind. The sentence, our common one-two structure for building thoughts, gives the mind just what it wants most: a two-piece idea. The two pieces are:

one | two
subject | predicate
what we're **talking** about | what we're **saying** about it

The person to whom we are talking needs to know **both**, and if either is absent, unclear, or otherwise disrupted, then we fail to communicate. The sentence is not an extra-human phenomenon of the world, it is made by the mind, it is an extension of the mind itself. In the sentence the mind extends itself out to the world, like an amoeba extending a pseudopod. The sentence is the mind, in language. So we can see the sentence both as a model of how the mind designs its own ideas for transmitting, and we can also see the sentence as a model of how we should write and speak if we want to be understood.

The sentence *is* the mind, in language.

From William Shakespeare's *Julius Caesar:*

	Cassius	is	aweary	of	the	world.
Parts of Speech:	n.	v.	adj.	prep.	adj.	n.
Parts of Sentence:	subject	pred.	subject complement			
Phrases:				-prepositional phrase-		
Clauses:	one independent clause, a simple declarative sentence					

This sentence from *Julius Caesar*, like all others, is a two-part thought. The first part is the subject, the one word, *Cassius*. The predicate gives us five words about the subject, and from the predicate we learn that Cassius *is aweary of the world*.

Clarity at all levels: This binary form must shape all levels of communication, not just the sentence level. We must know what this **sentence** is about, and what we are saying about it. We must know what this **paragraph** is about, and what we are saying about it. And we must know what this **essay** is about, and what we are saying about it. If the subject or the predicate component is damaged or missing at any of these levels, then one's communication to the other person fails.

SUBJECT

The noun or subject pronoun that the sentence is about.

Subject: (subj.) The **simple subject** of the sentence is the noun or subject pronoun that the sentence is about. *Wittgenstein* wrote *The Tractatus*. The **complete subject** includes the simple subject and all of its modifiers. *The perspicacious pundit, John Leonard,* excoriated the turgid movie's turbid script. Notice that only subject pronouns (*I, you, he, she, it, we, you, they*) can be sentence subjects. Remember the pronoun rule: a subject is a subject and an object is an object! *He and I* entered the competition.

Compound subject: A compound subject is a double subject: more than one noun or pronoun used as a double subject of the same clause: *Physics and astronomy* are my favorite subjects. *Einstein and Bohr* debated the quantum theory. A compound subject joined by the coordinating conjunction *and* is considered plural, and must take a plural verb. Jim *and* John *are* here. A compound subject joined by the coordinating conjunction *or* is singular. Jim *or* John *is* here. He *or* she *has* a duck, but he *and* she *have* a lion. Notice how logical this is: if Bach *and* Beethoven wrote symphonies, then two composers wrote, but if Bach *or* Beethoven wrote the *Eroica*, then only one composer wrote it. *And* really is a plural compound, and *or* really is a singular compound. Grammar is logical.

The verb and other words
that are about the subject.

Predicate: The predicate is the side of the sentence that says something about the subject. The **simple predicate** is the verb: Hamlet *went* over to the crater at the foot of the escarpment. The **complete predicate** is everything that is said about the subject: Hamlet *went to the crater and gathered three bags of comet dust.*

Compound verb: The subject of a sentence may take a compound verb as its predicate. William Blake's famous interrogative complex sentence, in his poem about the tiger, contains a compound verb in the dependent clause: "When the stars threw down their spears / And watered heaven with their tears: / Did He smile His work to see?" The subject *stars* has *threw and watered* as its compound verb. Note Blake's eccentric use of the colon after his dependent clause.

Subject/predicate set: The subject/predicate set is the simple combination of simple subject and simple predicate that is *always present as a nucleus in every idea*, in every sentence and in every clause. The sentence or clause may contain more than the subject/predicate set, but it will certainly contain that much. The sentence, remember, is therefore our model of clarity, our model of clear thought. With its subject/predicate set nucleus, the *sentence is a mind-made model of the mind.* In Charles Dickens's famous first sentence to his novel of the French Revolution, *A Tale of Two Cities*, there are sixteen clauses, each with its own subject/predicate set!

It was the best of times, it was the worst of times, it was the age of wisdom, it was the age of foolishness, it was the epoch of belief, it was the epoch of incredulity, it was the season of Light, it was the season of Darkness, it was the spring of hope, it was the winter of despair, we had everything before us, we had nothing before us, we were all going direct to Heaven, we were all going direct the other way—in short, the period was so far like the present period, that some of its noisiest authorities insisted on its being received, for good or for evil, in the superlative degree of comparison only.

- Charles Dickens, *A Tale of Two Cities*

Ideas have number. The formal logic of every idea begins with subject/verb agreement. Every sentence is either about something—or about some things! Do you remember that verbs have **number**, that they can be either singular or plural? Well, nouns and pronouns also have number, and will also be either singular or plural. In a sentence, a plural subject must be accompanied by a likewise plural verb (genes transmute), and a singular subject must be accompanied by a likewise singular verb (gene transmutes), or else there is a contradiction (genes transmutes). Both verb and subject indicate number; they express that the sentence is either a thought about something singular, or else it is a thought about something plural. It cannot logically be both. The subject should not tell you that the sentence is about something singular if the verb tells you that the sentence is about something plural. **The number of the subject must equal the number of the predicate**. In other words, you never want the subject and the verb to disagree about whether the subject is singular or plural, even if other distracting and confusing words or phrases come between the subject and its verb. In the following correct sentence, notice how the singular subject and its singular verb agree, ignoring the intervening prepositional phrase: The *top* of the mountains *is* covered by rainbows.

Español: In Spanish every sentence has a subject/predicate set, but the subject and its predicate will often be one verb! Of course in English we can have a one-word imperative sentence, such as "Jump!" But the English sentence gives little information about the subject. English verbs do not vary through conjugations significantly: I jump, you jump, he she or it jumps, we jump, you jump, they jump. In Spanish on the other hand, *each person of the verb is different*, and so the verb includes the subject! The Spanish verb *tener* means to have:

tengo, I have	**tenemos**, we have
tienes, you have	**teneis** you have
tiene, he/she/it has	**tienen**, they have

So whereas in English we could never say, "Has a book," because that would be a sentence **fragment** lacking a subject, in Spanish we can say "Tiene un libro," and the verb will stand alone as a combination subject-predicate! This inclusion of subjects within verbs gives Spanish efficiency and a possibility for emphasis by including a separate pronoun.

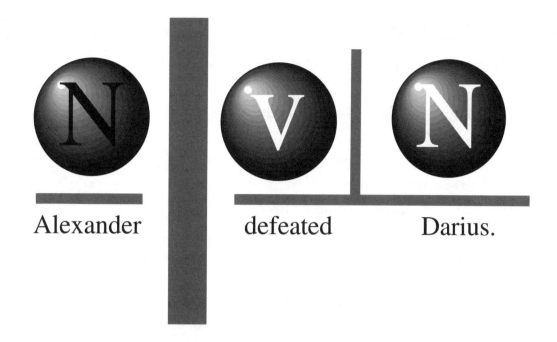

Alexander   defeated   Darius.

DIRECT OBJECT

A noun or object pronoun that receives the action of the action verb.

     Direct object: A direct object is a noun or **object** pronoun (*me, you, him, her, it, us, you, them*) that receives the action of the action verb. When there is a direct object, we call the action verb **transitive**; when the action verb does act on a direct object, we call the action verb **intransitive**. Only action verbs can be transitive or intransitive; linking verbs are neither. Notice that subject pronouns may not be used as direct objects, because a subject is a subject. Only an object is an object. The direct object is the object of direct action. We hold these *truths* to be self-evident.

FOUR-LEVEL ANALYSIS

From Marjorie Kinnan Rawlings's *The Yearling:*

	The	sand	burned	his	bare	calloused	soles.
Parts of Speech:	adj.	n.	v.	pron.	adj.	adj.	n.
Parts of Sentence:		subject	predicate				direct object
Phrases:			no prepositional, appositive, or verbal phrases				
Clauses:			one independent clause, a simple declarative sentence				

From William Shakespeare's *The Taming of the Shrew:*

	Where	did	you	study	all	this	goodly	speech?
Parts of Speech:	adv	v.	pron	v.	adj.	adj.	adj.	n.
Parts of Sentence:	pred.		subject	pred.				direct object
Phrases:	no prepositional, appositive, or verbal phrases							
Clauses:	one independent clause, a simple interrogative sentence							

Here is a fun sentence by William Shakespeare. In Kate's sentence, the subject splits the predicate's helping verb from its main verb, and the direct object is modified by a cascade of adjectives.

Be sure to focus closely on the difference between the direct object and the subject complement, which we will study in a few pages. You need to be able to see, instantly, that your sentence is either an action verb sentence that might have a direct object, or a linking verb sentence that might have a subject complement.

In your mind, keep those two pairs memorized: action verbs with direct objects, and linking verbs with subject complements. The importance of these two pairs will be increasingly clear to you as we learn more.

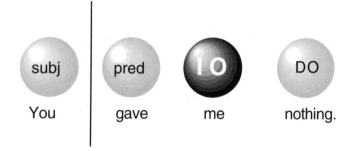

subj   pred   IO   DO

You   gave   me   nothing.

INDIRECT OBJECT

A noun or object pronoun that is indirectly affected by the action verb, and that is located between the action verb and the direct object.

Indirect object: An indirect object is a noun or **object** pronoun located between the action verb and the direct object. The structure is S—AV—**IO**—DO. The indirect object is indirectly affected by the action verb's action on the direct object. Notice that if there is an indirect object, there must be a direct object, and so the action verb is still transitive. We gave *him* the business. Heisenberg gave modern *physics* the Uncertainty Principle.

We use the indirect object as an alternative to using a prepositional phrase. We can either say "The forest brigade gave an ultimatum to the rebels," or we can use the indirect object instead: "The forest brigade gave the rebels an ultimatum."

FOUR-LEVEL ANALYSIS

From William Shakespeare's *Hamlet:*

	I	never	gave	you	aught.
Parts of Speech:	pron.	adv.	v.	pron.	n.
Parts of Sentence:	subject		action v predicate	indirect object	direct object
Phrases:	no prepositional, appositive, or verbal phrases				
Clauses:	one independent clause, a simple declarative sentence				

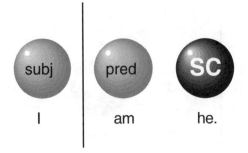

subj | pred | SC
I | am | he.

SUBJECT COMPLEMENT

A noun, subject pronoun, or adjective that is linked to the subject by a linking verb and tells more about the subject.

Subject complement: A subject complement a noun, subject pronoun, or adjective that complements the subject; it is linked to the subject by a linking verb. The subject complement, in a sense, renames the subject. Gauguin was Van Gogh's *friend*. Notice that the subject complement does precisely what its name implies; it complements (completes) the subject because it makes our knowledge of the subject more complete than it would otherwise have been. Note that only a subject pronoun can be a subject complement, because a *subject is a subject*.

To compliment someone is to praise him or her; to complement something is to complete it, as the subject complement completes the subject.

FOUR-LEVEL ANALYSIS

From William Shakespeare's *Julius Caesar:*

	It	was	Greek	to	me.
Parts of Speech:	pron.	v.	n.	prep.	pron.
Parts of Sentence:	subject	predicate	subject complement		
Phrases:				-prepositional phrase-	
Clauses:	one independent clause, a simple declarative sentence				

This is uttered by Casca in Act I, ii. The linking verb is the basis of the equation.

complement

Predicate nominative: *A predicate nominative* is a subject complement that is a noun or subject pronoun. It was *she and I* who came to visit. It is *I*, Hamlet.

Predicate adjective: *Predicate adjective* is a term sometimes used to describe a subject complement made out of an adjective. I am *sleepy*.

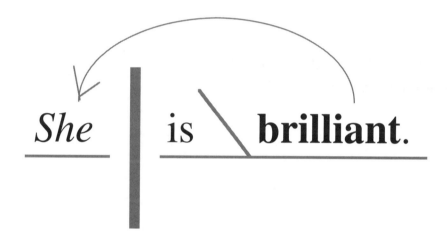

Why call them "subject complements"?: I call predicate adjectives and predicate nominatives *subject complements* because it allows me to explain pronoun usage so easily. I can say that anything called a **subject** takes a subject pronoun, and anything called an **object** takes an object pronoun. **A subject is a subject and an object is an object**. This seems to illustrate the simple truth of pronoun usage. Subjects of verbs and subject complements take subject pronouns.

Object complement: An object complement is a noun, object pronoun, or adjective that completes the meaning of the direct object. They elected him *president*. They painted the house *blue*.

The Boolean (If, then) logic of sentence analysis: When you analyze the parts of a clause, begin by looking for a one-two thought: a subject/predicate set. Find the subject and its verb. Is the verb action or linking? **If it's an action verb**, **then** there might be a direct object. If there is a direct object, then look between the direct object and the action verb for an indirect object. **If it's a linking verb**, **then** there might be a subject complement. Once you have completed the clause, go to the next clause and repeat the process. Everything hinges on whether the verb is action or linking.

Find the subject/predicate set.

Is the verb ACTION or LINKING?

> **If** the verb is *action*, **then**
> > Do not look for a subject complement.
> > Look for a direct object.
> > **If** you find a direct object, **then**
> > > Look for an indirect object.

> **If** the verb is *linking*, **then**
> > Do not look for a direct object.
> > Look for a subject complement.

Look for the next subject/predicate set and repeat.

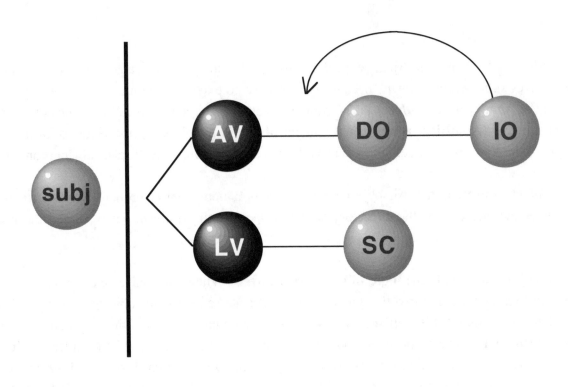

Wuthering Direct Objects, and Wuthering Subject Complements: Look at this quotation from Emily Brontë's *Wuthering Heights*, and study the direct objects, which are in bold, and the subject complements, which are circled. See how the direct objects switch pronouns to object case? See that the first subject complement is a predicate nominative, and the second one is a predicate adjective? Can you see how direct objects only go with action verbs, and subject complements only go with linking verbs? Do you realize that you yourself make direct objects, indirect objects, and subject complements all day long, in everything you say and write?

Possibly, some people might suspect **him** of a degree of underbred pride; I have a sympathetic **chord** within that tells **me** it is nothing of the sort; I know, by instinct, his reserve springs from an aversion to showy displays of feeling—to manifestations of mutual kindliness....I bestow my own **attributes** over liberally on him. Mr. Heathcliff may have entirely dissimilar **reasons** for keeping his hand out of the way when he meets a would-be **acquaintance**, to those which actuate **me**. Let me hope my constitution is almost peculiar.

Now that you understand the parts of the sentence, go back to the parts of speech section and review pronoun usage!

In these sentences, each word in **bold** contains important Latin or Greek stems. First, identify the part of speech of the bold word, then identify the part of sentence of the word in italics, using the following abbreviations: subject, subj.; predicate, pred.; direct object, D.O., indirect object, I.O.; and subject complement, S.C. Your blank might look like: ___adv. D.O.___

1. The **pathetic** creature received *sympathy*.   _____

2. The unexpected **anomaly** was *amorphous* in shape.   _____

3. This is the *difference* between **astronomy** and agronomy?   _____

4. Does a **diffident** person have *self-confidence*?   _____

5. Does **cacophony** hurt the *ear*?   _____

6. The **heterogeneous** mixture had a noisome *odor*.   _____

7. Should *science* give us **prescience**?   _____

8. Would you like a *photograph* of my **autograph**?   _____

9. Is this treaty **bilateral** or *multilateral*?   _____

10. The shiny red **tractor** attracted many *buyers*.   _____

11. Please **inscribe** *something* insane in my annual.   _____

12. *He* refused **to cooperate** with the copilot.   _____

13. The **audiophile** has a wonderful *collection* of recordings.   _____

14. The **crystalline** *substance* began to evaporate.   _____

15. Did the **neolithic** *age* come before the paleolithic age?   _____

16. Can you find a *hexagram* and a **hexagon**?   _____

17. It's an ***infraction*** of the rules to fracture someone's nose. _____

18. The **platypus** has a plate-like *bill*.   _____

19. The Greek **pantheon** of gods was not *monotheistic*.   _____

20. Can an ambulatory hospital *patient* **somnambulate**?   _____

In these sentences, each word in **bold** contains important Latin or Greek stems. First, identify the part of speech of the bold word, then identify the part of sentence of the word in italics, using the following abbreviations: subject, subj.; predicate, pred.; direct object, D.O.; indirect object, I.O.; and subject complement, S.C. Your blank might look like: ___adv.   D.O.___

1.	The **pathetic** creature received *sympathy*.	adjective, D.O
2.	The unexpected **anomaly** was *amorphous* in shape.	noun, S.C
3.	This is the *difference* between **astronomy** and agronomy?	noun, S.C.
4.	Does a **diffident** person have *self-confidence*?	adjective, D.O.
5.	Does **cacophony** hurt the *ear*?	noun, D.O.
6.	The **heterogeneous** mixture had a noisome *odor*.	adjective, D.O.
7.	Should *science* give us **prescience**?	noun, D.O.
8.	Would you like a *photograph* of my **autograph**?	noun, D.O.
9.	Is this treaty **bilateral** or *multilateral*?	adjective, S.C.
10.	The shiny red **tractor** attracted many *buyers*.	noun, D.O.
11.	Please **inscribe** *something* insane in my annual.	verb, D.O.
12.	*He* refused **to cooperate** with the copilot.	noun, subj.
13.	The **audiophile** has a wonderful *collection* of recordings.	noun, D.O.
14.	The **crystalline** *substance* began to evaporate.	adjective, subj.
15.	Did the **neolithic** *age* come before the paleolithic age?	adjective, subj.
16.	Can you find a *hexagram* and a **hexagon**?	noun, D.O.
17.	It's an ***infraction*** of the rules to fracture someone's nose.	noun, S.C.
18.	The **platypus** has a plate-like *bill*.	noun, D.O.
19.	The Greek **pantheon** of gods was not *monotheistic*.	noun, S.C.
20.	Can an ambulatory hospital *patient* **somnambulate**?	verb, subj.

GoBack definitions
Level II
Parts of Sentence

For purposes of consistency when playing **GoBack**, you can use these definitions for some of the major terms in the parts of sentence. Be sure to review the **GoBack** definitions from the Parts of Speech, because the game will be cumulative.

Sentence: a group of words that has a subject and its predicate, and makes a complete thought

Fragment: an incomplete thought

Subject: the noun or subject pronoun that the sentence is about.

Predicate: the simple predicate is the verb.

Direct object: The noun or object pronoun that receives the action of the action verb.

Indirect object: The noun or object pronoun between the action verb and the direct object, that is indirectly affected by the action

Subject complement: The noun, subject pronoun, or adjective, that is linked to the subject by a linking verb, and that tells more about the subject.

Predicate nominative: A subject complement that is a noun or pronoun.

Predicate adjective: A subject complement that is an adjective.

3

parts of speech

---

parts of the sentence

---

phrases

---

clauses

The birds flew over the green treetops.

Phrase: A phrase is like a flying formation of birds: it is something made of some things. It is a part of speech made of some words. A phrase is not a complete idea, because it is *a group of words that contains no subject/predicate set and that only acts as a single part of speech*.

We might use a simple adjective in a sentence, or we might use a prepositional phrase instead, or we might use a participle phrase instead. The prepositional and participle phrases give us ways to make the adjective idea more elaborate, more developed.

A government
of the people,
by the people,
and for the people...

Difference between phrase and clause: Both phrases and clauses are groups of words, but a clause contains both a subject and its predicate, and a phrase does not. *I jumped* is a clause; *in the boat* is only a phrase. Phrases are found inside clauses; they are part of clauses.

Clauses have **subjects and predicates**.
Phrases **don't**.

67

Appositive phrase: An appositive is an interrupting definition. Typically, an appositive defines a noun, and thus forms an adjective. It is called an *appositive* because it is put (pos) beside (ap) what it defines. It is apposed. The idea of an appositive is, "WE INTERRUPT THIS SENTENCE TO BRING YOU A DEFINITION." An appositive may consist of only one word, or it may consist of an entire phrase. We usually enclose appositives and appositive phrases in commas, unless they are exceptionally short and clear by themselves:

Botticelli**,** **the Renaissance painter,** painted angels.

My friend **Hamlet** is a woodworking artist.

We always enclose **appositive states** and **appositive years** in commas

Athens**,** **Greece,** is the site of the Parthenon.

June 20**,** **1997,** is the date of departure.

Two commas: Notice that we put commas before **and after** appositives. Don't forget the second appositive commas, or you wind up with catastrophes in which the appositive becomes the subject of the verb, and the subject often becomes a noun of direct address! The result is ridiculous: Botticelli, the Renaissance painter painted angels. Appositives take two commas or none, unless the appositive is at the end of the sentence: I went to see the dancer, Gelsey Kirkland. The comma can make all the difference in the meaning of the sentence:

Botticelli**,** the Renaissance painter painted angels.

Botticelli**,** the Renaissance painter**,** painted angels.

Prepositional phrase: A prepositional phrase begins with a preposition (in the PRE position) and concludes with the **object of the preposition**. The preposition relates its object to another word in the sentence. If I say *the dog in the boat*, the preposition *in* shows a spatial relationship between its object *boat* and the noun *dog*. Prepositional phrases behave as modifiers; that is, they act like big adjectives or big adverbs. In the sentence, *The dog in the boat barked*, the prepositional phrase *in the boat* acts as an adjective to modify the noun *dog*.

The object of the preposition: The object of the preposition must be a noun or *object* pronoun (*me, you, him, her, it, us, you, them*). A subject is a subject and an object is an object. It is correct to say, "This is a present for you and me," but it is wrong to say "This is a present for you and I." Notice the object pronouns in the following correct prepositional phrases:

This letter is *for him and me.*
She and I went *with you and him.*
I asked a question *about her and us.*

There is no subject of preposition! It is not unusual for someone to make the mistake of using subject pronouns as objects of prepositions, especially when the object of preposition is compound. And so someone who would never say, "This remuneration is for I" will mysteriously and ridiculously say "This remuneration is for you and I." But we should always say for *me*: "This remuneration is for you and me" is correct grammar. An object is an object, period. Only object pronouns may be used as objects of prepositions, compounds notwithstanding.

She wrote this poem **for** you and **I**.

She wrote this poem **for** you and **me**.

Adjective prepositional phrases: Prepositional phrases that modify nouns or pronouns should be placed immediately after the noun or pronoun they modify. Otherwise, the phrase will be understood to modify the verb. Think through the logic of the following sentence: "On the beach, the dog barked at the **dog** *in the boat*." In "Hokku Poems" Richard Wright wrote, "With a twitching nose / A dog reads a telegram / On a wet tree trunk." Notice that this principle of placement means that no prepositional phrase at the beginning of a sentence can possibly modify a noun or pronoun.

mm

Misplaced modifiers: The **mm** proofreader's mark indicates a misplaced modifier, a serious error in grammar. Adjectives, adverbs, prepositional and participle phrases, and even clauses that act as modifiers must be placed next to or as close as possible to the things they modify. If we put the modifier by something else, it will modify something else. The result is often nonsense.

While Isaac **Denisen was chewing her gum,** a fly flew by.

While **chewing her gum, a fly** flew by.

Some more examples: If you say that "In an effort to be modest, Whitman's first edition of poetry lacked his name," that means that the *book* was being modest—a ridiculous idea. To correct the modification error, place the modifier next to the word you really intend to modify: "In an effort to be **modest, Whitman** omitted his name from the first edition of his poetry." The sentence, "An idealist, most of Plato's ideas are only ideals" means that ideas are idealists! Better would have been, "An idealist, Plato regarded his ideas as ideals." "Feeling alone and desperate, this was one of Dinesen's last letters" means that a letter felt desperate. Correct would have been, "Feeling alone and desperate, Dinesen wrote one of her last letters." If you say, "Whitman got to know omnibus drivers and ferryboat pilots at an early age," this could mean that he met very young drivers and pilots. If you put the modifier where it belongs, you get, "At an early age, Whitman got to know omnibus drivers and ferryboat pilots." Modifiers are like lights; they illuminate *things next to them*, and so you have to move them next to their intended targets:

VERBAL

A verb form used as a different part of speech.

Verbal phrase: A verbal is not a verb; it is a former verb now doing something else. Gerunds, participles, and infinitives are the three kinds of verbals. **Gerunds are nouns** (made of verbs); **participles are adjectives** (made of verbs); and **infinitives are nouns or modifiers** (made of verbs). In other words, when we change a verb into a different part of speech, we call it a *verbal*. Verbals are nouns, adjectives, or adverbs made out of verbs.

A verbal can be a single word, or it can join other words to become a phrase. As an example, if I take the verb *was thinking*, and saw off the helping verb *was* so that I only have *thinking* left, I can use this ex-verb as a noun! I can say, *"Thinking is my favorite behavior."* In that sentence, the subject *Thinking* is a verbal, a gerund. It is not yet a verbal phrase. I can make it a verbal phrase by adding words to it: *"Rapidly thinking thoughts is my favorite behavior."*

Why verbals are fun: Verbals are fun because they are so creative and energetic. We begin with verbs, and then we make nouns out of them, we make adjectives out of them, we make adverbs out of them, we saw off their helping verbs, and we devise quick ways to express things that would otherwise take paragraphs. Verbals are *not verbs* in sentences, they are ex-verbs, but they still have a verby quality, a verbiness, which gives them energy and force. With verbals, strange things can happen! Verbals are still verby enough that they can even have their own objects, even when they are being used as nouns! Example: *Brushing his face* was the Bigfoot's hobby. This gerund phrase *Brushing his face* is the subject of the sentence! Notice that *face* is the object of the noun/gerund *Brushing*!

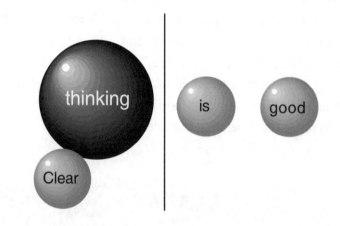

GERUND

A noun made from an -ing verb.

Gerund phrase: A gerund is a **noun** made out of an -ing verb, **or**, an -ing verb made into a noun. (Two ways of saying the same thing.) All kinds of **subjects and objects may be made out of gerunds** or gerund phrases. A gerund might be by itself, or it might join with other words to make a gerund phrase. *Thinking* is fun. *Thinking quickly* is fun. I quit *joking*.

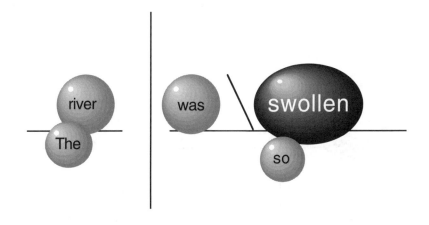

PARTICIPLE

An adjective made out of a verb.

Participle phrase: A participle is an **adjective** made out of a verb, **or**, an -ing, -ed, or -en verb made into an adjective. (Two ways of saying the same thing.) Participles always act as adjectives to modify nouns or pronouns. A participle might be by itself, or it might join with other words to make a participle phrase. In the model above, the partciple *swollen* is the subject complement, and since it is modified by an adverb, it is a participle phrase. In *The Wind in the Willows*, Kenneth Graham describes "the swollen river"; do you see the participle in that sentence? Is it a participle phrase? Yeats used participles in his poem "The Second Coming": "Turning and turning in the widening gyre / The falcon cannot hear the falconer." Look at this sentence from *The Wind in the Willows*, and see how many participles you can find:

Never in his life had he seen a river before—this sleek, sinuous, full-bodied animal, chasing and chuckling, gripping things with a gurgle and leaving them with a laugh, to fling itself on fresh playmates that shook themselves free, and were caught and held again.

- Kenneth Grahame, *The Wind in the Willows*

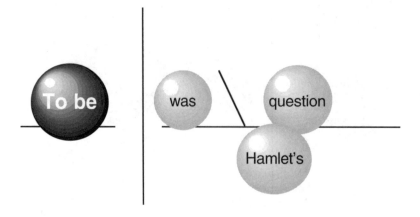

INFINITIVE

A noun or modifier
made from the to- form of the verb.

Infinitive phrase: An infinitive is a general form of the verb made into a **noun**, **adjective**, or **adverb**. This general form of the verb is usually expressed by beginning with the word *to*: to think, to dream, to snorkle, to excoriate. The infinitive is named for the fact that it is not (in) limited (fin) in tense/time. Since the infinitive is not limited to a tense, it is never used as a true predicate; we do not say, for example, "I to go home." Examples of infinitives include: *To think* is a pleasure. (noun) The philosopher *to read* is Plato. (adjective) He lives *to fish*. (adverb) To be is the question.

To be or not to be = 4 words!

To Think **is one word:** We think of an infinitive as *one word*. In our four-level analysis, the infinitive *to wander* is a single word, whereas a prepositional phrase like *to Boston* is two words.

Since an infinitive is only one word, it is best to word your sentences as to **avoid split infinitives**. Splitting an infinitive means inserting an adverb between the two words of the infinitive. If we take the infinitive *to see*, and split it with the adverb *vividly*, we have *to vividly see*, which is a split infinitive. It is better to put the adverb after the infinitive: to see vividly.

Split infinitives are hard **to ~~really~~ understand**.

The anomalous infinitive clause: Here is an exception to our "a subject is a subject and an object is an object" rule. It is also an exception to the idea that all predicates must have tense. This structure is known as the *infinitive clause*. It is actually possible for an infinitive to act as the predicate of an object pronoun, even though only subject pronouns usually take predicates! An example of an infinitive clause would be, "We wanted him to eat fish." In this sentence, the word *him* has to serve two purposes; it is the direct object of the main clause, and it is also the subject of the infinitive clause. In other words, when it comes to a showdown over who controls the case of the pronoun, the main clause wins; it overrules the infinitive clause. So really, this exception to the pronoun rule is logical. The infinitive clause gives us an outstanding example of the powerful flexibility and creativity that occurs in language.

A Question: Since infinitives can be either nouns or modifiers, can you think of a way to modify an infinitive with an infinitive?

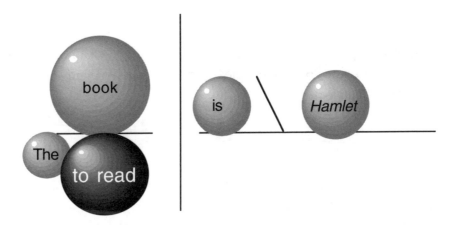

An infinitive can be an adjective. Here it modifies the subject.

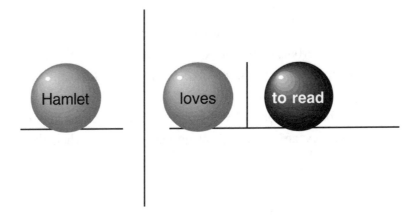

An infinitive can be a noun. Here it is the direct object.

Summary of Phrases

Prepositional phases are modifiers. They act like adjectives or adverbs. The adjective kind has to follow immediately the noun it modifies. We put a comma after multiple introductory prepositional phrases, but not after a single short one. Example: The philosopher *with the hemlock* did not feel thirsty.

• • •

Appositive phrases are interrupting definitions, and so the are adjectives. They take two commas or none. Example: Socrates, *the interrogative philosopher*, decided to drink the hemlock.

• • •

Verbal phrases are based on verbs that have been adapted to become other parts of speech.

• **Participles** are verbals that act as adjectives. They can end in various verby endings, but they will always be modifying a noun or pronoun. Example: *Shaking* fearfully, the frightened creature looked at the door.

• **Infinitives** are verbals that are nouns or modifiers and that begin with *to*, although sometimes the *to* is only understood to be there. Example: *To think* is fun.

• **Gerunds** are verbals ending in -ing and acting as nouns. A gerund can be the subject of a sentence or the direct object—anything that any noun can be. Example: *Thinking* is fun.

All of the verbals can appear by themselves in a sentence; they only become verbal *phrases* when they are modified by another word or when they have their own object.

From Robert Louis Stevenson's *Treasure Island:*

	The	figure	reappeared	and	began	to head	me	off.
Parts of Speech:	adj.	n.	v.	conj.	v.	----n.----	pron.	adv.
Parts of Sentence:		subject	--------compound predicate--------			------direct object ------		
Phrases:						----infinitive phrase----		
Clauses:		one independent clause, a simple declarative sentence						

This sentence, which has been shortened for brevity, is from *Treasure Island*. It has a nice compound verb as a predicate and also a beautiful infinitive phrase that serves as the direct object of the second verb. Notice that the infinitive, though it is a noun in the sentence, is still verby enough to have its own object, me, and to be modified by an adverb! So here, incredibly, we have a noun modified by an adverb!

Appositive phrase vs. parenthetical remark vs. nonessential clause vs. sharp break in thought: Students are often confused about how certain kinds of sentence interrupters differ from each other. Though each of these elements could be said to interrupt the sentence, they differ in other ways:

An **appositive phrase** is a *definition* inserted into a sentence: Smee, the rascally pirate, needs a mother.

A **parenthetical remark** is not a definition but a related comment or aside inserted into a sentence: Pirate Smee (How did *he* get into Neverland?) needs a mother.

A **nonessential clause** (See clause discussion below) is an adjective clause beginning with a relative pronoun: Pirate Smee, who probably needs a mother, is Hook's toady.

A **sharp break in thought** is one so unrelated to the sentence that you separate it with dashes: Pirate Smee—Get that alligator off my foot!—needs a mother.

For each of these sentences, first identify the part of speech of the word in **bold**, then identify the kind of phrase that is in italics.

1. The **orthopedist** went *on an expedition*. _____

2. Dr. Garcia, *the new mortician*, was **mortified** at the wound. _____

3. The **carnivorous** beasts *of the plains* lived well. _____

4. The **psychologist** viewed the parapsychologist *with suspicion*. _____

5. *Contradicting democratic philosophy,* **Ethnocentrism** injures all. _____

6. The geneticist's hobby was *to study **pathogenic** substances*. _____

7. **Prenatal** care is important *to those in natural environments*. _____

8. The **paleontologist** was an expert *on the Paleozoic era*. _____

9. To talk glibly gives only **cursory** attention *to the problem*. _____

10. The **cryptologist** worked all night *to break the enemy code*. _____

11. *Cracked lengthwise,* the object was discovered near the **cascade**. _____

12. *Decapitating criminals* was once a common form of punishment. _____

13. The **loquacious** bore answered *with a circumlocution*. _____

14. *From the beginning* the hero's sacrifice was a **sacrosanct** memory. _____

15. The **United** Planets soon celebrate *forming their union*. _____

16. The sky's **redness** streamed high *over the Himalayas*. _____

17. The **altimeter**, *rusted shut*, no longer measured the altitude. _____

18. Computer **graphics** enhance books *on politics and economics*. _____

19. The **isothermal** foothills escaped the extremes *of temperature*. _____

20. The new convert soon **reverted** *to his previous views*. _____

For each of these sentences, first identify the part of speech of the word in **bold**, then identify the kind of phrase that is in italics.

1. The **orthopedist** went *on an expedition*.   noun, prep.

2. Dr. Garcia, *the new mortician*, was **mortified** at the wound.   adjective, appos.

3. The **carnivorous** beasts *of the plains* lived well.   adjective, prep.

4. The **psychologist** viewed the parapsychologist *with suspicion*.   noun, prep.

5. *Contradicting democratic philosophy*, **Ethnocentrism** injures all.   noun, participle

6. The geneticist's hobby was *to study* **pathogenic** substances.   adjective, infinitive

7. **Prenatal** care is important *to those in natural environments*.   adjective, prep.

8. The **paleontologist** was an expert *on the Paleozoic era*.   noun, prep.

9. To talk glibly gives only **cursory** attention *to the problem*.   adjective, prep.

10. The **cryptologist** worked all night *to break the enemy code*.   noun, infinitive

11. *Cracked lengthwise*, the object was discovered near the **cascade**.   noun, participle

12. *Decapitating criminals* was once a common form of punishment.   noun, gerund

13. The **loquacious** bore answered *with a circumlocution*.   adjective, prep.

14. *From the beginning* the hero's sacrifice was a **sacrosanct** memory.   adjective, prep.

15. The **United** Planets soon celebrate *forming their union*.   adjective, gerund

16. The sky's **redness** streamed high *over the Himalayas*.   noun, prep.

17. The **altimeter**, *rusted shut*, no longer measured the altitude.   noun, participle

18. Computer **graphics** enhance books *on politics and economics*.   noun, prep.

19. The **isothermal** foothills escaped the extremes *of temperature*.   adjective, prep.

20. The new convert soon **reverted** *to his previous views*.   verb, prep.

GoBack definitions
Level III
Phrases

For purposes of consistency when playing **GoBack**, you can use these definitions for some of the major terms in the phrases. Remember to review Levels I and II before playing **GoBack**. Also, keep your thinking clear: remember that if you learn what these things are, you will benefit from it all of your life.

Phrase: A group of words that does not have a subject and its predicate.

Prepositional phrase: A phrase beginning with a preposition, used as a modifier.

Appositive: An interrupting definition.

Verbal: A verb form used as a noun, adjective, or adverb.

The three kinds of verbals: Gerunds, participles, and infinitives.

Gerund: An -ing verb form used as a noun.

Participle: A verb form of various endings used as an adjective.

Infinitive: The *to-* form of the verb, used as a noun or modifier.

parts of speech

parts of the sentence

phrases

clauses

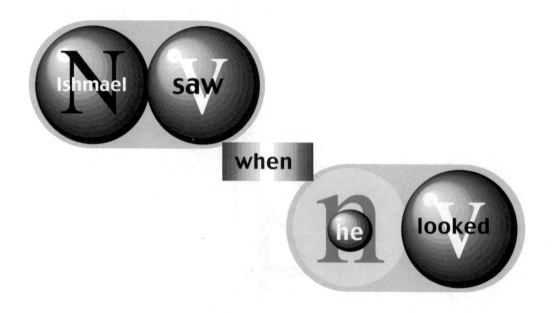

CLAUSE

A group of words that contains a subject and its predicate.

Clause that idea: Clauses are easy. The word *clause* comes from the same root as the words *claustrophobia*, *enclosure*, and *close*. The idea is that a clause is a closing: the subject opens the topic, and the predicate closes it; the subject asks, and the predicate answers. A clause is simply a **group of words that contains a subject *and* its predicate**, and this one-two structure opens and closes an idea. Every clause has this subject/predicate set at its center.

clause

$$\left[\text{subject, predicate}\right]$$

open,   close

The complete clause includes not only the subject and the verb, but all of the modifiers and phrases that go with them. A sentence might consist of only one clause, or it might contain several clauses, each with its own subject and predicate. How many clauses do you think you see in this passage from Henry David Thoreau's *Walden*?

I desire that there may be as many different persons in the world as possible; but I would have each one be very careful to find out and pursue his own way, and not his father's or his mother's or his neighbor's instead. The youth may build or plant or sail, only let him not be hindered from doing that which he tells me he would like to do.

I and D—Two Kinds of Clauses:

Independent clause (I): An independent clause is a clause that makes sense independently: *Ibsen was a gadfly.*

Dependent clause (D): A dependent (or *subordinate*) clause is a clause that does not make sense unless it can "hang on to" (de-down pend-hang) an independent clause. Dependent clauses are sometimes called *subordinate clauses*, and often begin with subordinating conjunctions. *If Ibsen was a gadfly . . .*

FOUR-LEVEL ANALYSIS

From William Shakespeare's *Julius Caesar:*

	When	**Caesar**	**says**	**"Do**	**this,"**	**it**	**is**	**performed.**
Parts of Speech:	conj.	n.	v.	v.	pron.	pron.	v.	v.
Parts of Sentence:		subject	predicate	---- object --- direct		subj.	--passive voice pred.--	
Phrases:	no prepositional, appositive, or verbal phrases							
Clauses:	------------------dependent clause------------- -------independent clause----- a complex declarative sentence							

This sentence is unusual because the direct object, *Do this*, of the introductory dependent clause is also a clause! See the subordinating conjunction?

Adjective dependent clause: An adjective clause (or relative clause) is a dependent clause used as an adjective: a (usually) short dependent clause that follows a noun or pronoun and modifies it. The adjective clause often interrupts the main clause, dividing the subject from the verb. Adjective clauses begin with relative pronouns. The man *who followed you* turned left. We watched the man *who turned left*. Whitman wrote, "I am he that walks with the tender and growing night."

The comma chameleon—punctuating essential and nonessential adjective clauses: Adjective clauses that are important to the meaning of the sentence need no commas around them, but adjective clauses that are unnecessary interruptions should be enclosed in commas. In other words, **if you do need the clause, you don't need the commas, and if you don't need the clause, then you do need the commas. You need one or the other.** If the clause is essential, then the commas aren't. Examples: The man who followed you turned left. The man, who happened to know Humphrey, coughed.

That versus ***which*:** Here is a good usage clue. The relative pronoun *that* often indicates an essential adjective clause: The book *that you lost* is on the shelf; whereas the relative pronoun *which* often indicates a nonessential adjective clause: The book, *which I enjoyed too*, is on the shelf.

Adverb dependent clause: Adverb clauses are dependent clauses that act as big adverbs. Adverb clauses usually begin with subordinating conjunctions. I jumped *when the fish expanded*.

Noun dependent clause: Noun clauses are dependent clauses that act as nouns. In the following sentence, the noun clause acts as a direct object to the action verb *wish*: I wish *that I liked music*.

Where dependent clauses go: Dependent clauses can not be used as sentences by themselves; they depend on (hang down from) an independent clause for meaning. The dependent clause may be placed before, after, or even in the middle of an independent clause:

> **If you find the white whale**, the voyage will be a success.
> The evil will collapse **when the white whale is destroyed**.
> The poet **who wrote the cantos** was exiled to Italy.
> I found **what I was looking for**.

Let's be very Thoreau: In *Walden*, Thoreau wrote some of the most beautiful sentences in American literature to convey some of the most profound ideas in American history. Look at this passage, and notice some of his dependent clauses, which will be in black. The independent clauses will be in gray: Do you see the subordinating conjunctions subordinating the second two clauses? What kind of dependent clause is the first one?

I am no more lonely than the loon in the pond **that laughs so loud**, or than Walden Pond itself. What company has that lonely lake, I pray? And yet is has not the blue devils, but the blue angels in it, in the azure tint of its waters. The sun is alone, except in thick weather, **when there sometimes appear to be two**, but one is a mock sun...

I have occasional visits in the long winter evenings, **when the snow falls fast** and the wind howls in the wood...

The difference between clause and sentence: A clause has both a subject and predicate, like a sentence, but a sentence always has a complete thought, whereas a clause might be incomplete. A sentence can consist of several clauses: If you find the Auden poem, I will scan its meter. In this sentence, there are two clauses; *If you find the Auden poem* is a dependent clause in which *you* is the subject and *find* is the simple predicate, and *I will scan its meter* is an independent clause in which *I* is the subject and *scan* is the simple predicate. So every sentence has at least one independent clause in it, but not every clause is a sentence because a dependent clause does not make a complete thought—it is dependent upon an independent clause.

We could express the relationship between clauses and sentences with Aristotelian syllogisms:

A. All sentences contain at least one independent clause.

B. "All men are created equal" is a sentence.

C. Therefore, "All men are created equal" contains at least one independent clause.

Or,

A. No dependent clause is a sentence by itself.

B. "If you can keep your head" is a dependent clause.

C. Therefore, "If you can keep your head" is not a sentence.

Four Sentence Structures

In the following discussion of how clauses can be combined into sentences, let the letter *I* stand for the independent clause, and let the letter *D* stand for the dependent clause. Let the letters *cc* stand for the coordinating conjunction (*and, but, or, nor, for, so, yet*).

I

Simple sentence: (Structure: **I**) A simple sentence is a sentence consisting simply of one independent clause. You can use a simple sentence to isolate an idea for attention. In his poem "The Disillusionment of Ten O'Clock" poet Wallace Stevens began with a simple sentence, "The houses are haunted / By white night gowns."

II

Compound sentence: (Structure: **I+I** or **I+I+I**, etc.) A compound sentence is a sentence compounded of two or more independent clauses. You can use a compound sentence to connect two related ideas of equal or nearly equal importance. Punctuate I;I or I,ccI. From Sylvia Plath's poem "The Moon and the Yew Tree": "It drags the sea after it like a dark crime; it is quiet / With the O-gape of complete despair." Randall Jarrell used a compound sentence in his poem "Death of the Ball turret Gunner": "From my mother's sleep I fell into the State, / And I hunched in its belly till my wet fur froze."

ID D,I

Complex sentence: (Structure: **I+D** or **D+I** or **D+I+D**, etc.) A complex sentence is a sentence that is complex because it consists of an independent clause joined to a dependent clause. You can use a complex sentence to show a primary idea that has a lesser idea in support of it. The independent clause will contain the primary idea. Punctuate **D,I** or **ID**. From poet Edward Arlington Robinson: "Whenever Richard Cory went down town, / We people on the pavement looked at him." In his poem "The Darkling Thrush," Thomas Hardy wrote, "I leant upon a coppice gate / When Frost was specter-gray."

IID DII

Compound-complex sentence: (Structure: **I+I+D** or **D+I+I**, etc.) A compound-complex sentence is a sentence that contains both compound clause structure and complex clause structure. You can use a compound-complex sentence to employ the strategies of compound and complex sentences at once. Punctuate a compound-complex sentence two clauses at a time, according to the rules for compound and complex sentences. Poet A.E. Housman wrote, "The time you won your town the race, / We chaired you through the marketplace; / Man and boy stood cheering by, / And home we brought you shoulder-high."

Summary of clause punctuation:

I,ccI (comma before coordinating conjunction in compound sentence)

I;I (semicolon between independent clauses if no coordinating conjunction)

ID (no comma after independent clause in complex sentence)

D,I (comma after dependent clause in complex sentence)

Note: this easy summary of clause punctuation gives a quick reference for punctuating independent clauses and adverbial dependent clauses. Adjective (relative) clauses are different; the relative clause is enclosed in commas if it is a nonessential interruption to the main idea, but it is not enclosed in commas if its presence in the sentence is essential or necessary.

I,ccI I;I
D,I ID

~~IccI~~ run-on!

~~I,I~~ comma splice!

DI?: Even though we often teach students to put a comma after the introductory adverbial dependent clause in a **D,I** complex sentence, that comma is often omitted in published material if the sentence seems clear and readable without the comma. The teacher may wish to emphasize to students that at the professional level this comma is regarded as discretionary.

Comma splice error: A comma splice is the error of joining two independent clauses with a comma. **(I,I)** The archaeologist went to Cairo, we went home. To correct this error, either insert a coordinating conjunction after the comma, or change the comma to a semicolon.

Run-on sentence error: A run-on sentence is the error of joining two independent clauses with only a coordinating conjunction or with nothing. **(IccI or II)** This causes the two ideas in the compound sentence to blur together, losing their clear identities. The archaeologist went to Cairo but we went home. The archaeologist went to Cairo we went home. Remember that poets and novelists will sometimes deliberately use run-on sentences; Wallace Stevens did in his sentence, "The house was quiet and the world was calm." Ernest Hemingway was famous for it.

Four Purposes of Sentences/Ideas:

The sentence purposes are so well named that they are virtually self-defining. Each does precisely what its name implies:

declarative sentence: A declarative sentence is a sentence that *declares* (states). I will.

interrogative sentence: An interrogative sentence is a sentence that *interrogates* (asks). Will you? T.S. Eliot's J. Alfred Prufrock asked, "Do I dare to eat a peach?"

imperative sentence: An imperative sentence is a sentence that *imperiously* commands. Go away. Dylan Thomas wrote, "Do not go gentle into that good night."

exclamatory sentence: An exclamatory sentence is a sentence that *exclaims*. I will!

The world
dictates
the grammar.

The world dictates the grammar. Grammar serves meaning, and not conversely. You cannot seek within grammar for the all causes of grammatical structure; these causes are often external. A sentence will not be simple, complex, or compound because of the rules of grammar; it will have clause structure suitable to the ideas.

There may be short, simple sentences because the moment to be communicated—say, Cornwall's dying gasps in Shakespeare's *King Lear*— requires a series of terrible silences, that position themselves tragically *between* the sentences: "I have received a hurt. Follow me, lady. Turn out that eyeless villain; throw this slave upon the dunghill. Regan, I bleed apace. Untimely comes this hurt; give me your arm." There is nothing, internal to grammar, which dictates the use of these staccato, clipped sentences; rather, it is Cornwall's pain, his inability to utter more than a few words at a breath, which explains the syntax. Cornwall has been stabbed, and in his only thirty-one wounded words there are seven clauses, five periods, two commas, and two semicolons. The passage has an average of only four words per clause. It is not Cornwall's words that communicate his agony, but rather the *interwords* that dictate his constricted grammar, forcing itself into the gaps between his death spasms:

"I have received a hurt/////////////Follow me/////////////////lady/////////////////Turn out that eyeless villain////////////throw this slave upon the dunghill/////////////Regan////////////I bleed apace////////////////// Untimely comes this hurt///////////////////give me your arm."

Clearly, the secret of Cornwall's grammar cannot be internally analyzed within the system of grammar itself; the grammar is not a function of itself but of the character's experience: his small gasps of sentence are all he can manage between his large gasps of death.

The example of Cornwall vividly illustrates another insufficiently contemplated aspect of language study, the extraordinary meaning and power of punctuation. In every period and comma of Cornwall's death there is an abyss.

I have received a hurt.
Follow me, lady.
Turn out that eyeless villain.
throw this slave upon the dunghill.
Regan, I bleed apace.
Give me your arm.

GoBack definitions
Level IV

For purposes of consistency when playing GoBack, you can use these definitions for some of the major terms in the clauses. Be sure to review the definitions from the first three levels.

Clause: A group of words that has a subject and its predicate

Independent clause: A clause that is a complete thought

Dependent clause: A clause that is not a complete thought, but needs to be connected to an independent clause.

The four clause structures: Simple, compound, complex, compound-complex.

Simple sentence: A sentence with one independent clause.

Compound sentence: A sentence with two or more independent clauses.

Complex sentence: A sentence with an independent clause attached to a dependent clause.

Compound-complex sentence: A sentence with a compound structure and a complex structure

The four sentence purposes: declarative, imperative, interrogative, exclamatory.

Declarative sentence: A sentence that declares or makes a statement.

Imperative sentence: A sentence that is imperious, that makes a command.

Interrogative sentence: A sentence that interrogates, that asks a question.

Exclamatory sentence: A sentence that exclaims, that has an exclamation point.

Review: As a way to review, try inventing an alien grammar. Create a language like English, except that 5-10 of the rules are different. Here is a sample:

Alien Grammar

Your ship crashes and you find yourself in a strange, alien land, with green clouds and yellow mountains. Navy blue streams traverse the landscape, and pink fish jump from the water. A crisp, cool wind blows the mauve trees to the west, or is it the east? The three suns shine down from the crimson sky, casting a triple shadow. Strange, yes, but the strangest part is yet to come: the grammar.

In this land, the language is just like English, except that certain rules are different. For example:

1. Singular nouns all end in -lo, and plural nouns all end in *-lolo,* not *-s.* The subject complement suffix is attached after the singular/plural suffix.
2. Adjectives immediately follow nouns, and end in *-la.*
3. Adverbs immediately follow what they modify, and end in *-loo.*
4. The first word of every sentence is the verb, unless the sentence is interrogative. Verbs begin with the hissing sound *sss-.*
5. There are no object pronouns, only subject pronouns; everything is thought to be alive.
6. All subject pronouns begin with the prefix *lee-*
7. Direct objects and objects of verbals begin with the prefix *lum-.*
8. Subject complements begin with *lim-* and end with *-mil.*
9. The preposition begins with the prefix *ner-* is the last word of the prepositional phrase.
10. Interrogative sentences begin with the word *hooop.*
11. The second person pronoun is never spoken, out of respect. This missing word is indicated by the humming sound, *mmmm.*
12. The definite article is *rach* and the indefinite article is *roop.*

As you gaze around in mute stupefaction, a creature flops flappily across the ground to you, peers intensely into your eyes, his nose almost touching yours. He blinks, and says in Floppy:

> **Hooop sssare what rach hecklo limmmmmmmil. Ssssaw neverloo beforeloo leeI lumanythinglo strangela soloo as mmmm. Hooop sssare mmmm roop limmonsterlomil. Hooop sssis why mmmm noselo mmmm eyelolo nirbelow. Ssshave leeI lumscalelolo nicela tummylo myla neron. Hooop ssswould ssslike mmmm to pat lumheadlo myla.**

Translate the alien's language into ordinary English. Then translate a well known saying in English into Floppy. You might choose a famous paragraph from a historical document, or a humorous dialogue in a television commercial.

What the heck are you? I never saw anything so strange as you
before. Are you a monster? Why is your nose below your eyes? I
have nice scales on my tummy. Would you like to pat my head?

Punctuation Rules
A Concise Summary

Here is a summary and reference section for any students or teachers who would like to have a concise review of common punctuation rules. Keep in mind that punctuation requires a knowledge of all four levels of grammar.

A note of caution: even though it is important for the student writer to learn and apply standard and sensible rules of punctuation, it is also important to realize that any strict set of rules is partly subjective and arbitrary; great writers you read will frequently violate—usually for artistic reasons—any set of rules of punctuation or grammar that we might formulate. Hemingway, for example, made an art form out of the run-on sentence. But notice that if you did not know what the standard punctuation was, you would be blind to the creative artistic maneuvering of the great writer.

In addition, punctuation preferences and standards vary. Some style manuals would have you omit the final comma before the coordinating conjunction in a list, whereas others, such as Strunk and White's *Elements of Style*, would ask you to retain it. You will also see differing preferences about the proper construction of dashes, which can be made like this - like this--like this -- or even like this—depending partly on whether you are using a typewriter or computer. In the end, you try to pick sensible principles for punctuating—principles that bring order to your ideas. The principles of punctuation I prefer are given below, for you to use or adapt. They are the principles upon which the punctuation tests in this text are based.

In thinking about the importance of punctuation, it is useful to remember the words of Oscar Wilde, when asked what he had done today, he said:

I spent the whole morning putting in a comma, and the whole afternoon taking it out.

comma: (,)

after introductory participle phrases: Falling quickly, he sang.

after introductory interjections: Yes, I do.

after informal salutations: Dear Dante,

after long introductory prepositional phrases:
In the chill early morning wind, we moved forward.

after multiple introductory prepositional phrases:
At the beginning of the competition, she learned anxiety.

after introductory dependent clauses (D,I): If you go, I go.

after the day and year: January 3, 1987, was cold.

after the city and state: Florence, Italy, is windy.

around nonessential (nonrestrictive) clauses:
The dog, which had a nice smile, turned back.

around nonessential participle phrases:
My friend, laughing with delight, produced the chicken.

around most appositives: Hamlet, my good friend, is visiting.

around nouns of direct address: Yes, Hamlet, I will.

around parenthetical expressions: I always, bless me, sneeze.

before coordinating conjunctions in I,ccI compound sentences:
I have some mutton, and he has some jerky.

between all items in a list: tall, dark, handsome, and smart

between adjectives preceding a noun: A smart, friendly man

between contrasts introduced by *not*: It's here, not there.

between name and degree or title: Marcus Aurelius, Ph.D.

inside closing quotation marks: "Shut up," he explained.

NOT after a short prepositional phrase: In May we departed.

NOT between compound subjects/predicates: Hamlet and Ophelia do.

NOT between subject and verb: Wrong: My good friend, is here.

semicolon: (;)

between independent clauses if no coordinating conjunction: I;I
I am an expert; he is a neophyte.

between items in a list if the items themselves contain commas:
We ordered bacon; fried, scrambled, and poached eggs; and grits.

between independent clauses joined by *however*, etc.
We all wanted to go; however, only Ishmael departed.

colon: (:)

before a list that is not a compound direct object or subject complement:
There are three categories: wishes, lies, and dreams.

before a long formal statement: To whom it may concern:

before a long quotation, as in a research paper.

between hours and minutes in time: 6:15
between Bible chapter and verse: Luke 4:16
after formal salutations: Dear Sir:
between titles and subtitles: *Walt Whitman: Poet of America*

italics: (*no* or <u>no</u>)   (italics and underlining are understood to be the same thing)
    title of a book: <u>A Tale of Two Cities</u> *Treasure Island*
    title of a magazine: *Life* <u>National Geographic</u>
    title of a work of art: <u>Mona Lisa</u> *David*
    title of a train or airplane: <u>Spirit of St. Louis</u> *The Hindenburg*
    words, letters, and numbers as such: the word *blubber*, the letter *a*, the number *5*
    foreign language words: *dejà vu*

    Underline (use italics) when you are referring to a word itself. Words, numbers, and letters *as such* must be placed in italics, which means—on a typewriter—that they must be underlined (NOT put in quotation marks!). In this way we distinguish the word *dog* from the animal, dog. We use *b*'s in spelling, and we use *3*'s in counting. See? We also place foreign language words in italics/underline: Homer begins his story *in medias res*, in the middle of things. This technique will be especially important when you are analyzing poetry or literature and are making reference to the words, letters, or sounds contained in the writing.

    Underline titles. The titles of books, newspapers, ships, trains, works of art, major musical compositions, and other important titles are always to be placed in italics, both in the body of a research paper and in the Works Cited. If you are typing, this means that you underline the title, though in a published document *italics is the style in which the letters lean to the right*. In other words, when you see a title in a book, the title will look like this: *A Midsummer Night's Dream*, but in a research paper it will look like this: <u>A Midsummer Night's Dream</u>. Titles should **not** be placed in quotation marks or in upper case in lieu of italics. Less significant titles, such as the titles of chapters, articles, poems, or songs, do not deserve italics; these titles are only placed in quotation marks. In a Works Cited listing, book titles are only to be underlined; they are not also enclosed in quotation marks.

quotation marks: (" ")
    around a direct quotation: He said, "I am not a crook."
    commas and periods go inside quotes: "Chocolate," he said.
    colons and semicolons go outside quotes: He said, "Hi"; I left.
    title of short story, poem, song: "The Road Not Taken"
    title of article, chapter, or part of publication:
        The fourth chapter of My False Demise is entitled "Rumors."
    NOT to indicate cute, trite, or ungrammatical terms:
        Hi, "Buddies," how about a "pep talk!"

apostrophe: (')

    noun made into a possessive adjective: John's boat

    missing letter in a contraction: don't

    missing number in a year contraction: '47

    plurals of letters, numbers, signs, and words as such: a's 5's

    with an *s* **to show possession after a singular noun:** Dickens's

    alone to show possession after a plural noun ending in *s*: dogs'

    for quotations within quotations:

        John said, "Hamlet cried, 'Oops!' when he fell."

    in the contraction of *it* **and** *is*: it's

    NOT in the possessive pronoun *its*.

    NOT in plural centuries or decades: 1900s the 50s

hyphen: (-)

    word divided at end of line

    compound written numbers from twenty-one to ninety-nine

    fractions used as adjectives: a three-fourths majority

    prefixes before proper noun or proper adjective: Pre-Raphaelite

    compound nouns that include prepositional phrases: father-in-law

    compound adjective when it *precedes* **its noun:** a well-meant lie

    NOT in compound adjectives *after* **nouns:** It was well meant.

    do NOT use a hyphen (-) when you intend a dash (-- or —)

dash: (-- or —)

    abrupt break in thought: So I--wait a minute!--ate the fish.

    to show omitted words in dialogue:

        He said, "Come here, you young . . . ."

    To make a dash on a typewriter type two hyphens with NO spaces--like that.

    NOT to replace proper punctuation.

ellipsis: (. . .)

    to indicate words omitted from quotations

    Use three periods if the omission is within a sentence.

    Use four periods if the omission includes sentence ending.

    Type blank spaces between the periods of an ellipsis . . . see?


```
    The ellipsis, an elaboration: This comment must be in Courier font.  Learn
to use and properly construct the ellipsis.  We use an ellipsis, a series of
spaces and periods, to indicate that we have left out part of a quotation.  If
you are only quoting a phrase, you need no ellipsis at all: We saw by the
"dawn's early light."  We need not begin a short quote with an ellipsis if a
```

lower-case letter clearly indicates that the first word quoted was not the
first word of the sentence: Fitzgerald replied that he "needed no instructions
from Hemingway." We do begin a long quote with a three-period ellipsis if we
have left out the beginning of the sentence. A simple omission within a
sentence requires a three-period ellipsis with spaces before and after every
period: "But as for me . . . give me death." If you are omitting the end of a
question, you put the question mark after the ellipsis: We would ask "How many
angels can dance . . . ?" Finally, if we are omitting the final word or words
of a sentence (or more than one sentence), we must include a fourth period--
the one to end the sentence: "Mary had a little lamb. . . . And everywhere
that Mary went the lamb was sure to go." Notice the spacing; the extra period
occurs immediately after the final quoted word, with no intervening space. If
you are using documentary notes (as we do in our research papers) and you stop
quoting right after the ellipsis, then you put the extra period AFTER the
documentary note: As Mother Goose has noted, "Mary had a little lamb. Its
fleece was white . . ." (Goose 472).

parenthesis: (( ))

around parenthetical remarks added to a sentence:
He said I would be (I wish!) six feet tall.

brackets: ([ ])

around words inserted into quoted material:
Johnson notes, "At this time [Dickens] began to weaken."

When you insert words into quotations--usually for the purpose of
clarifying references or enhancing the flow of the sentences--you must enclose
your inserted words in brackets like [this] to show that these words were not
part of the original quote. Be sure to use [brackets] rather than
(parentheses) or <mathematical symbols>. Computer word processors usually have
brackets, but what if you are using a typewriter? Sometimes people carefully
add brackets with a pen after the paper is typed, since most typewriters do
not have brackets, but you can also make your own brackets on a typewriter by
using a combination of underlines and slants:

        slants and underlines /make the brackets/ like that.

question mark: (?)

at the end of an interrogative sentence: Do you have dogs?

inside closing quotes if part of quote: He asked, "Is there time?"

outside quotes if not part of quote: Did he say, "Remember me"?

period: (.)

at the end of a declarative sentence: I have three dogs.

at the end of a mild imperative sentence: Please go away.

after most abbreviations: Dr. Trelawney

inside closing quotation marks: He said, "Go away."

exclamation point: (!)

after an exclamatory sentence: The sky is falling!

after a strong imperative sentence: Get out!

NOT to express chronic cuteness: Hi! Guess what!!

virgule or slash (/)

When you are quoting poetry in a research paper, you don't have to return to a new line just because you reach the end of a line of the poem. Instead of returning to a new line, you may—if you wish—just insert a slash (/) at the point where the poem drops to a new line. Include one space before and after the slash: Mary had a little lamb, / Its fleece was white as snow, / And every where that Mary went / The lamb was sure to go. The slash will separate the lines of poetry for the reader. Of course, you can quote the lines in a column as they appear in the book also.

In other words, if you see this in a book:

> Mary had a little lamb,
> Its fleece was white as snow,
> And every where that Mary went
> The lamb was sure to go.

You can type it this way in your paper if you want to:

> Mary had a little lamb, / Its fleece was white as snow, / And every where that Mary went / The lamb was sure to go.

space: (or)

Type one space between words.

Type one space after a comma.

Type two spaces after the closing punctuation in each sentence:

```
Do it like this.  Not like this. See?
```

Indent *five* spaces for a new paragraph.

Indent *ten* spaces for a long quotation.

Leave a space between periods in an ellipsis: . . . not: ...
Leave NO spaces on either side of a dash or hyphen: pro-McGovern
Do *not* use only one single space between sentences.

Just give me some space:

Spaces: This section of <u>The Magic Lens</u> must again be in Courier type font, ragged right, in order to illustrate spacing matters that occur in research papers:

Always place two blank spaces after the period or other closing punctuation at the end of a sentence. We insert two blank spaces after all of the periods within each of the Works Cited listings. Place only a single blank space between two words in a sentence. Be sure to leave one blank space after commas, like that. If you don't,see what happens. The same rule applies to colons: leave one space afterwards; you also leave one blank space after semicolons, not two. You should leave a blank space after numbers followed by closing parentheses, 1) like that, rather than 2)like that. You do not leave a space before the punctuation , only after it.

When you type a three-period ellipsis, use four spaces to separate the three periods, like . . . this, rather than putting the periods together like...this. You should not leave blank spaces just inside quotation marks, parentheses, or brackets; these marks should be closed up against the words they enclose, (like this) rather than (like this). After an abbreviation's period, you use a single blank space: you would type "Mr. Dickens," not "Mr. Dickens." In parenthetical notes, leave a single space between the closing quotes and the parenthetical note "that follows, like this" (Jones 54). Leave two blank spaces between the period and the documentary note at the end of a long quotation.

Again: Do **not** put blank spaces inside quotation marks " like this " or within parentheses (like this); quotes and parentheses should be closed up around the words they enclose "like" (this).

I think of the blank space almost as one of the letters--it is the <u>null letter</u>, the act of placing a blank in the space. The blank space is a language object just as a letter or punctuation mark is a language object. The blank space has meaning; changes in spacing can cause changes in interpretation. Again: We normally put a single space between words in a sentence, a single space after colons and semicolons, a single space between Mr. and Name, and two blank spaces after the closing punctuation of each sentence.

Common English Grammar and Usage Problems

The following collection of common grammar errors and usage problems may be used as a general reference and as a reference for the Solecism Theater projects.

To **accept** is to take: I can accept no money for this harpoon.
To **except** is to omit: I can except no one from the rule except you.

To **affect** is to influence: Your idea will affect many people.
The verb **effect** means cause: Your idea will effect a new procedure.
The noun **effect** means result: Your idea will produce a good effect.

Use **afraid of** and **frightened by**, rather than **frightened of**: Ahab had been frightened by a whale, and was afraid of them ever since.

To **aggravate** is to make worse, not to irritate: It irritated me that she went out in the rain and aggravated her cold.

Use **all right**, not **alright**: We will be all right if the Spartans arrive.

An **allusion** is a reference: His comment was an allusion to the *Iliad*.
An **illusion** is a deception: The bas relief gave the illusion of depth.

In ordinary sentences, do not substitute the **ampersand (&)** or the mathematical **plus symbol (+)** for the coordinating conjunction **and**.

Bad is an adjective: The bad decision ruined the project.
Badly is an adverb: The bad swimmer did not swim badly.

The reason is not **because**; the reason is **that**: The reason we think carefully is that we regret our errors.

Something is **between** two: This secret is between you and me.
Something is **among** three or more: Divide the fish among the five dogs.

We **bring** toward, but we **take** away: If you take someone's lunch by mistake, you must bring it back to him or her.

Can means able to: You can repair a door if you know how.
May means are permitted to: Yes, you may leave the room.

Not **could of** or **should of**, but **could have** or **should have**: I could have read classics, and I should have read classics.
(We sometimes see **could've** as the contraction of **could have** and **should've** as the contraction of **should have**.)

Disinterested means without prejudice because of having no personal interest in something: We need a disinterested judge to try this case fairly. **Uninterested** means without interest in the sense of being bored: The boy was uninterested in the story, and began to daydream. A disinterested judge could find a case very interesting.

Use **done** only with a helping verb: I have done nothing to you.

Don't is the contraction of "do not": We don't like egocentrism.
Doesn't is the contraction of "does not": He doesn't like ethnocentrism.
Don't use **don't** for singular subjects: He don't like eggplant.

To **emigrate** is to migrate out: The family emigrated from Russia.
To **immigrate** is to migrate in: The family immigrated to Puerto Rico.

Use **farther** for distance: Her javelin went farther than his did.
Use **further** for time: We will consider this matter further.

Use **feel bad** rather than **feel badly**.

Use **fewer** for countable things: There are fewer players.
Use **less** for uncountable amount: There is less sugar.

If you are enumerating elements in your essay, use **first** and **second**, rather than **firstly** and **secondly**. The latter terms with their **-ly** suffix have a supercilious, pedantic ring to them that is undesirable. In fact, Thomas Hardy even satirized the use of such language in one of his poems, "Channel Firing." In the poem, a skeleton wakes up in the grave and muses satirically about someone he knows, "Parson Thirdly."

Fortuitous means by chance: A fortuitous circumstance occurred.
Fortunate means lucky: A fortunate condition resulted.

Good is an adjective: The good swimmer swam her fastest time.
Well is usually an adverb: The good swimmer swam well.
Well can sometimes be an adjective: He is not a well man.

Clothes, when put out to dry, are **hung**. People, when strung up to die, are **hanged**. Oedipus enters the palace to find that Jocasta has hanged herself.

Hopefully is an adverb meaning "full of hope"; it should not be used as a substitute for **I hope**: I hope that you will strive hopefully for knowledge.

Note the difference between **ideas** and **ideals**. **Ideas** are concepts, thoughts, and so forth. We could discuss the philosophical ideas of Friedrich Nietzsche. **Ideals** are standards, goals to be attained, ideas of excellence or perfection. Both ideas and ideals are mental, but we debate ideas while striving for the ideal.

It is best to use the word **impact** only as a noun, and not as a verb, in discussing the effect of individuals on history. When we say that x "impacted" y, this usage has an unfortunate, unpleasant medical connotation that is undesirable. The preferable word is **affected**. We affect others, rather than impact them, and when we affect them, this has an impact.

To **imply** is to suggest: He implied that we were to blame.
To **infer** is to deduce: We inferred that we were being blamed.

It's is the contraction of **it is**: It's fun to understand things.
its is a possessive pronoun: The alien chomped its jaws.

Use **kind of** rather than **kind of a**: It seemed to be some kind of nose.

Use **lend** as a verb: Lend me money for a harpoon.
Use **loan** as a noun: Give me a loan for a harpoon.

To **lie** (v.i.) is to rest: I will lie here in the shade.
To **lay** (v.t.) is to put: I will lay the book here on the rock.

Use **like** as a preposition: We have good books like these.
Use **as** as a conjunction: We have good books, as you have.

Literally means actually, not figuratively. You could say, "We literally left within two minutes," but you could not say, "We literally vanished." If you did not physically vanish, then you did not literally vanish.

In the past we used the terms **man** and **mankind**, and even the possessive pronoun **his**, to refer to all human beings, both male and female. Today, our sensitivities have improved, and we try to avoid defaulting to the masculine gender when we intend to express something which also includes women. Other terms, such as **human beings**, **humanity**, **persons**, and even the compound pronouns such as **his or her** sound more accurate and more fair.

Myself and **yourself** should be used as reflexive or intensive pronouns rather than as direct objects. "I, myself, believed it" is correct usage, but "She asked John and myself if we had the loot" is not. It would be correct to say, "She asked John and me if we had the loot."

Nauseous means sickening: It was a nauseous sight.
Nauseated means sick at the stomach: I was nauseated by the sight.

Number is for countables: There were a number of soldiers there.
Amount is for uncountables: There was an enormous amount of tension.

Use **off** rather than **off of**: The ball bounced off the backboard.

Phenomenon is singular and **phenomena** is plural: The most interesting phenomenon of all the meteorological phenomena was the tornado.

Save **plus** for mathematics and use **in addition to** in most other situations: They wanted burgers. In addition to that, they wanted shakes.

Precipitate means hasty, and **precipitous** means steep: He made a precipitate decision to descend the precipitous path.

The phrase **relate to** is a vague colloquialism. Instead of saying that many people *relate to* J.D. Salinger's character Holden Caulfield, say that many people *understand* Holden, or that they find that Holden's struggles remind them of their own struggles, or something specific. To say we *relate to* Holden is vague. In what way do we relate? Do we feel the same alienation from conventional society that he feels? Do we have dreams similar to his dream of being the catcher in the rye? Do we love our little brothers and sisters? Do we feel that his language expresses our own view of the world? Do we feel ourselves losing our emotional our psychological health? There are so many thousands of relationships that simply to say one thing relates to another is almost to communicate nothing at all; you have to use a specific word that names that specific relationship.

Use **raise** transitively: They will attempt to raise the Titanic.
Use **rise** intransitively: She began to rise slowly through the air.

Use **regardless** rather than **irregardless**.

Respectfully is with respect: He spoke respectfully of his father.
Respectively is in sequence: He spoke of his father, his brother, and his sister, respectively.

Use **since** rather than **seeing as how**: Since you feel that way, I will do the work myself.

You **sit** (v.i.) down in a chair: She was sitting there on the porch.
You **set** (v.t.) down a book: She was setting the book on the step.

Someone is not they. Rather than saying, "Someone dropped their headphones," say, "Someone dropped a pair of headphones." Use **they** or **their** when you intend to refer to a group of people.

You **teach** people things, and you **learn** subjects: you do not learn people things: If you would like to learn algebra, I can teach you.

Than is a conjunction: We have more perplexities than you have.
Then is an adverb: We will go now; you go then.

Them should be used as an object pronoun, not as an adjective: And so, my friends, ask not when you can have them cookies, ask when you can have those cookies.

They're is the contraction of "they are": They're reading now.
Their is a possessive pronoun: They're reading their books.
There is a place: They're reading their books there.

Use **this** rather than **this here**: This dog bit me on this foot.

To is a preposition or an infinitive: She went to Boston to think.
Too is an adverb meaning "also" or "too much": I sleep too much, too.
Two is a number: Two twins twisted twine in the twilight.

Tortuous means full of twists: a tortuous highway.
Torturous means full of torture: a torturous ordeal.

Use **try to** rather than **try and**: Please try to help today.

Something is either **unique**, one of a kind, or it is not. There are no degrees of uniqueness, and so nothing can be **very** unique.

Use **way off** rather than **ways off**: He was a long way off.

Who is a subject pronoun: Who is here?
Whom is an object pronoun: To whom do you wish to speak?

Who refers to people: It was they who followed the truck.
That and **which** refer to objects: Which rock is that?

Who's is the contraction of **who** and **is**. Who's going to think?
Whose is a pronoun or adjective: Whose woods these are, I think I know.

Solecism Theater

(A Usage Mastery Project)

Student Instructions

Solecism Theater: In ancient Cilicia in the city of Soloi, the citizens spoke a corrupt form of Attic Greek, regarded by the Athenians as crude, foolish, and ungrammatical. This feeling of distaste for the Soloi-cisms spoken in Soloi has given us our word **solecism** (soh-leh-sism), which means a blunder in language, an ungrammatical usage, a misuse of language. **Solecism Theater** is a creative play-writing usage project in which students write short (3-5 minute) humorous plays which derive their humor from the contradictions and confusions of language usage errors.

Instructions: For one of the following three situations (or for one which you create), write a funny play of three to five minutes, which dramatically and vividly illustrates the difference between standard English usage and solecism. This is not a solemn scholarly assignment: make your play original, witty, or satirical. Have fun. Notice that titles are not provided for any of the play situations; you must write a creative title for your play.

Here's the catch: *Every sentence* must illustrate either correct usage or incorrect usage. Try to include a variety of different common usage errors in your play, and try to show the same usage in both correct and incorrect forms. Note that some misunderstandings (*they're*, *their*, *there*) become most noticeable in written language, so if you include them, you will need to creatively write your play so that the audience will understand what is happening when the play is performed.

Open Book: Solecism Theater is not a test of your usage knowledge. In writing your solecism play, you may use the usage discussion in this text as an open-book reference, or you may use other published usage discussions if your teacher allows.

Performance: After you write your play, you will be given an opportunity to perform it in class. You may need to have other students help you perform your play. Feel free to incorporate clever props and costumes.

Someone Dropped Their Banana:
A Sample Solecism Play
MC Thompson

Fred and Joe enter. Fred looks down, and picks up a banana.

Fred:	Look, someone dropped their banana.
Joe:	How did you know many people own that banana?
Fred:	Hopefully, they don't!
Joe:	It makes those people feel *hopeful* to not own the banana?
Fred:	Are you trying to aggravate me?
Joe:	No, I'm not trying to make you worse; you said it was "their banana," I just want to know who they are, and why they're so hopeful about their banana.
Fred:	I ain't never said they were hopeful about no banana.
Joe:	Oh, so you admit you said it.
Fred:	I ain't never said it.
Joe:	Let me get this straight: You said the people don't own a banana hopefully.
Fred:	I'll not discuss this farther. I said someone dropped their banana.
Joe:	You won't discuss this farther?
Fred:	Right.
Joe:	Then how close do you want me to stand, so we can talk about it?
Fred:	I want you to stand a-ways over there, and leave me alone.
Joe:	But you said you didn't want to discuss it farther.
Fred:	I ain't gonna discuss it no farther.
Joe:	Then why are you sending me farther?
Fred:	You're trying to aggravate me, for sure.
Joe:	No, I'm just trying to improve you.
Fred:	Now, what're you inferring?
Joe:	I can't infer anything, you have me confused.
Fred:	If you ask me, you are literally a bird.
Joe:	I am a mammal.
Fred:	I see I can't learn you nothing.
Joe:	What do you want to learn about me?
Fred:	Your nonsense is making me feel nauseous.
Joe:	No, I think you look fine.
Fred:	I didn't say nothing about how I look!
Joe:	You said you made me sick.
Fred:	I didn't never say that.
Joe:	That's right, you did.
Fred:	See here, even with a lot of dark, rotten places, I'm gonna eat this banana.
Joe:	I didn't realize you were sick. What disease do you have?
Fred:	I ain't got no disease!
Joe:	I'm so sorry to hear it. Where do you have these dark, rotten places, on your stomach? Let me see.
Fred:	I never said I had no dark, rotten place, I said there were rotten places on the banana.
Joe:	You mean you got a skin disease from a banana?
Fred:	This conversation is literally splitting my head.
Joe:	Oh, no! Now I understand why you said you were nauseous.

Fred runs away screaming, and Joe sits down, peels the banana, and eats it.

Write a 3-5 minute Solecism Play based on one of the following situations or on one which you create. Remember to write a creative title for your play.

Situation 1: Two individuals meet on the street. One can utter no correct sentence, and the other can utter no incorrect sentence. Their humorous interchange revolves around one person trying to correct the other's spoken grammar, but the latter is so used to hearing incorrect grammar, that he doesn't realize he's being corrected, and keeps missing the point that it's his own language which is at issue.

Situation 2: Two individuals are surreptitiously whispering and writing notes in a class as the teacher is lecturing on problems of English usage. Neither student is paying any attention to the lecture, and both are holding up their notes for the other to see. The two students each have serious spoken and written usage problems. The juxtaposition of the students' usage errors with the teacher's lecture on those very problems makes an amusing and ironic story.

Situation 3: Two friends meet by surprise. One can speak no sentence without a pronoun error (of agreement, or case, or reference), and the other can speak no sentence without a subject/verb disagreement. Provide your own topic for their conversation.

Situation 4: On a distant planet in 2071, a citizen in the American colony goes out to eat at a fast food joint, where only the latest crazes in colonial fast foods are served. The person taking fast food orders can ask no question which is free of usage errors, and the citizen tries to answer the questions correctly, but the food order is incredibly fouled up as a result of the exasperating language problem. No matter how hard the order taker and the citizen try to communicate, things only become worse.

Situation 5: Two friends write to each other. One friend writes a one-page letter in which no sentence is without a usage problem. The letter contains a wide variety of different usage problems and common punctuation errors, some of which are also problems of spoken language. The second friend writes back, discussing the same matters in correct usage.

Situation 6: In the presence of a group of people, two individuals have a misunderstanding caused by a classic pronoun reference error: one of the two makes the "adolescent *they*" error in every single sentence, and the second always thinks that *they* or *their* refers to the group of people nearby, which causes a major misunderstanding to develop!

ℒoops

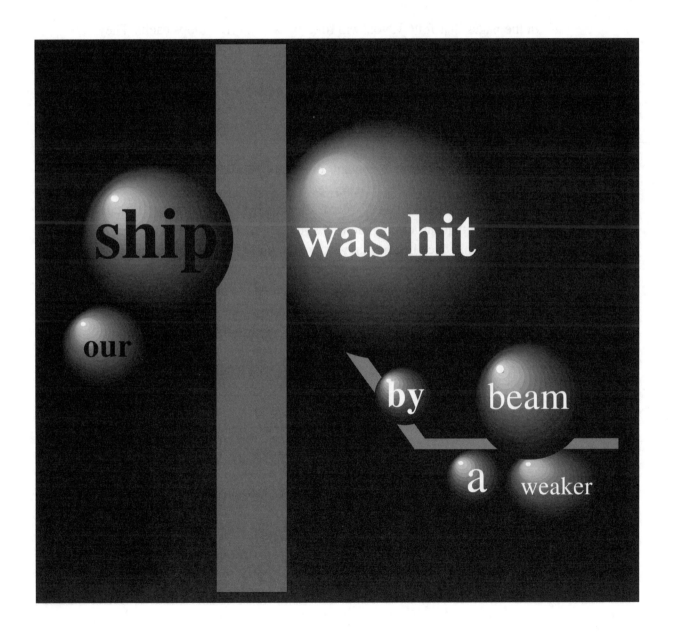

Introduction to the Loops

In the pages that follow, you will find two sets of five loops each. They are called loops, not chapters, because chapters tend to move forward in a linear way, introducing new material along the path, whereas these loops do not really introduce new ideas; rather, they let us explore new expressions of things we have begun to know, increasing our comprehension rather than our content.

After each group of five loops, there are major tests available. One is a four-level grammar test, which contains one hundred questions and is largely based on the four-level analysis sentences that come at the beginning of each loop. The second is a P as *f* of G Punctuation Test, a very difficult punctuation test that can only be done if you really know what you are doing with punctuation, which means that you have to know your grammar.

Within the loops there are lots of options for individual or group assignments. These options will introduce you to some famous grammar and to the styles of writers, and will give you a chance to have some fun applying the grammar you are learning.

The Martian visitors will have landed by Thursday.

Parts of speech: *The* is an adjective (definite article) modifying the plural common noun *visitors*; *Martian* is a proper adjective that also modifies *visitors*; *will* and *have* are helping verbs that help the main verb *landed* form the future perfect tense; *by* is a preposition, and *Thursday* is a proper noun that is also the object of the preposition *by*.

Parts of the sentence: The subject is *visitors*, and *will have landed* is the verb/simple predicate.

Phrases: The sentence contains two phrases. The first is a verb phrase, *will have landed*, that consists of a main verb and two helping verbs. We often show the tense of a verb by creating a phrase: *will fly, has flown, will have flown*, etc. The second phrase in this sentence is a prepositional phrase, *by Thursday*. This phrase modifies the verb. Remember that prepositional phrases are always modifiers.

Clauses: This is a simple, declarative sentence based on a single subject and predicate. It is simple because it contains one clause, and it is declarative because it makes a statement.

• • •

Perfect tense: Remember that the perfect tenses are called *perfect* after the Latin verb *perficere*, to finish. If I *will have landed* by Thursday, I *will have finished* by then.

Proper adjective: *Martian* is a proper adjective, capitalized because it derives from the proper noun, *Mars*.

Remember: There is a Four-Level Analysis sentence at the beginning of each loop, and it is these very sentences that are used in the Grammar Review Test. Be sure to study these sentences carefully.

	The	Martian	visitors	will	have	landed		by	Thursday.
Parts of Speech:	adj.	adj.	n.	v.	v.	v.		prep.	n.

Parts of Sentence: subject   ------predicate-----

Phrases: --prep. phrase--

Clauses: one independent clause, simple declarative sentence

This sentence illustrates the logic of prepositional phrase modification. We know that prepositional phrases are modifiers, so every prepositional phrase is either an adjective or an adverb. Which one is this? One way to tell is to remember the preposition placement rule: any prepositional phrase that modifies a noun must be place immediately after it. So *by Thursday* can not modify *visitors*, it can only modify the verb. By this same rule the phrase would modify the verb if the phrase came at the beginning of the sentence.

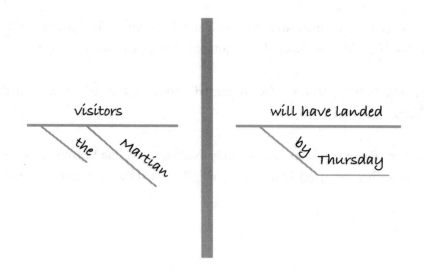

Questions for individual thought or small group discussion:

synthesis: making connections

You look up a verb in the dictionary and find that, in addition to a definition, the dictionary entry contains the letters *v.t.* in italics. What does that tell you about how that verb is to be used? How many forms of knowledge have to come together in your brain to enable you to look up and comprehend the abbreviation *v.t.*?

divergence: thinking of alternatives

Grammar is a way of thinking about language, but another way of saying that is that *grammar helps you to organize ideas*. Think of as many ways as you can in which grammar helps you to organize ideas, and consider this question one level at a time, beginning with parts of speech, then parts of the sentence, then phrases, and then clauses.

analysis: breaking down into components

Why are the parts of speech called the parts of speech?

aesthetics: artistic qualities

Which sentence do you think is more beautiful:

"I only regret that I have but one life to give for my country."

"These are the times that try men's souls."

Why?

Use the grammar clues to solve this Mystery Sentence:

A children's story contains a compound declarative sentence distinguished by three independent clauses. A coordinating conjunction is used twice to join the three clauses together. Each clause contains a contraction of the first person singular subject pronoun and the helping verb *will*. The third clause contains a second person singular possessive adjective, a direct object, and an adverb. The first two clauses contain only subjects and verbs. What is the sentence?

---

1. I'll huff, and I'll puff, and I'll blow your house down.

From Nathaniel Hawthorne's
The Scarlet Letter

A throng of bearded men, in sad-colored garments and gray, steeple-crowned hats, intermixed with women, some wearing hoods, and others bareheaded, was assembled in front of a wooden edifice, the door of which was heavily timbered with oak and studded with iron spikes.

What is the style of this first paragraph from Nathaniel Hawthorne's classic? How many sentences are in the paragraph? How many words in the sentence? Is there a direct object? What is the subject/predicate set? How many adjectives are in the paragraph? What generalizations could you make about the style of the paragraph? What do you notice about, and how can you explain, the following consonants:

A throng of bearded men, in sad-colored garments and gray, steeple-crowned hats, intermixed with women, some wearing hoods, and others bareheaded, was assembled in front of a wooden edifice, the door of which was heavily timbered with oak and studded with iron spikes.

1. Write a simple declarative sentence that has a compound subject consisting of one common noun and one proper noun, that has a verb consisting of a main verb and a helping verb, that contains a direct object, and that contains an indefinite article.

2. Write a complex declarative sentence that contains a dependent clause beginning with a subordinating conjunction followed by an independent clause which includes a subject complement.

---

1. Ahab and the mariners have hunted a beautiful creature.
2. If you didn't climb the mast, Starbuck is a liar.

Loop One Writing Lab
Prepositional Phrases

1. Describe a peaceful woodland scene, with an animal moving through or across it. You can choose any animal you like. The description should be between fifty and a hundred words long.

2. After you finish, read your paragraph, then go back and strike through the prepositional phrases.

3. See if you can think of a different way to include the information that used to be in the prepositional phrases.

4. Write your own definition of *preposition* and *prepositional phrase*.

"O, what a rogue and peasant slave am I."

-William Shakespeare

Perhaps Shakespeare's greatest play, *Hamlet*, contains this classic line of self-doubt, when Hamlet cries in soliloquy: "Oh, what a rogue and peasant slave am I!" Analyze the four levels of grammar in Hamlet's sentence.

Parts of speech: *Oh* is an interjection; *what* is an adjective modifying the noun *rogue*; the indefinite article *a* is also an adjective modifying *rogue*; *and* is a coordinating conjunction joining the nouns *rogue* and *slave* into a compound; *peasant* is here used as an adjective to modify the noun *slave*; *am* is a present tense linking verb; *I* is a first person singular subject pronoun.

Parts of the sentence: The subject of this sentence is *I*; its predicate is the linking verb *am*: the linking verb connects the subject to a compound subject complement, the two nouns *rogue* and slave; which are predicate nominatives. The sentence is notable for its effective inversion, putting the despised subject of Hamlet's sentence, himself, last, to echo in the silence of the period.

Phrases: There are no prepositional, appositive, or verbal phrases.

Clauses: This is a simple declarative sentence, consisting of only one clause, since it has only one subject/predicate set.

FOUR-LEVEL ANALYSIS

	Oh,	what	a	rogue	and	peasant	slave	am	I.
Parts of Speech:	interj.	adj.	adj.	n.	conj.	adj.	n.	v.	pron.
Parts of Sentence:				---- compound subject complement----				pred.	subj.
Phrases:				-------------no phrase-------------					
Clauses:			one independent clause, simple declarative sentence						

113   156

For the next ten sentences, identify the **part of speech** of the word in **bold**:

1. Do **bacilli** and fungi have nuclei in their cells? _____

2. Can a system of justice **ever** be unjust? _____

3. The **luminous** moonlight illuminated the *Pequod.* _____

4. The **superannuated** doorman celebrated his fiftieth anniversary. _____

5. At the satellite's **apogee** we could not find it with binoculars. _____

6. The senior class president **befriended** the venerable man. _____

7. **On** his solo transcontinental flight, he enjoyed the solitude. _____

8. Basic instructions are **included** with each new bassoon. _____

9. The interrogation was **derogatory** in tone. _____

10. Several members of **Parliament** had a parley in the parlor. _____

For the next ten sentences, identify the **part of sentence** of the word in **bold**:

11. The **plenipotentiary** met twice with the potentate. _____

12. The surge of the sea portended the **resurgence** of violence. _____

13. The philologist delighted in inventing witty **neologisms**. _____

14. The grammar in the telegram was not **correct**. _____

15. During the holy man's incantation, the spirit began **to appear**. _____

16. There **were** no regal ceremonies in the interregnum. _____

17. The doctor's prognosis gave **Diogenes** renewed hope. _____

18. The musician's androgynous **appearance** was widely imitated. _____

19. The secret agent spilled the deadly chemical **agent**. _____

20. There may be little **time** to act or react. _____

For the next ten sentences, identify the phrase in **bold**:

1. Bulgakov, **the anarchist's friend**, had a severe case of anemia.   _____

2. **Complaining loudly**, the absentee landlord was abducted   _____

3. We advised the adventurer **to admire his adversary**.   _____

4. The melodeon played a sappy melody **during the melodrama**.   _____

5. The pilot tried **to study aeronautics and aerodynamics**.   _____

6. The albino stared **at the white pages** of the blank album.   _____

7. Luciferase is the enzyme **in the luminous organs** of the firefly.   _____

8. Does Franklin's epitaph contain a witty epigram **for posterity**?   _____

9. **At the exhumation**, the rich humus was removed.   _____

10. **Viewing microbes** is a favorite habit of biologists.   _____

For the next ten sentences, identify the sentence structure (disregard bold type).

11. The bonny lass discovered the **bonanza** by accident.   _____

12. We learned, and the **superstructure** was constructed in three days.   _____

13. They left when chlorine damaged the **chlorophyll** in the plants.   _____

14. He held the **cyanotype** to the light and she admired the blue lines.   _____

15. The **cytologist** watched the leucocytes and erythrocytes.   _____

16. She folded the **diploma** and handed it to the waiting diplomat.   _____

17. His **dyslexia** made it hard to pronounce words, but he succeeded.   _____

18. The **ecologist** was fascinated with living things in the ecosystem.   _____

19. The senator had **hypoglycemia**, not anemia, when this occurred.   _____

20. A specialist in dysentery and **enteritis** explained the rare ailment.   _____

For the next ten sentences, identify the **part of speech** of the word in **bold**:

1. Do **bacilli** and fungi have nuclei in their cells?   noun

2. Can a system of justice **ever** be unjust?   adverb

3. The **luminous** moonlight illuminated the *Pequod.*   adjective

4. The **superannuated** doorman celebrated his fiftieth anniversary.   adjective

5. At the satellite's **apogee** we could not find it with binoculars.   noun

6. The senior class president **befriended** the venerable man.   verb

7. **On** his solo transcontinental flight, he enjoyed the solitude.   preposition

8. Basic instructions are **included** with each new bassoon.   adjective

9. The interrogation was **derogatory** in tone.   adjective

10. Several members of **Parliament** had a parley in the parlor.   noun

For the next ten sentences, identify the **part of sentence** of the word in **bold**:

11. The **plenipotentiary** met twice with the potentate.   subject

12. The surge of the sea portended the **resurgence** of violence.   direct object

13. The philologist delighted in inventing witty **neologisms**.   object of a gerund

14. The grammar in the telegram was not **correct**.   subject complement

15. During the holy man's incantation, the spirit began **to appear**.   direct object

16. There **were** no regal ceremonies in the interregnum.   predicate

17. The doctor's prognosis gave **Diogenes** renewed hope.   indirect object

18. The musician's androgynous **appearance** was widely imitated.   subject

19. The secret agent spilled the deadly chemical **agent**.   direct object

20. There may be little **time** to act or react.   subject complement

For the next ten sentences, identify the **bold** phrase and its part of speech:

1.	Bulgakov, **the anarchist's friend**, had a severe case of anemia.	appositive, adjective
2.	**Complaining loudly**, the absentee landlord was abducted.	participle, adjective
3.	We advised the adventurer **to admire his adversary**.	infinitive, noun
4.	The melodeon played a sappy melody **during the melodrama**.	prepositional, adverb
5.	The pilot tried **to study aeronautics and aerodynamics**.	infinitive, noun
6.	The albino stared **at the white pages** of the blank album.	prepositional, adverb
7.	Luciferase is the enzyme **in the luminous organs** of the firefly.	prepositional, adjective
8.	Does Franklin's epitaph contain a witty epigram **for posterity**?	prepositional, adjective
9.	**At the exhumation**, the rich humus was removed.	prepositional, adverb
10.	**Viewing microbes** is a favorite habit of biologists.	gerund, noun

For the next ten sentences, identify the sentence structure (disregard bold type).

11.	The bonny lass discovered the **bonanza** by accident.	simple
12.	We learned, and the **superstructure** was constructed in three days.	compound
13.	They left when chlorine damaged the **chlorophyll** in the plants.	complex
14.	He held the **cyanotype** to the light, and she admired the blue lines.	compound
15.	The **cytologist** watched the leucocytes and erythrocytes.	simple
16.	She folded the **diploma** and handed it to the waiting diplomat.	simple
17.	His **dyslexia** made it hard to pronounce words, but he succeeded.	compound
18.	The **ecologist** was fascinated with living things in the ecosystem.	simple
19.	The senator had **hypoglycemia**, not anemia, when this occurred.	complex
20.	A specialist in dysentery and **enteritis** explained the rare ailment.	simple

For each of the following sentences, circle the letter of each answer that is true. The answer can be any combination, including all or none. This exercise will teach you the real process of punctuation as a function of grammar.

1. In October the Allies advanced and the Axis gathered its resources.
   - a. a comma after the prepositional phrase
   - b. a comma after the dependent clause
   - c. a comma after the independent clause
   - d. an apostrophe in the contraction
   - e. commas before and after the appositive

2. In San Antonio Texas the tumbleweed covered Ricardos field.
   - a. a comma after the city
   - b. a comma after the state appositive
   - c. an apostrophe in the plural noun
   - d. an apostrophe in the possessive noun
   - e. a comma after the dependent clause

3. A very large moon shone as Alexander the Macedonian conqueror rode forward.
   - a. a comma between adjectives
   - b. a comma after the dependent clause
   - c. a comma after the independent clause
   - d. commas around the appositive
   - e. commas around the noun of direct address

4. Hamlet Whitmans book Leaves of Brass is about a train called The Occident Express.
   - a. italics on the train title
   - b. an apostrophe in the possessive noun
   - c. quotation marks around the book title
   - d. italics on the book title
   - e. commas around the appositive

5. The well planned party and the serene weather rejuvenated twenty seven friends.
   - a. comma between adjectives that precede the noun.
   - b. a hyphen in the compound adjective
   - c. a comma after the dependent clause
   - d. a hyphen in the compound number
   - e. an apostrophe in the possessive noun

Answer Key

1. In October the Allies advanced, and the Axis gathered its resources.
       a. a comma after the prepositional phrase   d. an apostrophe in the contraction
       b. a comma after the dependent clause   e. commas before and after the appositive
       c. a comma after the independent clause

   The sentence needs an I,ccI comma to make the sentence compound rather than run-on.

2. In San Antonio, Texas, the tumbleweed covered Ricardo's field.
       a. a comma after the city   **d. an apostrophe in the possessive noun**
       b. a comma after the state appositive   e. a comma after the dependent clause
       c. an apostrophe in the plural noun

   The state is an appositive, and needs a comma both before and after it, since it is an interrupting definition. We also need an apostrophe for the possessive noun.

3. A very large moon shone as Alexander, the Macedonian conqueror, rode forward.
       a. a comma between adjectives   **d. commas around the appositive**
       b. a comma after the dependent clause   e. commas around the noun of direct address
       c. a comma after the independent clause

   We need commas around the appositive, but not before the second clause, since this is an ID complex sentence. If it were reversed, then it would need the D,I comma.

4. Hamlet Whitman's book, *Leaves of Brass,* is about a train called *The Occident Express.*
       a. italics on the train title   **d. italics on the book title**
       b. an apostrophe in the possessive noun   **e. commas around the appositive**
       c. quotation marks around the book title

   Book titles and all major vessels of transport titles should be in italics (or underlined, same thing.)

5. The well-planned party and the serene weather rejuvenated twenty-seven friends.
       a. comma between adjectives that precede the noun.   **d. a hyphen in the compound number**
       b. a hyphen in the compound adjective   e. an apostrophe in the possessive noun
       c. a comma after the dependent clause

Our ship was hit by a weaker beam.

Parts of speech: *Our* is a possessive pronoun modifying the noun *ship*; *ship* is a singular common noun; *was hit* consists of the helping verb *was* and the main verb *hit*; *was hit* is past tense, passive voice action verb; *by* is a preposition; *a* and *weaker* are adjectives modifying the singular common noun *beam*. The adjective *a* is an indefinite article.

Parts of the sentence: The subject is *ship*, and the verb is *was hit*. There is no direct object, indirect object, or subject complement.

Phrases: The sentence contains a prepositional phrase, *by a weaker beam*. The preposition is *by*, and the object of the preposition is *beam*. The purpose of a prepositional phrase is to modify; this particular prepositional phrase modifies the verb. In other words, this prepositional phrase acts like an adverb, even though the phrase contains no adverb.

Clauses: The sentence only contains one clause; it is therefore a simple sentence in structure. The entire sentence is the clause—an independent clause. Within the clause there is a prepositional phrase which is discussed above. Just as the heart can be within the body, so that a person has both a heart and a body, a phrase can be within a clause, so that a sentence can have both a phrase and a clause. In other words, a clause can have a phrase inside it.

• • •

Degrees of adjectives: Some adjectives can be expressed in three degrees. Examples are *good, better, best*; *tall, taller, tallest*; *bad, worse, worst*; and *weak, weaker, weakest*. The names of the three degrees are the **positive** degree (weak), the **comparative** degree (weaker), and the **superlative** degree (weakest). The adjective *weaker* in the sentence above is in the comparative degree.

Active Voice: The sentence above is expressed in passive voice. Often a sentence will have more power if it is reworded to use the active voice. This means that the subject of the sentence will be acting, not acted on. *A weaker beam hit our ship* is the active voice version of the sentence.

	Our	ship	was	hit	by	a	weaker	beam.
Parts of Speech:	pron.	n.	v.	v.	prep.	adj.	adj.	n.
Parts of Sentence:	subject		--predicate--					
Phrases:					----------prepositional phrase---------			
Clauses:	one independent clause, simple declarative sentence							

The key concept to understand in this sentence is that the action verb is passive voice. We have the option of saying either that the beam hit the ship (active voice) or that the ship was hit by the beam (passive voice). Remember that active voice will be preferred in most of the things that you write. A linking verb is neither active voice nor passive voice; these terms apply only to action verbs.

BINARY DIAGRAM

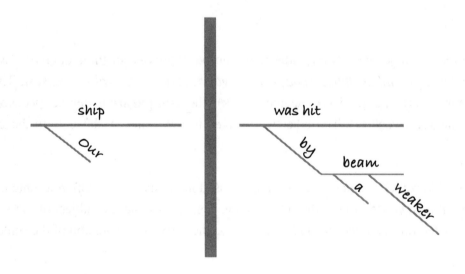

Questions for individual thought or small group discussion:

emotion: feelings

How many names of emotions can you think of? Can you give names to some of the subtle, in-between emotions, e.g. *wistful*? Think of more examples, decide what part of speech each example is, and imagine what someone's face would look like if he or she were experiencing that emotion.

synthesis: making connections

What writing function do adjectives, prepositional phrases, adverbs, participle phrases, and infinitive phrases share?

divergence: thinking of alternatives

How many descriptive adjectives can you think of that are not the names of colors but that describe visual properties, e.g.,. *shiny*. Keep thinking of examples until you think of some excellent words that are rarely used.

analysis: breaking down into components

A traditional sentence diagram has a long horizontal line, dividing the bottom from the top, and a vertical line, dividing the left from the right. What is the difference between these two lines, and which do you think is more important?

Use the grammar clues to solve this Mystery Sentence:

This sentence from a nursery rhyme begins with four alliterated one-syllable interjections in a row, followed by a first person singular subject pronoun, an present tense transitive action verb, a definite article, a singular common noun, a preposition that does not show a relationship of time or of space, an indefinite article, and a three-syllable proper noun.

Fee, fi, fo fum, I smell the blood of an Englishman.

From Frederick Douglass's
Narrative of the Life of Frederick Douglass

From this time I was most narrowly watched. If I was in a separate room any considerable length of time, I was sure to be suspected of having a book, and was at once called to give an account of myself. All this, however, was too late. The first step had been taken. Mistress, in teaching me the alphabet, had given me the *inch*, and no precaution could prevent me from taking the *ell*.

What characterizes the style of this first paragraph from Frederick Douglass's classic autobiography? How many sentences are in the paragraph? How long are the sentences? Are there many direct objects or subject complements? How many adjectives or adverbs are in the paragraph? Do you see any verbals? What generalizations could you make about the style of the paragraph? Are there needless words in the paragraph, or does every word tell?

How does the writing style of Douglass's paragraph compare to Nathaniel Hawthorne's style in the passage we read in Loop One?

1. Write a compound exclamatory sentence which uses a coordinating conjunction and punctuation to separate the clauses, and which contains one clause with a compound predicate. One of the clauses should contain two adverbs.

2. Write a simple interrogative sentence with a future tense verb, an infinitive phrase, and a prepositional phrase.

---

1. Nervously, we laughed aloud in the sun, but the white whale turned and swam toward our raft!

2. Will Queequeg try to jump into the sea?

Loop Two Writing Lab
The Paragraph

1. Write a well-organized paragraph on the subject of your choice. The paragraph should contain at least five sentences.

2. Divide the paragraph into its individual sentences and rearrange them so that the paragraph is as disorganized and confusing as possible. Do this without altering the sentences themselves.

3. Think carefully about what the difference is between paragraphs one and two.

4. Write a well-organized paragraph on the subject, "What Connects One Idea to Another?"

"Take me home to Aunt Em!"

-L. Frank Baum

One of the most popular stories ever written, L. Frank Baum's classic about Dorothy and the Wizard of Oz has become a permanent fixture in modern culture. This sentence, uttered with Toto in her arms, reflects Dorothy's profound desire to go home.

Parts of speech: *Take* is a singular present tense action verb; *me* is a first person singular object pronoun; *home* is an adverb modifying *take*; *to* is a preposition showing the relationship between its object *Aunt Em* and the verb; *Aunt Em* is a proper noun, which is probably best considered as a single entity.

Parts of the sentence: The subject of the sentence is an understood *you*; that subject's predicate is *take*; *me* is the direct object of the action verb.

Phrases: There is an adverbial prepositional phrase *to Aunt Em*, that modifies the verb.

Clauses: This is a simple imperative sentence; it might be argued that it is an exclamatory sentence, which in a sense is true, but its essence as a command seems to be primary.

FOUR-LEVEL ANALYSIS

	(you)	Take	me	home	to	Aunt Em!
Parts of Speech:		v.	pron.	adv.	prep.	n.
Parts of Sentence:	(subj.)	pred.	direct object			
Phrases:					----prepositional phrase----	
Clauses:		one independent clause, simple imperative sentence				

For each of the next ten sentences, identify the **part of speech** of the word in **bold**:

1. **Polychrome** sculptures have more colors than monochrome ones. _____

2. The **formation** of troops in formal uniforms was impressive. _____

3. Three consecutive sequels were of no **consequence**. _____

4. **His** hypoglycemia made him watch his diet. _____

5. The patient's hemophilia made it difficult to stop **the** hemorrhage. _____

6. The expedition's Ultima Thule was the **North** Pole. _____

7. She felt that it was **infra dig** to eat fried chicken with her fingers. _____

8. Leukemia produces an **excessive** number of leucocytes. _____

9. If **hemolysis** breaks down red blood cells, what does analysis do? _____

10. Did mesons strike Mesopotamia in the **Mesozoic** Era? _____

For each of the next ten sentences, identify the **part of sentence** of the word in **bold**:

11. Would **you** walk a millimeter to drink a milligram of milk? _____

12. The memo helped **him** remember the commemoration ceremony. _____

13. Don't digress; discuss **progress** with members of congress. _____

14. The collaborators spent laborious **nights** in the laboratory. _____

15. The mycardiograph showed his myocardium is **strong**. _____

16. The evacuation left **vacancies** in the vacation resort. _____

17. The oligarchy gave national **policy** a renewed secrecy. _____

18. Did the fructose from the apples raise his glucose **level**? _____

19. Unfortunately, the neurosis **developed** into a psychosis. _____

20. The celebrity's **pulchritude** was only equaled by his turpitude. _____

For the next ten sentences, identify the phrase in **bold**:

1. A pleochroic crystal shows colors **from different directions**. _____

2. **Quivering with anger**, the podiatrist treated the injured arthropod. _____

3. The sorority was located **between two fraternities**. _____

4. **Careful searching** showed not one phenomenon but several. _____

5. The valedictory address contained valid arguments **to think about**. _____

6. **Finally trapped**, the parapsychologist told a parable with a paradox. _____

7. Von Helmsmit, **the old baron**, was dominant over his dominion. _____

8. Do workers **in this country** want a meritocracy or an ergatocracy? _____

9. Rhizophagous animals dig up and feed **on delicious rhizomes**. _____

10. Saprogenic bacteria caused the material **to decay rapidly**. _____

For the next ten sentences, identify the sentence structure (disregard the bold type):

11. The **schism** in the party healed, and they won the election. _____

12. When he's in **Mesopotamia**, he uses the **hippodrome**. _____

13. Did his **chromosome** problem have a **psychosomatic** cause? _____

14. The **Sporozoa** are **Protozoa**; they multiply by **sporogenesis**. _____

15. The people in the **station** voted to preserve the **status quo**. _____

16. As we climbed, **rhododendron** bloomed on the high mountainsides. _____

17. The **taxidermist** was interested in a new **taxonomy** of species. _____

18. The new **volunteer** had a **malevolent** expression, if you ask me. _____

19. As the candidate tried to **fraternize**, the local politicians laughed. _____

20. **Trichinosis** is a disease; it is caused by the **trichina** worm. _____

For each of the next ten sentences, identify the **part of speech** of the word in **bold**:

1. **Polychrome** sculptures have more colors than monochrome ones.   adjective

2. The **formation** of troops in formal uniforms was impressive.   noun

3. Three consecutive sequels were of no **consequence**.   noun

4. **His** hypoglycemia made him watch his diet.   pronoun

5. The patient's hemophilia made it difficult to stop **the** hemorrhage.   adjective

6. The expedition's Ultima Thule was the **North** Pole.   adjective

7. She felt that it was **infra dig** to eat fried chicken with her fingers.   noun

8. Leukemia produces an **excessive** number of leucocytes.   adjective

9. If **hemolysis** breaks down red blood cells, what does analysis do?   noun

10. Did mesons strike Mesopotamia in the **Mesozoic** Era?   adjective

For each of the next ten sentences, identify the **part of sentence** of the word in **bold**:

11. Would **you** walk a millimeter to drink a milligram of milk?   subject

12. The memo helped **him** remember the commemoration ceremony.   direct object

13. Don't digress; discuss **progress** with members of congress.   direct object

14. The collaborators spent laborious **nights** in the laboratory.   direct object

15. The mycardiograph showed his myocardium is **strong**.   subject complement

16. The evacuation left **vacancies** in the vacation resort.   direct object

17. The oligarchy gave national **policy** a renewed secrecy.   indirect object

18. Did the fructose from the apples raise his glucose **level**?   direct object

19. Unfortunately, the neurosis **developed** into a psychosis.   predicate

20. The celebrity's **pulchritude** was only equaled by his turpitude.   subject

For the next ten sentences, identify the **bold** phrase and its part of speech:

1. A pleochroic crystal shows colors **from different directions**.   prepositional, adverb

2. **Quivering with anger**, the podiatrist treated the injured arthropod.   participle, adjective

3. The sorority was located **between two fraternities**.   prepositional, adverb

4. **Careful searching** showed not one phenomenon but several.   gerund, noun

5. The valedictory address contained valid arguments **to think about**.   infinitive, adjective

6. **Finally trapped**, the parapsychologist told a parable with a paradox.   participle, adjective

7. Von Helmsmit, **the old baron**, was dominant over his dominion.   appositive, adjective

8. Do workers **in this country** want a meritocracy or an ergatocracy?   prepositional, adjective

9. Rhizophagous animals dig up and feed **on delicious rhizomes**.   prepositional, adverb

10. Saprogenic bacteria caused the material **to decay rapidly**.   infinitive, adverb

For the next ten sentences, identify the sentence structure (disregard the bold type):

11. The **schism** in the party healed, and they won the election.   compound

12. When he's in **Mesopotamia**, he uses the **hippodrome**.   complex

13. Did his **chromosome** problem have a **psychosomatic** cause?   simple

14. The **Sporozoa** are **Protozoa**; they multiply by **sporogenesis**.   compound

15. The people in the **station** voted to preserve the **status quo**.   simple

16. As we climbed, **rhododendron** bloomed on the high mountainsides.   complex

17. The **taxidermist** was interested in a new **taxonomy** of species.   simple

18. The new **volunteer** had a **malevolent** expression if you ask me.   complex

19. As the candidate tried to **fraternize**, the local politicians laughed.   complex

20. **Trichinosis** is a disease; it is caused by the **trichina** worm.   compound

For each of the following sentences, circle the letter of each answer that is true. The answer can be any combination, including all or none. This exercise will teach you the real process of punctuation as a function of grammar.

1. With a subtle sort of smile the president said All citizens are created equal.
   a. a comma after the prepositional phrases
   b. an apostrophe in the contraction
   c. a comma before the direct quotation
   d. quotation marks around the direct quotation
   e. a period inside the closing quotation marks

2. When the poet wrote The Divine Comedy he created a new poetic form.
   a. a comma after the independent clause
   b. an apostrophe in the possessive noun
   c. a comma after the dependent clause
   d. italics on the poem title
   e. quotation marks around the poem title

3. A two thirds Roman majority wanted circuses bread and gladiatorial entertainment.
   a. a hyphen in the compound adjective
   b. a colon at the beginning of the list
   c. a comma after the plural common noun
   d. a list comma before the coordinating conjunction
   e. a comma after the dependent clause

4. Reaching blindly outward the hoary translucent apparition gained its footing.
   a. a comma after the prepositional phrase
   b. comma between adjectives preceding the noun
   c. a comma after the participle phrase
   d. a comma after the gerund phrase
   e. an apostrophe in the contraction

5. Ola is the Spanish word for wave it is an easy noun to learn.
   a. quotation marks around the Spanish noun
   b. italics on the Spanish noun
   c. a comma after the independent clause
   d. a comma after the dependent clause
   e. a semicolon after the independent clause

Answer Key

1. With a subtle sort of smile, the president said, "All citizens are created equal."
   a. a comma after the prepositional phrases   **d. quote marks around direct quotation**
   b. an apostrophe in the contraction   **e. period inside the closing quote marks**
   c. a comma before the direct quotation

   A comma after multiple introductory prepositional phrases. Our standard is to put the period inside the closing quotes, although corporations and the British often put it outside.

2. When the poet wrote *The Divine Comedy,* he created a new poetic form.
   a. a comma after the independent clause   **d. italics on the poem title**
   b. an apostrophe in the possessive noun   e. quotation marks around the poem title
   c. a comma after the dependent clause

   We need a D,I comma after the introductory dependent clause in this complex sentence, and with a poem as long and important as Dante's Divine Comedy, we should put the title in italics; after all, it makes an entire book.

3. A two-thirds Roman majority wanted circuses, bread, and gladiatorial entertainment.
   a. a hyphen in the compound adjective   **d. list comma before coordinating conj.**
   b. a colon at the beginning of the list   e. a comma after the dependent clause
   c. a comma after the plural common noun

   A hyphen makes two-thirds *a compound adjective, but if we said "it increased by two thirds," we wouldn't want the hyphen because then* thirds *would be a noun, and* two *would only be its modifying adjective. We prefer to put the list comma before the coordinating conjunction.*

4. Reaching blindly outward the hoary, grizzled apparition gained its footing.
   a. a comma after the prepositional phrase   d. a comma after the gerund phrase
   b. comma between adjectives preceding the noun   e. an apostrophe in the contraction
   c. a comma after the participle phrase

   No comma after a single introductory prepositional phrase if no confusion is present. We separate multiple adjectives that precede and modify a noun—not including articles.

5. *Ola* is the Spanish word for *wave*; it is an easy noun to learn.
   a. quotation marks around the Spanish noun   d. a comma after the dependent clause
   b. italics on the Spanish noun   **e. semicolon after the independent clause**
   c. a comma after the independent clause

   We would actually put both Ola *and* wave *in italics; the first is a foreign language word and also a word as such, and the second is a word as such. We put an I;I semicolon between the two independent clauses in this compound sentence, since there is no coordinating conjunction between the clauses.*

Explosions and cataclysms rocked the night thunderously.

Parts of speech: *Explosions* and *cataclysms* are plural common nouns joined by the coordinating conjunction *and*; *rocked* is a past tense transitive action verb; *the* is an adjective (definite article) modifying the noun *night*; and *thunderously* is an adverb which modifies the verb *rocked*.

Parts of the sentence: *Explosions and cataclysms* is the compound subject of the verb *rocked*; *night* is the direct object of the verb *rocked*, since it receives the action of the verb: the night gets rocked. There are no indirect objects or subject complements. Remember that there can be no direct object unless there is an action verb, and there can be no subject complement unless there is a linking verb.

Phrases: There are no prepositional, verbal, or appositive phrases.

Clauses: This is a simple sentence because it contains only one subject/predicate set, the set *Explosions and cataclysms/rocked*. Notice that even though there are two subjects, they are both subjects of the same verb, and so both belong in the same clause. In order for the two subjects to be in two clauses, they would each have to have their own verb.

• • •

Adverb: the adverb *thunderously* is separated from the verb it modifies by two intervening words. Adverbs have a way of turning up at various locations in sentences.

Punctuation: There should be no comma between the two nouns in the compound subject. Compound sentences sometimes use commas, but compound subjects or verbs do not. Another way of saying this is that if a part of a sentence is compound, it is usually not interrupted with a comma.

Explosions and cataclysms rocked the night thunderously.

Parts of Speech:	n.	conj.	n.		v.	adj.	n.	adv.
Parts of Sentence:	--------------subject--------------				predicate		direct object	
Phrases:	no prepositional, appositive, or verbal phrases							
Clauses:	one independent clause, simple declarative sentence							

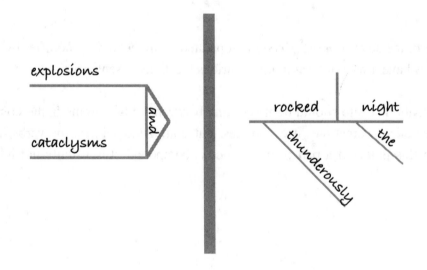

129   178

Questions for individual thought or small group discussion:

evaluation: judging value with criteria

Which would be worse, writing characterized by good grammar and poor diction, or writing characterized by good diction and poor grammar? Explain.

intuition: ideas from the blue

Language is, among other things, sound. Poets and novelists alike have long recognized that the sounds of words can amplify the emotional power of language. Pick several vowels and several consonants—what images or experiences do the sounds of these letters remind you of? Allow your mind to be free and suggestible, responsive to the sheer elemental sounds of language.

aesthetics: artistic qualities

What do you think some people mean by "clean, clear writing"? What would the opposite be? Why would clean, clear writing be considered pleasing?

divergence: thinking of alternatives

What if verbals did not exist? How many benefits of having verbals can you think of?

Use the grammar clues to solve this Mystery Sentence:

This sentence from American history begins with a plural demonstrative pronoun, followed by a plural present tense linking verb, then a definite article, then a one-syllable plural common noun; this is followed by a relative clause beginning with a relative pronoun which is also sometimes a singular demonstrative pronoun, a plural present tense action verb, a possessive adjective based on the plural of the noun *man*, and a direct object made of a one-syllable plural common noun rhyming with *rolls*.

These are the times that try men's souls. - Thomas Paine

From Robert Louis Stevenson's

Treasure Island

I remember him as if it were yesterday, as he came plodding to the inn door, his sea-chest following behind him in a handbarrow; a tall, strong, heavy, not-brown man; his tarry pigtail falling over the shoulders of his soiled blue coat; his hands ragged and scarred, with black, broken nails; and the sabre cut across one cheek, a dirty, livid white.

What can be said about the style of this paragraph from Robert Louis Stevenson's classic sea novel? How many sentences are in the paragraph? What is the sentence structure? Does Stevenson avoid adjectives? What generalizations could you make about the style of the paragraph?

How does Stevenson's writing style compare to Frederick Douglass's or Nathaniel Hawthorne's styles in the selections we saw in Loop One and Loop Two?

Why do you think Stevenson chose this unusual sentence structure?

1. Write a sentence that contains a properly used semicolon and a participle phrase.

2. Write a simple declarative sentence that begins with a first person singular subject pronoun, followed by a singular transitive action verb, then a common noun, followed by a preposition, an adjective definite article, a singular common noun, a preposition modifying that noun, a definite article, and the four-word proper name of a nation, the last two words of which are a prepositional phrase.

---

1. Rapidly filling with water, the Pequod began to sink; members of the crew glanced at each other.
2. I pledge allegiance to the flag of the United States of America.

Loop Three Writing Lab
Sentence Structure

1. Write a paragraph of 50-100 words, in which every sentence is a simple, declarative sentence.

2. Rewrite the paragraph, using various techniques, to make it one sentence.

3. Compare the two versions of the same paragraph.

4. Write a statement about the effect of sentence structure on the feeling of a paragraph.

It's a sin to kill a mockingbird.

-Harper Lee

A novel by Harper Lee, *To Kill a Mockingbird*, is known by a statement that is made by one of the novel's characters, Atticus Finch: "It's a sin to kill a mockingbird." Analyze the grammar of Atticus's words.

Parts of speech: *It's* is a contraction of the third person singular personal pronoun *It* and the present tense linking verb *is*; *a* is an adjective (indefinite article) modifying the singular common noun *sin*; *to kill* is an infinitive adjective modifying *sin*; *a* is an adjective modifying the singular common noun *mockingbird*.

Parts of the sentence: The subject of this sentence is *It*, and the predicate is *is*; since *is* is a linking verb, we must look to see if there is a subject complement: yes, *sin* is a subject complement linked to the subject *It* by the linking verb *is*.

Phrases: The sentence contains a famous phrase: "to kill a mockingbird." It is an infinitive phrase, and the entire phrase, not just *to kill*, is an adjective modifying *sin*. Within the phrase, *mockingbird* serves as an object to the infinitive *to kill*, as though *to kill* were a verb. Actually, infinitives are never used as verbs in sentences (I to see you!).

Clauses: Since the sentence contains only one subject/predicate set, *It/is*, it is a simple sentence by structure. By purpose, the sentence is declarative.

FOUR-LEVEL ANALYSIS

	It's	a	sin	to kill	a	mockingbird.
Parts of Speech:	pron./v.	adj.	n.	adj.	adj.	n.
Parts of Sentence:	subj./pred.		subject complement			
Phrases:				------------infinitive phrase-------------		
Clauses:	one independent clause, simple declarative sentence					

Identify the **part of speech** in **bold** in these sentences:

1. In the tropics the leafy **heliotropes** turn toward the sun. _____

2. A gastrologist studies the stomach; a **gastronome** prepares food. _____

3. The aged arthropod suffered **from** arthritis and arthralgia. _____

4. The popular ventriloquist had a heart operation on his **left** ventricle. _____

5. **Dorsiventral** leaves have distinct upper and lower surfaces. _____

6. The universe is sometimes referred to as the **macrocosm**. _____

7. Are right-handed people really more **dexterous**? _____

8. **Brachypterous** insects have short wings. _____

9. **Brachiate** trees have widely spreading branches in pairs, like arms. _____

10. The branchiopods are marine crustaceans that breathe **through** gills. _____

Identify the **part of sentence** in **bold** in these sentences:

11. The hyperkinetic boy did not possess **telekinesis**, fortunately. _____

12. The species *Homo sapiens* **belongs** to the Chordata phylum. _____

13. **Reproduction** by budding is also called blastogenesis. _____

14. If fingerprinting is dactylography, is sign language **dactylology**? _____

15. If you press your closed **eyelids**, you will see phosphenes. _____

16. What **is** the difference between a pentagram and a pentagon? _____

17. Perlite is a volcanic **glass** that resembles obsidian. _____

18. The voracious carnivore devoured the small **herbivore**. _____

19. The hologram gave the **scientists** a new view of the structure. _____

20. The diploid **structure** divided into two haploid structures. _____

Identify the type of **phrase** that is in **bold**:

1. Ishmael, **a member of the Anglican church**, is an Anglophile. _____

2. **To gain insight**, the anthropologist studies human cultures. _____

3. **Resembling birds**, the pterosaur and pterodactyl were dinosaurs. _____

4. Pithecanthropus skeletons were found **to be fragile**. _____

5. Her calligraphy is ornate, like the music **of the calliope**. _____

6. The austral winds raised storms **over the Australian outback**. _____

7. **Trembling nervously**, a boy held the cephalopod in both hands. _____

8. The physician asked the chiropractor **to practice chiromancy**. _____

9. The survivor **of the holocaust** made a caustic comment. _____

10. **With a laugh**, the extraterrestrial admired the subterranean grottoes. _____

Identify the **sentence structure** of each of these sentences. Disregard the bold.

11. The **cataract** and **cataclysm** caused **catastrophe** in the **catacombs**. _____

12. The lying criminal **perjured** himself, but the **jury** listened. _____

13. A **confluence** of **influences** made her **fluent** in Spanish, and it did. _____

14. The senator's **adherents** laughed, and the speech was **incoherent**. _____

15. The corrupt ruler was **deposed** when his **deposits** were discovered. _____

16. His **mundane** conversation bored her to tears; it was too much. _____

17. Is a **democracy** a **meritocracy** or a **plutocracy** for the **aristocracy**? _____

18. His **egomania** kept him from noticing the **kleptomania** of his guest. _____

19. Because he was **victimized** by his own ignorance, he paid a price. _____

20. The **anthology** article discussed the **anthozoans**; it was good. _____

Identify the **part of speech** in **bold** in these sentences:

1. In the tropics the leafy **heliotropes** turn toward the sun.   noun

2. A gastrologist studies the stomach; a **gastronome** prepares food.   noun

3. The aged arthropod suffered **from** arthritis and arthralgia.   preposition

4. The popular ventriloquist had a heart operation on his **left** ventricle.   adjective

5. **Dorsiventral** leaves have distinct upper and lower surfaces.   adjective

6. The universe is sometimes referred to as the **macrocosm**.   noun

7. Are right-handed people really more **dexterous**?   adjective

8. **Brachypterous** insects have short wings.   adjective

9. **Brachiate** trees have widely spreading branches in pairs, like arms.   adjective

10. The branchiopods are marine crustaceans that breathe **through** gills.   preposition

Identify the **part of sentence** in **bold** in these sentences:

11. The hyperkinetic boy did not possess **telekinesis**, fortunately.   direct object

12. The species *Homo sapiens* **belongs** to the Chordata phylum.   predicate

13. **Reproduction** by budding is also called blastogenesis.   subject

14. If fingerprinting is dactylography, is sign language **dactylology**?   subject complement

15. If you press your closed **eyelids**, you will see phosphenes.   direct object

16. What **is** the difference between a pentagram and a pentagon?   predicate

17. Perlite is a volcanic **glass** that resembles obsidian.   subject complement

18. The voracious carnivore devoured the small **herbivore**.   direct object

19. The hologram gave the **scientists** a new view of the structure.   indirect object

20. The diploid **structure** divided into two haploid structures.   subject

Identify the type of **bold** phrase and give its part of speech:

1. Ishmael, **a member of the Anglican church**, is an Anglophile. appositive, adjective

2. **To gain insight**, the anthropologist studies human cultures. infinitive, adverb

3. **Resembling birds**, the pterosaur and pterodactyl were dinosaurs. participle, adjective

4. Pithecanthropus skeletons were found **to be fragile**. infinitive, adverb

5. Her calligraphy is ornate, like the music **of the calliope**. prepostional, adjective

6. The austral winds raised storms **over the Australian outback**. prepositional, adverb

7. **Trembling nervously**, a boy held the cephalopod in both hands. participle, adjective

8. The physician asked the chiropractor **to practice chiromancy**. infinitive, noun

9. The survivor **of the holocaust** made a caustic comment. prepositional, adjective

10. **With a laugh**, the extraterrestrial admired the subterranean grottoes. prepositional, adverb

Identify the **sentence structure** of each of these sentences. Disregard the bold.

11. The **cataract** and **cataclysm** caused **catastrophe** in the **catacombs**. simple

12. The lying criminal **perjured** himself, but the **jury** listened. compound

13. A **confluence** of **influences** made her **fluent** in Spanish, and it did. compound

14. The senator's **adherents** laughed, and the speech was **incoherent**. compound

15. The corrupt ruler was **deposed** when his **deposits** were discovered. complex

16. His **mundane** conversation bored her to tears; it was too much. compound

17. Is a **democracy** a **meritocracy** or a **plutocracy** for the **aristocracy**? simple

18. **Egomania** kept him from noticing the **kleptomania** of his guest. simple

19. Because he was **victimized** by his own ignorance, he paid a price. complex

20. The **anthology** article discussed the **anthozoans**; it was good. compound

For each of the following sentences, circle the letter of each answer that is true. The answer can be any combination, including all or none. This exercise will teach you the real process of punctuation as a function of grammar.

1. The Red River Valley is a nice tune to know when youre in the desert.
   - a. italics on the song title
   - b. quotation marks around the song title
   - c. a comma after the dependent clause
   - d. a comma after the independent clause
   - e. an apostrophe in the contraction

2. Wow its fun to see three countries in a five day trip.
   - a. a comma after the interjection
   - b. an apostrophe in the possessive pronoun
   - c. an apostrophe in the contraction
   - d. a comma after the independent clauses
   - e. a hyphen in the compound adjective

3. In the Jamestown colony the incidence of pneumonia was down by one third.
   - a. comma after the introductory prepositional phrase
   - b. a hyphen in the fraction
   - c. a comma after the dependent clause
   - d. commas around the appositive
   - e. commas around the parenthetical remark

4. On December 4 1866 Wassily Kandinsky the abstract painter was born.
   - a. a comma after the day
   - b. a comma after the year appositive
   - c. a comma after the participle phrase
   - d. commas around the appositive
   - e. a comma after the dependent clause

5. Caught by the swift current Dagoo gazed through the porthole.
   - a. a comma after the dependent clause
   - b. comma after the introductory prepositional phrases
   - c. a comma after the participle phrase
   - d. commas around the appositive
   - e. a semicolon between the clauses

Answer Key

1. "The Red River Valley" is a nice tune to know when you're in the desert.
   a. italics on the song title
   b. quotation marks around the song title
   c. a comma after the dependent clause
   d. a comma after the independent clause
   e. an apostrophe in the contraction

   For the title of a song, a chapter, or an article, we use quotation marks; for the title of a book, an epic poem, or a major vessel of transport, we use italics. Remember that italics and underline are considered to be the same thing. On a typewriter, or when we are writing a research paper on the computer in `Courier type font,` *underline is better because Courier looks bad in italics. See:*

   I read *War and Peace* this week.
   `I read ` *`War and Peace`* ` this week.`
   `I read ` <u>`War and Peace`</u> ` this week.`

2. Wow, it's fun to see three countries in a five-day trip.
   a. a comma after the interjection
   b. an apostrophe in the possessive pronoun
   c. an apostrophe in the contraction
   d. a comma after the independent clauses
   e. a hyphen in the compound adjective

   It's *is the contraction of* it *and* is; *it needs an apostrophe.*

3. In the Jamestown colony the incidence of pneumonia was down by one third.
   a. comma after the introductory prepositional phrase
   b. a hyphen in the fraction
   c. a comma after the dependent clause
   d. commas around the appositive
   e. commas around the parenthetical remark

   No punctuation needed. Here the fraction is an adjective and a noun, rather than a compound adjective.

4. On December 4, 1866, Wassily Kandinsky, the abstract painter, was born.
   a. a comma after the day
   b. a comma after the year appositive
   c. a comma after the participle phrase
   d. commas around the appositive
   e. a comma after the dependent clause

   The sentence has two appositives, the year and then the definition of Kandinsky. Each one needs two commas to separate it from what it interrupts. The danger is always forgetting the second appositive comma.

5. Caught by the swift current, Dagoo gazed through the porthole.
   a. a comma after the dependent clause
   b. comma after the introductory prepositional phrases
   c. a comma after the participle phrase
   d. commas around the appositive
   e. a semicolon between the clauses

   We can't pick answer b because there is only one prepositional phrase at the beginning of the sentence, but it modifies a participle, so the answer is c.

The Andromedans attacked savagely, and we fell back.

Parts of speech: *The* is an adjective modifying the proper noun *Andromedans*; *attacked* is an intransitive action verb modified by the adverb *savagely*; *and* is a coordinating conjunction which joins two clauses; *we* is a pronoun (a personal, first-person plural pronoun, antecedent unknown); *fell* is the verb of the subject *we*; and *back* is an adverb modifying *fell*.

Parts of the sentence: This is an easy sentence to analyze because it simply contains two subject/predicate sets with a few modifiers. The first subject/predicate set is *Andromedans /attacked*, and the second set is *we/fell*. There are no direct objects, indirect objects, or subject complements.

Phrases: The sentence contains no prepositional, verbal, or appositive phrases.

Clauses: This is a compound sentence because it contains two independent clauses. The first clause is *The Andromedans attacked savagely*, and the second clause is *we fell back*. The two independent clauses are joined by a comma and a coordinating conjunction. Remember that when a compound sentence is joined by a coordinating conjunction (*and, but, or, nor, for, so, yet*), the comma is required. Without the comma the sentence would be a run-on sentence—a major error.

• • •

Compounds: Remember that the most important issue in compounds—whether it is compound adjectives, compound subjects, compound direct objects, or a compound sentence like this one where two independent clauses are joined together into a compound—is not have we punctuated the compound correctly but should this be a compound in the first place. We make compounds so that sentences will reflect the real world, where things sometimes come in pairs. This includes ideas, events, and objects.

The Andromedans attacked savagely, and we fell back.

Parts of Speech:	adj.	n.	v.	adv.	conj.	pron.	v.	adv.

Parts of Sentence:	subject	predicate

Phrases: no prepositional, appositive, or verbal phrases

Clauses: -------------independent clause-------------   --independent clause--

two independent clauses, I,ccI compound declarative sentence

This sentence illustrates the proper construction of an I,ccI compound sentence, with the comma before the coordinating conjunction that joins the two clauses together.

BINARY DIAGRAM

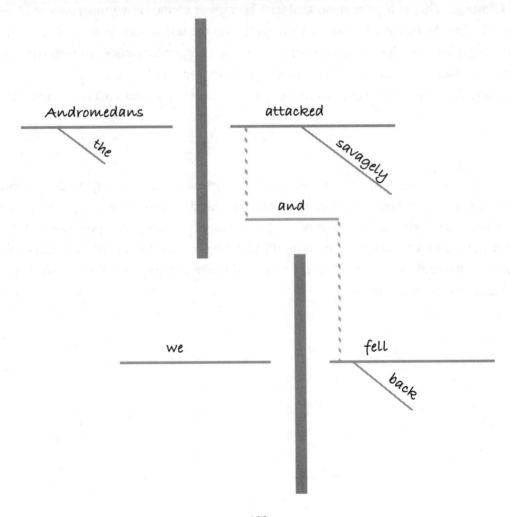

Questions for individual thought or small group discussion:

analysis: breaking down into components

The word *paragraph* is composed of two ancient stems, *para*, meaning beside, and *graph*, meaning write. Explain, in terms of these stems, why the name paragraph is an excellent name for what a paragraph does.

evaluation: judging value with criteria

One of our alternatives in writing is to choose between the indirect object and the prepositional phrase. We can say *I present Mort this medal* or *I present this medal to Mort*. If you were addressing an awards banquet, which construction would you prefer to use, and why?

intuition: ideas from the blue

Pick a color adjective, a motion adjective, and a temperature adjective. Imagine a scene which those three adjectives suggest.

synthesis: making connections

What two parts of speech do you think have most in common? What two parts of sentence do you think have most in common? Give your reasons. What grammar structure reminds you most of something in mathematics?

Use the grammar clues to solve this Mystery Sentence:

This interrogative sentence from a children's nursery rhyme begins with a two-syllable proper noun, repeated twice and used as the noun of direct address, followed by an adverb modifying an adjective that rhymes with the first word of the sentence, then an interrogative adverb, a helping verb, a second person singular possessive pronoun, a two-syllable common noun, and a main verb.

Mary, Mary, quite contrary, how does your garden grow?

From Henry David Thoreau's

Walden

The adventurous student will always study classics, in whatever language they may be written and however ancient they may be. For what are the classics but the noblest recorded thoughts of man? They are the only oracles which are not decayed, and there are such answers to the most modern inquiry in them as Delphi and Dodona never gave. We might as well omit to study Nature because she is old. To read well, that is, to read true books in a true spirit, is a noble exercise, and one that will task the reader more than any exercise which the customs of the day esteem. It requires a training such as the athletes underwent, the steady intention almost of the whole life to this object. Books must be read as deliberately and reservedly as they were written.

What do you notice about the style of this paragraph from Henry David Thoreau's classic essay? How long are Thoreau's sentences? Does he use big words, or rely on common words? What is the central purpose of this paragraph? Which sentence do you think is the best expression of his theme? How many verbals does Thoreau use?

1. Write a compound imperative sentence that has no pronouns, but has a noun of direct address and two interjections.

2. Write a simple declarative sentence that has a compound infinitive as the subject of a linking verb, with a subject complement (predicate nominative form) following the verb.

1. Yes, Dagoo, jump; O, jump!
2. To read or not to read is the dilemma.

Loop Four Writing Lab
Verbals

1. Write twenty-five words, using only sentences and no sentence fragments, containing as many verbals as you can possibly fit in.

2. Rewrite the passage, trying to replace every verbal with a common noun.

3. Compare the two versions of the same paragraph.

4. Write a statement explaining what you learned about verbals.

"I'm sure those are not the right words."

-Lewis Carroll

In Wonderland, Alice says this after trying unsuccessfully to recite a poem about a crocodile. The grammar is very interesting.

Parts of speech: *I'm* is the contraction of the subject pronoun *I* and the singular present tense linking verb *am*; *sure* is an adjective modifying *I*; *those* is a plural demonstrative pronoun; *are* is a plural present tense linking verb *are*: *not* is an adverb modifying *are*; *the* is an adjective definite article modifying the plural common noun *words*; and *right* is also an adjective modifying *words*.

Parts of the sentence: *I* is the subject of the linking verb predicate *am*, which links the subject to a subject complement predicate adjective *sure*; in the second clause, *those* is the subject of the linking verb *are* which links its subject to the subject complement predicate nominative *words*.

Phrases: There are no prepositional, appositive, or verbal phrases.

Clauses: This short sentence has a main clause, *I'm sure*, followed by an adverbial clause *those are not the right words* that modifies the adjective *sure*.

FOUR-LEVEL ANALYSIS

	I'm	sure	those	are	not	the	right	words.
Parts of Speech:	pron./v.	adj.	pron.	v.	adv.	adj.	adj.	n.
Parts of Sentence:	subj./pred.	subject complement	subj.	pred.				subject complement
Phrases:		----no prepositional, appositive, or verbal phrases----						
Clauses:		an ID complex declarative sentence						

Identify the **part of speech** in **bold** in each sentence below:

1. The linguini-loving linguist knew the **lingua franca**. _____

2. **Motile** microorganisms have powers of spontaneous motion. _____

3. The navy **circumnavigated** the globe by precise navigation. _____

4. The **undulant** waves soon inundated the low regions. _____

5. The famous **polyglot** spoke seventeen languages. _____

6. A hazy corona circled the moon the night **before** the coronation. _____

7. The goddess of the golden dawn, Aurora, held the **auriferous** rocks. _____

8. At the party the **literati** discussed the glories of literature. _____

9. The rational person will not **rationalize** his wrongs away. _____

10. Singing was an emotional **catharsis** for the vocalist. _____

Identify the **part of sentence** in **bold** in each sentence below:

11. There **was** a disparity between his story and the facts. _____

12. Are the rewards of the job **commensurate** with the duties? _____

13. We can choose either harmony or **acrimony**. _____

14. The quintet played **Mozart** to a group of quinquagenarians. _____

15. The **sociopath** used his knowledge of sociology to evil purposes. _____

16. Ovoviviparous fish produce **eggs** that hatch inside the mother. _____

17. The **dysphasia** resulted from injury to the brain's speech center. _____

18. His resignation **obviated** the need for impeachment proceedings. _____

19. Are you studying these phenomena or this **phenomenon**? _____

20. Histology is the **study** of the structure of plant and animal tissues. _____

For each sentence, identify the type of **phrase** in **bold**:

1. The atmometer measures the rate **of evaporation** of water.   _____

2. **Completely fascinated**, the cardiologist saw the electrocardiogram.   _____

3. **For a technician**, the Soviet cosmonaut had cosmopolitan tastes.   _____

4. The order **to attack quickly** was countermanded by his counterpart.   _____

5. The craniotomy was performed **by a skilled brain surgeon**.   _____

6. As if **to make a point**, the cyclone hurled the bicycle fifty yards.   _____

7. Agnostics are not usually attracted **to Gnosticism**.   _____

8. Over the years, his habits had ossified **beyond hope of change**.   _____

9. Beetles, **xylophagous insects**, had eaten the antique xylophone.   _____

10. The costermonger and fishmonger shouted out prices **to passersby**.   _____

For each sentence, identify the **sentence structure**. Disregard bold type.

11. **September** was the seventh month of the Roman calendar.   _____

12. I know; the flood of immigration stirred the public **xenophobia**.   _____

13. The **cardiovascular** system responded as the exercise increased.   _____

14. The storm **forecast** filled her with **foreboding**, but it was not enough.   _____

15. When she looked, the **smallish** object had a faint, **greenish** tint.   _____

16. Their assault on the summit was **hopeless**, **bootless**, and **fruitless**.   _____

17. As you know, we think high fashion is a **barometer** for new trends.   _____

18. The geologist studied the **ferrous** rock with care, but he missed it.   _____

19. The **quasi-military** operation into Cambodia has failed; it is true.   _____

20. We visited **Polynesia**, **Micronesia**, and **Melanesia** and came home.   _____

Identify the **part of speech** in **bold** in each sentence below:

1. The linguini-loving linguist knew the **lingua franca**.   noun

2. **Motile** microorganisms have powers of spontaneous motion.   adjective

3. The navy **circumnavigated** the globe by precise navigation.   verb

4. The **undulant** waves soon inundated the low regions.   adjective

5. The famous **polyglot** spoke seventeen languages.   noun

6. A hazy corona circled the moon the night **before** the coronation.   preposition

7. The goddess of the golden dawn, Aurora, held the **auriferous** rocks.   adjective

8. At the party the **literati** discussed the glories of literature.   noun

9. The rational person will not **rationalize** his wrongs away.   verb

10. Singing was an emotional **catharsis** for the vocalist.   noun

Identify the **part of sentence** in **bold** in each sentence below:

11. There **was** a disparity between his story and the facts.   predicate

12. Are the rewards of the job **commensurate** with the duties?   subject complement

13. We can choose either harmony or **acrimony**.   direct object

14. The quintet played **Mozart** to a group of quinquagenarians.   direct object

15. The **sociopath** used his knowledge of sociology to evil purposes.   subject

16. Ovoviviparous fish produce **eggs** that hatch inside the mother.   direct object

17. The **dysphasia** resulted from injury to the brain's speech center.   subject

18. His resignation **obviated** the need for impeachment proceedings.   predicate

19. Are you studying these phenomena or this **phenomenon**?   direct object

20. Histology is the **study** of the structure of plant and animal tissues.   subject complement

For each sentence, identify the type of **bold** phrase and its part of speech:

1. The atmometer measures the rate **of evaporation** of water.   prepositional, adjective

2. **Completely fascinated**, the cardiologist saw the electrocardiogram.   participle, adjective

3. **For a technician**, the Soviet cosmonaut had cosmopolitan tastes.   prepositional, adverb

4. The order **to attack quickly** was countermanded by his counterpart.   infinitive, adjective

5. The craniotomy was performed **by a skilled brain surgeon**.   prepositional, adverb

6. As if **to make a point**, the cyclone hurled the bicycle fifty yards.   infinitive, adverb

7. Agnostics are not usually attracted **to Gnosticism**.   prepositional, adverb

8. Over the years, his habits had ossified **beyond hope of change**.   prepositional, adverb

9. Beetles, **xylophagous insects**, had eaten the antique xylophone.   appositive, adjective

10. The costermonger and fishmonger shouted out prices **to passersby**.   prepositional, adverb

For each sentence, identify the **sentence structure**. Disregard bold type.

11. **September** was the seventh month of the Roman calendar.   simple

12. I know; the flood of immigration stirred the public **xenophobia**.   compound

13. The **cardiovascular** system responded as the exercise increased.   complex

14. The storm **forecast** filled her with **foreboding**, but it was not enough.   compound

15. When she looked, the **smallish** object had a faint, **greenish** tint.   complex

16. Their assault on the summit was **hopeless**, **bootless**, and **fruitless**.   simple

17. As you know, we think high fashion is a **barometer** for new trends.   complex

18. The geologist studied the **ferrous** rock with care, but he missed it.   compound

19. The **quasi-military** operation into Cambodia has failed; it is true.   compound

20. We visited **Polynesia**, **Micronesia**, and **Melanesia** and came home.   simple

For each of the following sentences, circle the letter of each answer that is true. The answer can be any combination, including all or none. This exercise will teach you the real process of punctuation as a function of grammar.

1. In December Baltimore lost its best player when a bizarre event occurred.
   a. a comma after the prepositional phrase
   b. a comma after the month
   c. an apostrophe in the possessive pronoun
   d. an apostrophe in the contraction
   e. a comma between the clauses

2. Because the wind was roaring we remained on the beach.
   a. a comma after the participle phrase
   b. a comma after the dependent clause
   c. a comma after the independent clause
   d. a semicolon between the clauses
   e. a comma after the prepositional phrase

3. The well intentioned athlete ran two miles uphill one downhill and one level.
   a. a hyphen in the compound adjective
   b. a colon before the list
   c. a comma after the adjective uphill
   d. a list comma after the adjective downhill
   e. a comma between the clauses

4. Flying across the Pacific was Noonans greatest dream.
   a. a comma after the introductory participle phrase
   b. a comma after the dependent clause
   c. an apostrophe in the possessive noun
   d. commas around the appositive phrase
   e. commas around the parenthetical remark

5. Yes the English lost twenty five fighters in the Battle of Britain.
   a. a comma after the introductory adverb
   b. a comma after the interjection
   c. a comma after the dependent clause
   d. a hyphen in the compound adjective
   e. a comma before the prepositional phrase

Answer Key

1. In December Baltimore lost its best player when a bizarre event occurred.
   a. a comma after the prepositional phrase
   b. a comma after the month
   c. an apostrophe in the possessive pronoun
   d. an apostrophe in the contraction
   e. a comma between the clauses

   No punctuation needed; this is a complex sentence with an ID clause structure. If it read the other way around: "When a bizarre event occurred, Baltimore lost its best player," then it would be a D,I structure and would need the comma.

2. Because the wind was roaring we remained on the beach.
   a. a comma after the participle phrase
   b. a comma after the dependent clause
   c. a comma after the independent clause
   d. a semicolon between the clauses
   e. a comma after the prepositional phrase

   This is a D,I complex sentence that begins with a subordinating conjunction to introduce the dependent clause.

3. The well-intentioned athlete ran two miles uphill, one downhill, and one level.
   a. a hyphen in the compound adjective
   b. a colon before the list
   c. a comma after **uphill**
   d. a list comma after **downhill**
   e. a comma between the clauses

   Again, though some style manuals will now abandon the list comma before the coordinating conjunction, we feel it best to retain it.

4. Flying across the Pacific was Noonan's greatest dream.
   a. a comma after the introductory participle phrase
   b. a comma after the dependent clause
   c. an apostrophe in the possessive noun
   d. commas around the appositive phrase
   e. commas around the parenthetical remark

   Even though this sentence begins with a gerund phrase (which contains a prepositional phrase), we will not put a comma after it because it is the subject of the sentence, and we do not separate the subject from its predicate.

5. Yes, the English lost twenty-five fighters in the Battle of Britain.
   a. a comma after the introductory adverb
   b. a comma after the interjection
   c. a comma after the dependent clause
   d. a hyphen in the compound adjective
   e. a comma before the prepositional phrase

   An interjection, since it has no grammatical function, is not connected to anything, so it can be separated with a comma without doing violence to the kinds of relationships that other parts of speech have.

Every planet has a magnetic field around it.

Parts of speech: *Every* is an adjective modifying the singular common noun *planet*; *has* is a present tense active voice transitive action verb; *a* is an adjective (indefinite article) modifying the singular common noun *field*; *magnetic* is also an adjective modifying the noun *field*; *around* is a preposition; and *it* is a third person singular pronoun which takes the place of the noun *planet*. In other words, *planet* is the antecedent of *it*.

Parts of the sentence: The subject is *planet*; the simple predicate is *has*; and the direct object is *field*.

Phrases: The sentence contains only one prepositional phrase, *around it*. The phrase modifies the verb *has*, telling where.

Clauses: The sentence contains only one clause, and it is therefore a simple sentence.

• • •

Subject/Verb Agreement: The adjective *every* before a subject takes a singular verb. This is true regardless of intervening prepositional phrases: *Every* one of the planets *has* a magnetic field around it. Every one/has, not Every one/have.

To have: The verb *has* is sometimes mistaken for a linking verb, since it sounds so much like *is*. But notice that the sentence doesn't link the planet to the field: it isn't an equation; the field isn't something the planet IS; the field is something the planet has. The planet has a field, just as a man has a duck. The field and the duck are objects which receive the action of the verb, they are not subject complements which are linked to (identified with) the subject. Possession, in other words, is a form of action.

Every	planet	has	a	magnetic	field	around	it.

Parts of Speech:

adj.	n.	v.	adj.	adj.	n.	prep.	pron.

Parts of Sentence:

	subject	predicate			direct object		

Phrases:

--prepositional--

Clauses:

one independent clause, simple declarative sentence

Prepositional phrases are always modifiers: adjectives or adverbs. How do we know that this phrase is an adverb and not an adjective? We can hear the logic: it *has* it *around* it, sounds more right than *a field around it*. And the phrase tells where the planet *has* it.

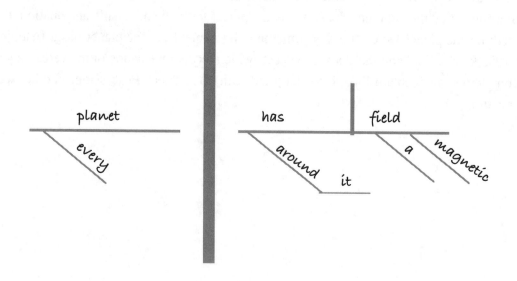

Questions for individual thought or small group discussion:

analysis: breaking down into components

The word **participle** comes from the Latin word *participium*, meaning a participation—a sharing. In what sense is there a participation in the relationship between a noun or pronoun and its participle?

aesthetics: artistic qualities

You are in telepathic communication with a friendly alien on a distant desert planet. The mind-pal can understand the words of your thoughts but cannot see visions through your eyes. What nouns, adjectives, and adverbs can you use to help your friend understand what rain is like, as we experience it through our senses? Answer this question by listing first the nouns, then the adjectives, and then the adverbs which communicate the experience of rain.

evaluation: judging value with criteria

Would our language be improved or diminished if we were to eliminate pronoun cases? In other words, suppose we eliminated the object case him-her-me-us-them pronouns and always used subject case I-he-she-etc. pronouns, so that there was never any confusion. *I saw he today. I saw he and she today.* Would our language be improved or diminished? Would new confusions arise?

divergence: thinking of alternatives

Now that you know more about grammar, how many specific benefits can you think of that come from this knowledge? List as many as you can.

Use the grammar clues to solve this Mystery Sentence:

A famous sentence from Shakespeare begins with a compound infinitive in which the second infinitive in the compound is negated by an adverb and ends with a clause that contains a demonstrative pronoun as a subject, a present tense linking verb, a definite article, and a singular common noun as a subject complement.

To be or not to be, that is the question. (Hamlet)

From George Orwell's

1984

Don't you see that the whole aim of Newspeak is to narrow the range of thought? In the end we shall make thoughtcrime literally impossible, because there will be no words in which to express it. Every concept that can ever be needed will be expressed by exactly *one* word, with its meaning rigidly defined and all its subsidiary meanings rubbed out and forgotten.

What can you say about the style of this paragraph from George Orwell's classic novel of a nightmarish totalitarian society? How would you characterize the tone of Orwell's paragraph? Was Orwell implying that control of grammar would be control of society? What is the relationship between individuality and language? How many clauses are there in this paragraph? What is the most common sentence structure?

1. Write a five clause compound sentence that has nine words or fewer.

2. Write a clause of ten words or more that has one noun, one verb, but no conjunctions, no interjections, and no prepositions.

---

1. Look, I came; I saw; I conquered; I am.

2. Very slowly, the tired, dirty, disheveled band trudged far away.

Loop Five Writing Lab
Disruptions of Normal Order

1. Write five separate sentences that begin with subjects and then have transitive action verbs and direct objects.

2. Revise each sentence so that the direct object precedes the subject and verb.

3. Compare the two versions of the sentences.

4. Write a statement explaining what you learned about the effect of inverting normal sentence order.

"In our last conflict, four of his five wits went halting off."

-William Shakespeare

This scathing line, spoken by Beatrice in Act I scene i of Shakespeare's comedy *Much Ado About Nothing*, shows Beatrice's contempt for the mean intelligence of her rival, Benedick, with whom she is destined to fall in love, like it or not. Its creative wording gives new life to the tired phrase, *lost his wits*.

Parts of speech: *In* is a preposition; *our* is a possessive pronoun that also has some force as an adjective; *last* is an adjective modifying the singular common noun *conflict*; *four* is a noun; *of* is a preposition showing the relationship between *wits* and *four*; *his* is a possessive pronoun; *went* is a plural past tense verb; *halting* is an adverb which modifies the verb and is modified by another adverb *off*. If you try to say that *went halting* is the verb, how would you answer the question, what tense is it?

Parts of the sentence: The subject of this sentence is *four*; the subject's simple predicate is the action verb *went*. If you try to say that *wits* is the subject, than what is the object of the preposition—an adjective?

Phrases: There are two prepositional phrases, *in our last conflict* which modifies the verb, and *of his five wits* which modifies *four*.

Clauses: This is a simple declarative sentence, consisting of only one clause, since it has only one subject/predicate set.

FOUR-LEVEL ANALYSIS

In our last conflict, four of his five wits went halting off.

	In	our	last	conflict	four	of	his	five	wits	went	halting	off
Parts of Speech:	prep.	pron.	adj.	n.	n.	prep.	pron.	adj.	n.	v.	adv.	adv.

Parts of Sentence: subject ... predicate

Phrases: -----prepositional phrase----- --prep. phrase--

Clauses: one independent clause, simple declarative sentence

212

For each sentence, identify the **part of speech** of the word in **bold**.

1. We **convened** at the Hilton on Third Avenue.   _____

2. The **ichthyologist** removed the petrified ichthyosaur bones.   _____

3. The **gravamen** of the charges is that he left his post under fire.   _____

4. The calorimeter measured the heat of the **calorific** reaction.   _____

5. **Heliophiles** catch few solar rays at the winter solstice.   _____

6. The ophthalmologist treats the diseases of **the** eye.   _____

7. There were nucleotides in the chromosomes **of** the cell nucleus.   _____

8. He tried **to sate** his insatiable appetite for pizza.   _____

9. Male proterandrous insects appear earlier in the season **than** females. _____

10. The montane vistas of Montevideo **are** like those in Montana.   _____

For each sentence, identify the **part of sentence** of the word in **bold**.

11. A kilometer, one thousand meters, is 0.62137 **miles** in length.   _____

12. Myriad **explanations** exist of unidentified flying objects.   _____

13. At the first sign of tachycardia, he **was rushed** to the hospital.   _____

14. Is nuclear fission the **opposite** of nuclear fusion?   _____

15. The cumulus clouds accumulated as the sun baked the **sea**.   _____

16. The meteorologist reported that the meteorite did no **damage**.   _____

17. The hibernal winds did not reach the hibernating **bear**.   _____

18. The dilemma **was** whether to study the dicotyledon or diencephalon. _____

19. The **bathymetry** of the Pacific was easily studied with a bathyscaph. _____

20. Barnacles and other cirripeds covered the marina's **pilings**.   _____

For each sentence, identify the type of **phrase** in **bold**, and give its part of speech.

1. The gloomy soul was unable **to overcome her melancholy**. _____

2. **Suddenly stumbling**, the vice president greeted the vice consul. _____

3. Agent Orange was a toxic defoliant used **in the Vietnam War**. _____

4. **To provide relief**, we filled the atomizer with a new scent. _____

5. **In morphological terms**, orbicular leaves are circular and flat. _____

6. Her multifarious nefarious deeds landed her **in prison**. _____

7. The ignis fatuus seemed to ignite and hover **over the swamp**. _____

8. We could do nothing **to mollify the man's anger**. _____

9. Quickly delineate your proposal **for the new rapid transit system**. _____

10. Hemiplegia, **a partial paralysis**, is a serious condition. _____

For each sentence, identify the **sentence structure**. Disregard the bold.

11. The obsessed **oologist** painted his house; it was robin's-egg blue. _____

12. As we became aware of the ship's **retrograde** motion, we sank. _____

13. The **pneumococcus** bacteria gave him **pneumonia**, and it was bad. _____

14. Skeletons of the microscopic **radiolarians** show **radial** symmetry. _____

15. The sponge expels water through its **osculum**; this is well known. _____

16. As you saw, the **immense** wall was **impervious** to cannon fire. _____

17. The **convection** current distributed the heat of the flames. _____

18. Houdini accomplished feats of **prestidigitation**, but he was doomed. _____

19. The **gymnasium** is the perfect place for **gymnastics**, or so I think. _____

20. An Amoeba's **cytoplasm** includes **endoplasm** and **ectoplasm**. _____

For each sentence, identify the **part of speech** of the word in **bold**.

1. We **convened** at the Hilton on Third Avenue.   verb

2. The **ichthyologist** removed the petrified ichthyosaur bones.   noun

3. The **gravamen** of the charges is that he left his post under fire.   noun

4. The calorimeter measured the heat of the **calorific** reaction.   adjective

5. **Heliophiles** catch few solar rays at the winter solstice.   noun

6. The ophthalmologist treats the diseases of **the** eye.   adjective

7. There were nucleotides in the chromosomes **of** the cell nucleus.   preposition

8. He tried **to sate** his insatiable appetite for pizza.   noun

9. Male proterandrous insects appear earlier in the season **than** females. conjunction

10. The montane vistas of Montevideo **are** like those in Montana.   verb

For each sentence, identify the **part of sentence** of the word in **bold**.

11. A kilometer, one thousand meters, is 0.62137 **miles** in length.   subject complement

12. Myriad **explanations** exist of unidentified flying objects.   subject

13. At the first sign of tachycardia, he **was rushed** to the hospital.   predicate

14. Is nuclear fission the **opposite** of nuclear fusion?   subject complement

15. The cumulus clouds accumulated as the sun baked the **sea**.   direct object

16. The meteorologist reported that the meteorite did no **damage**.   direct object

17. The hibernal winds did not reach the hibernating **bear**.   direct object

18. The dilemma **was** whether to study the dicotyledon or diencephalon.   predicate

19. The **bathymetry** of the Pacific was easily studied with a bathyscaph.   subject

20. Barnacles and other cirripeds covered the marina's **pilings**.   direct object

For each sentence, identify the type of **phrase** in **bold**.

1. The gloomy soul was unable **to overcome her melancholy**.   infinitive, adverb

2. **Suddenly stumbling**, the vice president greeted the vice consul.   participle, adjective

3. Agent Orange was a toxic defoliant used **in the Vietnam War**.   prepositional, adverb

4. **To provide relief**, we filled the atomizer with a new scent.   infinitive, adverb

5. **In morphological terms**, orbicular leaves are circular and flat.   prepositional, adverb

6. Her multifarious nefarious deeds landed her **in prison**.   prepositional, adverb

7. The ignis fatuus seemed to ignite and hover **over the swamp**.   prepositional, adverb

8. We could do nothing **to mollify the man's anger**.   infinitive, adjective

9. Quickly delineate your proposal **for the new rapid transit system**.   prepositional, adjective

10. Hemiplegia, **a partial paralysis**, is a serious condition.   appositive, adjective

For each sentence, identify the **sentence structure**. Disregard the bold.

11. The obsessed **oologist** painted his house; it was robin's-egg blue.   compound

12. As we became aware of the ship's **retrograde** motion, we sank.   complex

13. The **pneumococcus** bacteria gave him **pneumonia**, and it was bad.   compound

14. Skeletons of the microscopic **radiolarians** show **radial** symmetry.   simple

15. The sponge expels water through its **osculum**; this is well known.   compound

16. As you saw, the **immense** wall was **impervious** to cannon fire.   complex

17. The **convection** current distributed the heat of the flames.   simple

18. Houdini accomplished feats of **prestidigitation**, but he was doomed.   compound

19. The **gymnasium** is the perfect place for **gymnastics**, or so I think.   compound

20. An Amoeba's **cytoplasm** includes **endoplasm** and **ectoplasm**.   simple

For each of the following sentences, circle the letter of each answer that is true. The answer can be any combination, including all or none. This exercise will teach you the real process of punctuation as a function of grammar.

1. The Neotitanic the fastest cruise ship on the planet can reach fifty two knots.
    a. quotation marks around the ship title
    b. italics on the ship title
    c. commas around the dependent clause
    d. commas around the appositive
    e. a hyphen in the compound number

2. Taken by surprise the yellow spider jumped at the arachnologist.
    a. a comma after the dependent clause
    b. a comma after the gerund phrase
    c. a comma after the participle phrase
    d. commas around the appositive
    e. quotation marks around the subject

3. The new usher who happens to have the letter *m* on his cap is short.
    a. a comma after the compound subject
    b. commas around the appositive
    c. commas around the nonessential clause
    d. a semicolon between the independent clauses
    e. italics on the letter as such

4. The Virginia colony needed three things salt pepper and catsup.
    a. a semicolon between the clauses
    b. a colon after the plural noun
    c. a comma after salt
    d. a list comma before the coordinating conjunction
    e. commas around the parenthetical remark

5. Did you read the story Digital Literature in this months Electrica Magazine?
    a. quotation marks around the story title
    b. italics on the story title
    c. commas around the appositive
    d. italics on the magazine title
    e. an apostrophe in the possessive noun

Answer Key

1. The *Neotitanic*, the fastest cruise ship on the planet, can reach fifty-two knots.
   - a. quotation marks around the ship title
   - **b. italics on the ship title**
   - c. commas around the dependent clause
   - **d. commas around the appositive**
   - **e. a hyphen in the compound number**

   Remember to put two commas around an appositive. This sentence is a good example of the confusion that can happen if you forget the second appositive comma.

2. Taken by surprise, the yellow spider jumped at the arachnologist.
   - a. a comma after the dependent clause
   - b. a comma after the gerund phrase
   - **c. a comma after the participle phrase**
   - d. commas around the appositive
   - e. quotation marks around the subject

   A comma goes after an introductory participle phrase, meaning, one that introduces a sentence.

3. The new usher, who happens to have the letter *m* on his cap, is short.
   - a. a comma after the compound subject
   - b. commas around the appositive
   - **c. commas around the nonessential clause**
   - d. a semicolon between the independent clauses
   - e. italics on the letter as such

   You can tell by the wording that this clause is not essential to the sentence, but is just extra information. It is optional, and is an interruption. That is why it gets commas around it. We always put words, letters, and numbers as such in italics.

4. The Virginia colony needed three things: salt, pepper, and catsup.
   - a. a semicolon between the clauses
   - **b. a colon after the plural noun**
   - **c. a comma after salt**
   - **d. list comma before coordinating conj.**
   - e. commas around the parenthetical remark

   Here we need the colon because the list follows and explains the direct object. If it read "The Virginia colony needed salt, pepper, and catsup," then we would not need the colon because the list would just be a compound direct object, and we never want to put a comma between the action verb and the direct object!

5. Did you read the story, "Digital Literature," in this month's *Electrica Magazine*?
   - **a. quotation marks around the story title**
   - b. italics on the story title
   - **c. commas around the appositive**
   - **d. italics on the magazine title**
   - **e. an apostrophe in the possessive noun**

   Articles are in quotes, magazine titles are in italics.

Grammar Review Test

Loop 1-5

Prepare for Usage Questions

The Grammar Review Test is based on the five four-level analyses that are the first pages of each of the five loops. Questions on the test come from all four levels of grammar: parts of speech, parts of the sentence, phrases, and clauses.

In addition to containing seventy-five questions based on four of the five sentences studied in class, the Grammar Review Test will also contain twenty-five other questions on usage, subject-verb agreement, clause punctuation, and other matters covered in the introductory lectures. A thorough review of all previous loops is recommended.

Students should be reminded that on a given question, more than one answer may be true; they should pick the *best*, most complete, answer.

Every planet has a magnetic field around it.

1. The word **every** is
    a. an adverb
    b. an adjective
    c. a preposition
    d. a conjunction

2. The word **planet** is
    a. a noun
    b. a pronoun
    c. an adjective
    d. an adverb

3. The word **magnetic**
    a. is a verb
    b. modifies **field**
    c. modifies **planet**
    d. is an adverb

4. The word **around** is
    a. a conjunction
    b. a preposition
    c. an adverb
    d. a pronoun

5. The word **it** is
    a. a noun and a subject
    b. an object of preposition
    c. a pronoun and a subject
    d. a pronoun

6. The word **field** is
    a. a noun and subject complement
    b. a noun and subject
    c. a noun and direct object
    d. a noun and indirect object

7. The sentence contains
    a. one article
    b. two articles
    c. three articles
    d. four articles

8. The sentence contains
    a. one adjective
    b. two adjectives
    c. three adjectives
    d. four adjectives

9. The sentence purpose is
    a. declarative
    b. interrogative
    c. imperative
    d. exclamatory

10. The sentence structure is
    a. simple
    b. compound
    c. complex
    d. compound-complex

11. The sentence subject is
    a. Every
    b. planet
    c. magnetic
    d. field

12. The verb/predicate is
    a. magnetic
    b. field
    c. around
    d. has

13. The verb is
    a. action and present tense
    b. action and past tense
    c. linking and present tense
    d. linking and past tense

14. The sentence contains
    a. one adverb
    b. two adverbs
    c. three adverbs
    d. none of the above

15. The verb is
    a. singular
    b. plural
    c. singular and transitive
    d. plural and transitive

16. The sentence contains
    a. one gerund
    b. one participle
    c. one infinitive
    d. none of the above

The Martian visitors will have landed by Thursday.

17. The subject is
    a. Martian
    b. visitors
    c. Thursday
    d. landed

18. The sentence contains
    a. one preposition
    b. two prepositions
    c. three prepositions
    d. no prepositions

19. The word **Martian** is
    a. a proper noun
    b. a proper adjective
    c. a common noun
    d. a common adjective

20. The word **Thursday** is
    a. an adjective
    b. a noun
    c. a pronoun
    d. an interjection

21. The sentence contains
    a. one verb
    b. two verbs
    c. three verbs
    d. four verbs

22. The sentence contains
    a. one clause
    b. two clauses
    c. one clause with one phrase
    d. one clause with no phrase

23. The sentence contains
    a. a subject complement
    b. a direct object
    c. no indirect object
    d. an indirect object

24. The sentence contains
    a. a gerund
    b. a participle
    c. an infinitive
    d. no verbal

25. The sentence contains
    a. one article
    b. two articles
    c. an infinitive
    d. none of the above

26. The phrase **by Thursday** modifies
    a. Martian
    b. visitors
    c. will have landed
    d. none of the above

27. The verb tense is
    a. present tense
    b. past
    c. future
    d. future perfect

28. The sentence purpose is
    a. declarative
    b. interrogative
    c. imperative
    d. exclamatory

29. The sentence structure is
    a. simple
    b. compound
    c. complex
    d. compound-complex

30. The word **by** relates
    a. Martian to visitors
    b. visitors to Thursday
    c. Martian to Thursday
    d. Thursday to landed

31. The sentence contains
    a. one interjection
    b. one conjunction
    c. both a and b
    d. neither a nor b

32. The sentence contains
    a. one dependent clause
    b. two dependent clauses
    c. three independent clauses
    d. no dependent clauses

The Andromedans attacked savagely, and we fell back.

33. The word **we** is
    a. a noun
    b. a pronoun
    c. an adjective
    d. a verb

34. The word **savagely** is
    a. an adjective
    b. a verb
    c. an adverb
    d. a preposition

35. The word **Andromedans** is
    a. a common noun
    b. a proper noun
    c. a proper adjective
    d. a common adjective

36. The verbs are
    a. present tense
    b. past tense
    c. future tense
    d. past perfect tense

37. The word **and** is
    a. a subordinating conjunction
    b. a coordinating conjunction
    c. a correlative conjunction
    d. none of the above

38. The sentence contains
    a. no direct object
    b. one direct object
    c. one subject complement
    d. one indirect object

39. The sentence contains
    a. one adjective
    b. two adjectives
    c. three adjectives
    d. none of the above

40. The antecedent of **we** is
    a. Andromedans
    b. attacked
    c. savagely
    d. unknown

41. The sentence contains
    a. one clause
    b. two clauses
    c. three clauses
    d. four clauses

42. The sentence contains
    a. no preposition
    b. one prepositions
    c. two prepositions
    d. three prepositions

43. The word **back** is
    a. a verb
    b. an adverb
    c. a preposition
    d. an adjective

44. The sentence purpose is
    a. declarative
    b. imperative
    c. exclamatory
    d. interrogative

45. The sentence structure is
    a. simple
    b. compound
    c. complex
    d. compound-complex

46. The first clause is
    a. independent
    b. dependent
    c. there is only one clause
    d. there is no clause

47. The sentence contains
    a. one interjection
    b. one preposition
    c. neither a nor b
    d. both a and b

48. The sentence contains
    a. one linking verb
    b. two linking verbs
    c. three linking verbs
    d. no linking verb

Explosions and cataclysms rocked the night thunderously.

49. The word **rocked** is
    a. a verb
    b. a past tense verb
    c. a past tense action verb
    d. none of the above

50. The word **thunderously** is
    a. an adjective
    b. an adverb
    c. a verb
    d. a preposition

51. The sentence contains
    a. no prepositional phrase
    b. one prepositional phrase
    c. two prepositional phrases
    d. three prepositional phrases

52. The word **Explosions** is
    a. a noun
    b. a pronoun
    c. a proper noun
    d. a common, plural noun

53. The word **and** is
    a. a subordinating conjunction
    b. a coordinating conjunction
    c. a correlative conjunction
    d. not a conjunction

54. The word **night** is
    a. a subject complement
    b. a direct object
    c. an indirect object
    d. a predicate nominative

55. The sentence contains
    a. a compound predicate
    b. a compound direct object
    c. a compound subject
    d. none of the above

56. The sentence contains
    a. one interjection
    b. one preposition
    c. one pronoun
    d. none of the above

57. The verb in the sentence is
    a. singular
    b. plural
    c. singular and past tense
    d. plural and past tense

58. The subject of the sentence is
    a. singular
    b. plural
    c. there is no subject
    d. none of the above

59. The sentence structure is
    a. simple
    b. compound
    c. complex
    d. compound-complex

60. The sentence contains
    a. one adjective
    b. two adjectives
    c. three adjectives
    d. no adjective

61. The sentence contains
    a. no gerund
    b. one gerund
    c. two gerunds
    d. three gerunds

62. The sentence purpose is
    a. declarative
    b. interrogative
    c. imperative
    d. exclamatory

63. The sentence contains
    a. one participle
    b. two participles
    c. three participles
    d. none of the above

64. The subject of the sentence is
    a. Explosions
    b. cataclysms
    c. Explosions and cataclysms
    d. none of the above

Our ship was hit by a weaker beam.

65. The subject is
    a. ship
    b. our
    c. hit
    d. beam

66. The word **by** is
    a. an adverb
    b. a conjunction
    c. a preposition
    d. a verb

67. The word **beam** is
    a. a noun
    b. a pronoun
    c. a verb
    d. an interjection

68. The verb is
    a. was
    b. hit
    c. both a and b
    d. none of the above

69. The adjective **weaker** is in the
    a. positive degree
    b. comparative degree
    c. superlative degree
    d. none of the above

70. The subject of the sentence
    a. is singular
    b. is plural
    c. there is no way to tell
    d. none of the above

71. The sentence contains
    a. no adverb
    b. one adverb
    c. two adverbs
    d. three adverbs

72. The sentence purpose is
    a. declarative
    b. imperative
    c. interrogative
    d. exclamatory

73. The verb in the sentence is
    a. active voice
    b. passive voice
    c. linking
    d. transitive

74. The sentence contains
    a. one gerund
    b. one participle
    c. one infinitive
    d. no verbal

75. The sentence is
    a. simple
    b. compound
    c. complex
    d. compound-complex

USAGE SECTION

76. Correct punctuation is:
    a. April 6, 1986 is here.
    b. April 6, 1986, is here.
    c. April 6 1986 is here.
    d. April 6; 1986 is here.

77. Correct punctuation is:
    a. When he lands, I'll depart.
    b. When he lands I'll depart.
    c. When he, lands, I'll depart.
    d. When he lands I'll, depart.

78. Appositives take
    a. no commas
    b. one comma
    c. two commas
    d. two commas or none

79. The Martian invaders had
    a. two many eyes.
    b. to many eyes.
    c. too many eyes.
    d. either b or c

80. Correct punctuation is
    a. Sam left, I went home.
    b. Sam left; and I went home.
    c. Sam left and I went home.
    d. Sam left, and I went home.

81. The Venusian dog
    a. bit it's tail too.
    b. bit its tail to.
    c. bit it's tail to.
    d. bit its tail too.

82. Correct usage is:
    a. Crick and Watson is here.
    b. Crick or Watson are here.
    c. Crick or Watson don't exist.
    d. Crick or Watson is here.

83. Correct punctuation is:
    a. Chicago Illinois is windy.
    b. Chicago, Illinois is windy.
    c. Chicago, Illinois, is windy.
    d. Chicago, Illinois, is, windy.

84. The term **it's** is
    a. a possessive pronoun
    b. an adjective
    c. a contraction
    d. none of the above

85. The ring of high mountains
    a. circle the city.
    b. circles the city.
    c. either a or b
    d. neither is correct

86. Correct punctuation is
    a. If you go, I will too.
    b. If you go; I will too.
    c. If you go I will too.
    d. If you go: I will too.

87. Every one of the colonists
    a. have their problems.
    b. has their problems.
    c. have his or her problems.
    d. has problems.

88. The lunar outpost
    a. has too many craters.
    b. has two many craters.
    c. has to many craters.

89. One of the lunar pods
    a. were for you.
    b. was for you.
    c. either a or b
    d. none of the above

90. Lunar children
    a. learn too fly early.
    b. learn two fly early.
    c. learn to fly early.
    d. all of the above.

91. A comma splice is:
    a. I will go, you will go.
    b. I will go, and you will go.
    c. I will go; you will go.
    d. When you go, I will go.

92. Which is correct:
    a. I will land, you may land.
    b. When I land; you land.
    c. You may land, when I land.
    d. When I land, you may land.

93. The bright blue android
    a. spoke to he and I.
    b. spoke to him and me.
    c. spoke to him and I.

94. They gave
    a. him and I a medal.
    b. he and me a medal.
    c. he and I a medal.
    d. him and me a medal.

95. Hamlet is sad because
    a. he don't have a choice.
    b. he don't has a choice.
    c. he doesn't have a choice.

96. Thousands of Venusians
    a. have they're own land.
    b. have there own land.
    c. have their own land.
    d. none of the above

97. Correct punctuation is
    a. John left when he could.
    b. John, left when he could.
    c. John left, when he could.
    d. John left; when he could.

98. It is
    a. he and I who ask.
    b. him and me who ask.
    c. him and I who ask.
    d. he and me who ask.

99. Correct is:
    a. It was him who saw she and I.
    b. It was he who saw she and I.
    c. It was him who saw her and me.
    d. It was he who saw her and me.

100. Which rule is not correct?
    a. I;I
    b. I,ccI
    c. D,I
    d. I,D

Every planet has a magnetic field around it.

1. The word **every** is
    a. an adverb
    b. an adjective
    c. a preposition
    d. a conjunction

2. The word **planet** is
    a. a noun
    b. a pronoun
    c. an adjective
    d. an adverb

3. The word **magnetic**
    a. is a verb
    b. modifies field
    c. modifies planet
    d. is an adverb

4. The word **around** is
    a. a conjunction
    b. a preposition
    c. an adverb
    d. a pronoun

5. The word **it** is
    a. a noun and a subject
    b. an object of preposition
    c. a pronoun and a subject
    d. a pronoun

6. The word **field** is
    a. a noun and subject complement
    b. a noun and subject
    c. a noun and direct object
    d. a noun and indirect object

7. The sentence contains
    a. one article
    b. two articles
    c. three articles
    d. four articles

8. The sentence contains
    a. one adjective
    b. two adjectives
    c. three adjectives
    d. four adjectives

9. The sentence purpose is
    a. declarative
    b. interrogative
    c. imperative
    d. exclamatory

10. The sentence structure is
    a. simple
    b. compound
    c. complex
    d. compound-complex

11. The sentence subject is
    a. Every
    b. planet
    c. magnetic
    d. field

12. The verb/predicate is
    a. magnetic
    b. field
    c. around
    d. has

13. The verb is
    a. action and present tense
    b. action and past tense
    c. linking and present tense
    d. linking and past tense

14. The sentence contains
    a. one adverb
    b. two adverbs
    c. three adverbs
    d. none of the above

15. The verb is
    a. singular
    b. plural
    c. singular and transitive
    d. plural and transitive

16. The sentence contains
    a. one gerund
    b. one participle
    c. one infinitive
    d. none of the above

The Martian visitors will have landed by Thursday.

17. The subject is
    a. Martian
    b. visitors
    c. Thursday
    d. landed

18. The sentence contains
    a. one preposition
    b. two prepositions
    c. three prepositions
    d. no prepositions

19. The word **Martian** is
    a. a proper noun
    b. a proper adjective
    c. a common noun
    d. a common adjective

20. The word **Thursday** is
    a. an adjective
    b. a noun
    c. a pronoun
    d. an interjection

21. The sentence contains
    a. one verb
    b. two verbs
    c. three verbs
    d. four verbs

22. The sentence contains
    a. one clause
    b. two clauses
    c. one clause with one phrase
    d. one clause with no phrase

23. The sentence contains
    a. a subject complement
    b. a direct object
    c. no indirect object
    d. an indirect object

24. The sentence contains
    a. a gerund
    b. a participle
    c. an infinitive
    d. no verbal

25. The sentence contains
    a. one article
    b. two articles
    c. an infinitive
    d. none of the above

26. The phrase **by Thursday** modifies
    a. Martian
    b. visitors
    c. will have landed
    d. none of the above

27. The verb tense is
    a. present tense
    b. past
    c. future
    d. future perfect

28. The sentence purpose is
    a. declarative
    b. interrogative
    c. imperative
    d. exclamatory

29. The sentence structure is
    a. simple
    b. compound
    c. complex
    d. compound-complex

30. The word **by** relates
    a. Martian to visitors
    b. visitors to Thursday
    c. Martian to Thursday
    d. Thursday to landed

31. The sentence contains
    a. one interjection
    b. one conjunction
    c. both a and b
    d. neither a nor b

32. The sentence contains
    a. one dependent clause
    b. two dependent clauses
    c. three independent clauses
    d. no dependent clause

The Andromedans attacked savagely, and we fell back.

33. The word **we** is
    a. a noun
    b. a pronoun
    c. an adjective
    d. a verb

34. The word **savagely** is
    a. an adjective
    b. a verb
    c. an adverb
    d. a preposition

35. The word **Andromedans** is
    a. a common noun
    b. a proper noun
    c. a proper adjective
    d. a common adjective

36. The verbs are
    a. present tense
    b. past tense
    c. future tense
    d. past perfect tense

37. The word **and** is
    a. a subordinating conjunction
    b. a coordinating conjunction
    c. a correlative conjunction
    d. none of the above

38. The sentence contains
    a. no direct object
    b. one direct object
    c. one subject complement
    d. one indirect object

39. The sentence contains
    a. one adjective
    b. two adjectives
    c. three adjectives
    d. none of the above

40. The antecedent of **we** is
    a. Andromedans
    b. attacked
    c. savagely
    d. unknown

41. The sentence contains
    a. one clause
    b. two clauses
    c. three clauses
    d. four clauses

42. The sentence contains
    a. no preposition
    b. one prepositions
    c. two prepositions
    d. three prepositions

43. The word **back** is
    a. a verb
    b. an adverb
    c. a preposition
    d. an adjective

44. The sentence purpose is
    a. declarative
    b. imperative
    c. exclamatory
    d. interrogative

45. The sentence structure is
    a. simple
    b. compound
    c. complex
    d. compound-complex

46. The first clause is
    a. independent
    b. dependent
    c. there is only one clause
    d. there is no clause

47. The sentence contains
    a. one interjection
    b. one preposition
    c. neither a nor b
    d. both a and b

48. The sentence contains
    a. one linking verb
    b. two linking verbs
    c. three linking verbs
    d. no linking verb

Explosions and cataclysms rocked the night thunderously.

49. The word **rocked** is
    a. a verb
    b. a past tense verb
    c. a past tense action verb
    d. none of the above

50. The word **thunderously** is
    a. an adjective
    b. an adverb
    c. a verb
    d. a preposition

51. The sentence contains
    a. no prepositional phrase
    b. one prepositional phrase
    c. two prepositional phrases
    d. three prepositional phrases

52. The word **Explosions** is
    a. a noun
    b. a pronoun
    c. a proper noun
    d. a common, plural noun

53. The word **and** is
    a. a subordinating conjunction
    b. a coordinating conjunction
    c. a correlative conjunction
    d. not a conjunction

54. The word **night** is
    a. a subject complement
    b. a direct object
    c. an indirect object
    d. a predicate nominative

55. The sentence contains
    a. a compound predicate
    b. a compound direct object
    c. a compound subject
    d. none of the above

56. The sentence contains
    a. one interjection
    b. one preposition
    c. one pronoun
    d. none of the above

57. The verb in the sentence is
    a. singular
    b. plural
    c. singular and past tense
    d. plural and past tense

58. The subject of the sentence is
    a. singular
    b. plural
    c. there is no subject
    d. none of the above

59. The sentence structure is
    a. simple
    b. compound
    c. complex
    d. compound-complex

60. The sentence contains
    a. one adjective
    b. two adjectives
    c. three adjectives
    d. no adjectives

61. The sentence contains
    a. no gerund
    b. one gerund
    c. two gerunds
    d. three gerunds

62. The sentence purpose is
    a. declarative
    b. interrogative
    c. imperative
    d. exclamatory

63. The sentence contains
    a. one participle
    b. two participles
    c. three participles
    d. none of the above

64. The subject of the sentence is
    a. Explosions
    b. cataclysms
    c. Explosions and cataclysms
    d. none of the above

Our ship was hit by a weaker beam.

65. The subject is
    a. ship
    b. our
    c. hit
    d. beam

66. The word **by** is
    a. an adverb
    b. a conjunction
    c. a preposition
    d. a verb

67. The word **beam** is
    a. a noun
    b. a pronoun
    c. a verb
    d. an interjection

68. The verb is
    a. was
    b. hit
    c. both a and b
    d. none of the above

69. The adjective **weaker** is in the
    a. positive degree
    b. comparative degree
    c. superlative degree
    d. none of the above

70. The subject of the sentence
    a. is singular
    b. is plural
    c. there is no way to tell
    d. none of the above

71. The sentence contains
    a. no adverb
    b. one adverb
    c. two adverbs
    d. three adverbs

72. The sentence purpose is
    a. declarative
    b. imperative
    c. interrogative
    d. exclamatory

73. The verb in the sentence is
    a. active voice
    b. passive voice
    c. linking
    d. transitive

74. The sentence contains
    a. one gerund
    b. one participle
    c. one infinitive
    d. no verbal

75. The sentence is
    a. simple
    b. compound
    c. complex
    d. compound-complex

USAGE SECTION

76. Correct punctuation is:
    a. April 6, 1986 is here.
    b. April 6, 1986, is here.
    c. April 6 1986 is here.
    d. April 6; 1986 is here.

77. Correct punctuation is:
    a. When he lands, I'll depart.
    b. When he lands I'll depart.
    c. When he, lands, I'll depart.
    d. When he lands I'll, depart.

78. Appositives take
    a. no commas
    b. one comma
    c. two commas
    d. two commas or none

79. The Martian invaders had
    a. two many eyes.
    b. to many eyes.
    c. too many eyes.
    d. either b or c

80. Correct punctuation is
    a. Sam left, I went home.
    b. Sam left; and I went home.
    c. Sam left and I went home.
    d. Sam left, and I went home.

81. The Venusian dog
    a. bit it's tail too.
    b. bit its tail to.
    c. bit it's tail to.
    d. bit its tail too.

82. Correct usage is:
    a. Crick and Watson is here.
    b. Crick or Watson are here.
    c. Crick or Watson don't exist.
    d. Crick or Watson is here.

83. Correct punctuation is:
    a. Chicago Illinois is windy.
    b. Chicago, Illinois is windy.
    c. Chicago, Illinois, is windy.
    d. Chicago, Illinois, is, windy.

84. The term **it's** is
    a. a possessive pronoun
    b. an adjective
    c. a contraction
    d. none of the above

85. The ring of high mountains
    a. circle the city.
    b. circles the city.
    c. either a or b
    d. neither is correct

86. Correct punctuation is
    a. If you go, I will too.
    b. If you go; I will too.
    c. If you go I will too.
    d. If you go: I will too.

87. Every one of the colonists
    a. have their problems.
    b. has their problems.
    c. have his or her problems.
    d. has problems.

88. The lunar outpost
    a. has too many craters.
    b. has two many craters.
    c. has to many craters.

89. One of the lunar pods
    a. were for you.
    b. was for you.
    c. either a or b
    d. none of the above

90. Lunar children
    a. learn too fly early.
    b. learn two fly early.
    c. learn to fly early.
    d. all of the above.

91. A comma splice is:
    a. I will go, you will go.
    b. I will go, and you will go.
    c. I will go; you will go.
    d. When you go, I will go.

92. Which is correct:
    a. I will land, you may land.
    b. When I land; you land.
    c. You may land, when I land.
    d. When I land, you may land.

93. The bright blue android
    a. spoke to he and I.
    b. spoke to him and me.
    c. spoke to him and I.

94. They gave
    a. him and I a medal.
    b. he and me a medal.
    c. he and I a medal.
    d. him and me a medal.

95. Hamlet is sad because
    a. he don't have a choice.
    b. he don't has a choice.
    c. he doesn't have a choice.

96. Thousands of Venusians
    a. have they're own land.
    b. have there own land.
    c. have their own land.
    d. none of the above

97. Correct punctuation is
    a. John left when he could.
    b. John, left when he could.
    c. John left, when he could.
    d. John left; when he could.

98. It is
    a. he and I who ask.
    b. him and me who ask.
    c. him and I who ask.
    d. he and me who ask.

99. Correct is:
    a. It was him who saw she and I.
    b. It was he who saw she and I.
    c. It was him who saw her and me.
    d. It was he who saw her and me.

100. Which rule is not correct?
    a. I;I
    b. I,ccI
    c. D,I
    d. I,D

Student Name:_____ Date:_____
Period:_____ Loop 1-5 Grammar Review TEST

	A B C D		A B C D		A B C D		A B C D
1.	0 0 0 0	26.	0 0 0 0	51.	0 0 0 0	76.	0 0 0 0
2.	0 0 0 0	27.	0 0 0 0	52.	0 0 0 0	77.	0 0 0 0
3.	0 0 0 0	28.	0 0 0 0	53.	0 0 0 0	78.	0 0 0 0
4.	0 0 0 0	29.	0 0 0 0	54.	0 0 0 0	79.	0 0 0 0
5.	0 0 0 0	30.	0 0 0 0	55.	0 0 0 0	80.	0 0 0 0
6.	0 0 0 0	31.	0 0 0 0	56.	0 0 0 0	81.	0 0 0 0
7.	0 0 0 0	32.	0 0 0 0	57.	0 0 0 0	82.	0 0 0 0
8.	0 0 0 0	33.	0 0 0 0	58.	0 0 0 0	83.	0 0 0 0
9.	0 0 0 0	34.	0 0 0 0	59.	0 0 0 0	84.	0 0 0 0
10.	0 0 0 0	35.	0 0 0 0	60.	0 0 0 0	85.	0 0 0 0
11.	0 0 0 0	36.	0 0 0 0	61.	0 0 0 0	86.	0 0 0 0
12.	0 0 0 0	37.	0 0 0 0	62.	0 0 0 0	87.	0 0 0 0
13.	0 0 0 0	38.	0 0 0 0	63.	0 0 0 0	88.	0 0 0 0
14.	0 0 0 0	39.	0 0 0 0	64.	0 0 0 0	89.	0 0 0 0
15.	0 0 0 0	40.	0 0 0 0	65.	0 0 0 0	90.	0 0 0 0
16.	0 0 0 0	41.	0 0 0 0	66.	0 0 0 0	91.	0 0 0 0
17.	0 0 0 0	42.	0 0 0 0	67.	0 0 0 0	92.	0 0 0 0
18.	0 0 0 0	43.	0 0 0 0	68.	0 0 0 0	93.	0 0 0 0
19.	0 0 0 0	44.	0 0 0 0	69.	0 0 0 0	94.	0 0 0 0
20.	0 0 0 0	45.	0 0 0 0	70.	0 0 0 0	95.	0 0 0 0
21.	0 0 0 0	46.	0 0 0 0	71.	0 0 0 0	96.	0 0 0 0
22.	0 0 0 0	47.	0 0 0 0	72.	0 0 0 0	97.	0 0 0 0
23.	0 0 0 0	48.	0 0 0 0	73.	0 0 0 0	98.	0 0 0 0
24.	0 0 0 0	49.	0 0 0 0	74.	0 0 0 0	99.	0 0 0 0
25.	0 0 0 0	50.	0 0 0 0	75.	0 0 0 0	100.	0 0 0 0

Student Name:_____   Date: _____

Period:_____   Loop 1-5 Grammar Review TEST

#	A B C D		#	A B C D		#	A B C D		#	A B C D
1.	0 + 0 0		26.	0 0 + 0		51.	+ 0 0 0		76.	0 + 0 0
2.	+ 0 0 0		27.	0 0 0 +		52.	0 0 0 +		77.	+ 0 0 0
3.	0 + 0 0		28.	+ 0 0 0		53.	0 + 0 0		78.	0 0 0 +
4.	0 + 0 0		29.	+ 0 0 0		54.	0 + 0 0		79.	0 0 + 0
5.	0 + 0 0		30.	0 0 0 +		55.	0 0 + 0		80.	0 0 0 +
6.	0 0 + 0		31.	0 0 0 +		56.	0 0 0 +		81.	0 0 0 +
7.	+ 0 0 0		32.	0 0 0 +		57.	0 0 0 +		82.	0 0 0 +
8.	0 0 + 0		33.	0 + 0 0		58.	0 + 0 0		83.	0 0 + 0
9.	+ 0 0 0		34.	0 0 + 0		59.	+ 0 0 0		84.	0 0 + 0
10.	+ 0 0 0		35.	0 + 0 0		60.	+ 0 0 0		85.	0 + 0 0
11.	0 + 0 0		36.	0 + 0 0		61.	+ 0 0 0		86.	+ 0 0 0
12.	0 0 0 +		37.	0 + 0 0		62.	0 0 0 +		87.	0 0 0 +
13.	+ 0 0 0		38.	+ 0 0 0		63.	+ 0 0 0		88.	+ 0 0 0
14.	0 0 0 +		39.	+ 0 0 0		64.	0 0 + 0		89.	0 + 0 0
15.	0 0 + 0		40.	0 0 0 +		65.	+ 0 0 0		90.	0 0 + 0
16.	0 0 0 +		41.	0 + 0 0		66.	0 0 + 0		91.	+ 0 0 0
17.	0 + 0 0		42.	+ 0 0 0		67.	+ 0 0 0		92.	0 0 0 +
18.	+ 0 0 0		43.	0 + 0 0		68.	0 0 + 0		93.	0 + 0 0
19.	0 + 0 0		44.	+ 0 0 0		69.	0 + 0 0		94.	0 0 0 +
20.	0 + 0 0		45.	0 + 0 0		70.	+ 0 0 0		95.	0 0 + 0
21.	0 0 + 0		46.	+ 0 0 0		71.	+ 0 0 0		96.	0 0 + 0
22.	0 0 + 0		47.	0 0 + 0		72.	+ 0 0 0		97.	+ 0 0 0
23.	0 0 + 0		48.	0 0 0 +		73.	0 + 0 0		98.	+ 0 0 0
24.	0 0 0 +		49.	0 0 + 0		74.	0 0 0 +		99.	0 0 0 +
25.	+ 0 0 0		50.	0 + 0 0		75.	+ 0 0 0		100.	0 0 0 +

Cut a copy on dotted lines, punch out +'s with a hole punch, tape back together, avoiding holes.

Punctuating Grammar

P as ƒ of G

Loops Six-Ten

Instructions for the **Punctuating Grammar** Test

This test is designed to test your understanding of punctuation as a means of displaying the grammatical structure of a sentence. We group words together to form grammatical "objects" such as subjects, predicates, phrases, and clauses, and we group these objects to form communicable ideas which we call *sentences*. When we speak, we separate the grammatical objects with pauses and intonations, but when we are writing, we need a visible way to show where one grammatical object ends and the next begins. We call this visible way of displaying the grammar of a sentence *punctuation*.

There are fifty questions in this test, and each question is worth two points, for a total of one hundred points.

In this test, each question has five possible choices, A through E. **The correct answer to the question can be any combination of choices, including all and none. In order to get the two points of credit for the question, you must get the entire correct combination. There is no partial credit.**

The reason there is no partial credit is that though the content of these sentences is imaginative and unusual, the grammar of the sentences is not. The grammar is quite elementary and ordinary, and it is reasonable to expect that any good student with an understanding of elementary grammar would be able to understand and punctuate the sentences.

The choices offered are not necessarily accurate descriptions of the sentence in the question. If a choice is "a comma after the dependent clause," that does not mean that the sentence contains a dependent clause. You have to know whether there is one or not, just as if you were composing the sentence yourself.

A final point: In some sentences, it is possible that there is a mark of punctuation present for two good reasons. For example, in the sentence, *Oh, Hamlet, we all have epiphanies*, the first comma must be present both to separate the interjection and also to enclose the noun of direct address. In such a case, you should mark *both* of those reasons. This does not mean that you think there should be two commas in a row; it simply indicates that you are aware of both purposes for punctuating.

1. In March we collapsed and the Star League launched its forces.
   - a. a comma after the prepositional phrase
   - b. a comma after the dependent clause
   - c. a comma after the independent clause
   - d. an apostrophe in the contraction
   - e. commas before and after the appositive

2. In Chicago Illinois the meteors struck Johns house.
   - a. a comma after the city
   - b. a comma after the state appositive
   - c. an apostrophe in the plural noun
   - d. an apostrophe in the possessive noun
   - e. a comma after the dependent clause

3. A very red star exploded as Roger the Martian visitor glanced upward.
   - a. a comma between adjectives
   - b. a comma after the dependent clause
   - c. a comma after the independent clause
   - d. commas around the appositive
   - e. commas around the noun of direct address

4. Homer Johnsons book A Starship Returns is about a ship called Fractal.
   - a. italics on the ship title
   - b. an apostrophe in the possessive noun
   - c. quotation marks around the book title
   - d. italics on the book title
   - e. commas around the appositive

5. The well timed attack and the cold conditions caused thirty two deaths.
   - a. comma between adjectives that precede the noun.
   - b. a hyphen in the compound adjective
   - c. a comma after the dependent clause
   - d. a hyphen in the compound number
   - e. an apostrophe in the possessive noun

6. In a hostile tone of voice the Leader said Now its time to depart.
   - a. a comma after the prepositional phrases
   - b. an apostrophe in the contraction
   - c. a comma before the direct quotation
   - d. quotation marks around the direct quotation
   - e. a period inside the closing quotation marks

7. When the poet wrote The Planets Ring he created a new poetic form.
   - a. a comma after the independent clause
   - b. an apostrophe in the possessive noun
   - c. a comma after the dependent clause
   - d. italics on the poem title
   - e. quotation marks around the poem title

8. A two thirds majority wanted new space suits new food and new air.
   - a. a hyphen in the compound adjective
   - b. a colon at the beginning of the list
   - c. a comma after the plural common noun
   - d. a comma before the coordinating conjunction
   - e. a comma after the dependent clause

9. Stumbling clumsily forward the thin green Martian lost its balance.
   - a. a comma after the prepositional phrase
   - b. comma between adjectives preceding the noun
   - c. a comma after the participle phrase
   - d. a comma after the gerund phrase
   - e. an apostrophe in the contraction

10. Frdgkie is the Martian word for sand it is a difficult noun to pronounce.
    - a. quotation marks around the Martian noun
    - b. italics on the Martian noun
    - c. a comma after the independent clause
    - d. a comma after the dependent clause
    - e. a semicolon after the independent clause

11. America the Beautiful is a sad song to hear when youre lost in space.
    a. italics on the song title
    b. quotation marks around the song title
    c. a comma after the dependent clause
    d. a comma after the independent clause
    e. an apostrophe in the contraction

12. Gee its tiring to visit six planets in a two week tour.
    a. a comma after the interjection
    b. an apostrophe in the possessive pronoun
    c. an apostrophe in the contraction
    d. a comma after the independent clauses
    e. a hyphen in the compound adjective

13. On the Saturn colony the incidence of vacuuphobia is up by two thirds.
    a. comma after the introductory prepositional phrase
    b. a hyphen in the fraction
    c. a comma after the dependent clause
    d. commas around the appositive
    e. commas around the parenthetical remark

14. On January 4 1996 Ralph our finest moonpilot got bewildered.
    a. a comma after the day
    b. a comma after the year
    c. a comma after the participle phrase
    d. commas around the appositive
    e. a comma after the dependent clause

15. Trapped in the gravitational field Royce peered through his porthole.
    a. a comma after the dependent clause
    b. comma after the introductory prepositional phrases
    c. a comma after the participle phrase
    d. commas around the appositive
    e. a semicolon between the clauses

16. In July Neptune lost its largest moon when a massive meteor struck.
    a. a comma after the prepositional phrase
    b. a comma after the month
    c. an apostrophe in the possessive pronoun
    d. an apostrophe in the contraction
    e. a comma between the clauses

17. Because the gamma ray storm was severe we remained at pad nine.
    a. a comma after the participle phrase
    b. a comma after the dependent clause
    c. a comma after the independent clause
    d. a semicolon between the clauses
    e. a comma after the prepositional phrase

18. The zero gravity soccer field is two miles long one wide and one high.
    a. a hyphen in the compound adjective
    b. a colon before the list
    c. a comma after the adjective **long**
    d. a comma after the adjective **wide**
    e. a comma between the clauses

19. Flying into the endzone was the astrohalfbacks greatest fantasy.
    a. a comma after the introductory participle phrase
    b. a comma after the dependent clause
    c. an apostrophe in the possessive noun
    d. commas around the appositive phrase
    e. commas around the parenthetical remark

20. Yes the Defense League lost twenty five fighters in the asteroid belt.
    a. a comma after the introductory adverb
    b. a comma after the interjection
    c. a comma after the dependent clause
    d. a hyphen in the compound adjective
    e. a comma before the prepositional phrase

21. The Mu Pride the best train on the planet can reach mach twenty one.
    a. quotation marks around the train title
    b. italics on the train title
    c. commas around the dependent clause
    d. commas around the appositive
    e. a hyphen in the compound number

22. Taken by surprise the azure craterbull glared at the cratologist.
    a. a comma after the dependent clause
    b. a comma after the gerund phrase
    c. a comma after the participle phrase
    d. commas around the appositive
    e. quotation marks around the subject

23. The microchip vendor who happens to have the letter r on his helmet is tall.
    a. a comma after the compound subject
    b. commas around the appositive
    c. commas around the nonessential clause
    d. a semicolon between the independent clauses
    e. italics on the letter as such

24. The Venus colony needs three things oxygen silicon and rubidium.
    a. a semicolon between the clauses
    b. a colon after the plural noun
    c. a comma after **oxygen**
    d. a comma before the coordinating conjunction
    e. commas around the parenthetical remark

25. Did you read the article Blue Craters in this months Mars Magazine?
    a. quotation marks around the article title
    b. italics on the article title
    c. quotation marks around the magazine title
    d. italics on the magazine title
    e. an apostrophe in the possessive noun

26. On the Jupiter colony the black market in microchips is causing crime.
    a. comma after the introductory prepositional phrase
    b. a comma after the dependent clause
    c. commas around the parenthetical remark
    d. a semicolon between the independent clauses
    e. a hyphen in the compound adjective

27. The bugs that ate the platinum landing pads are hard to exterminate.
    a. commas around the appositive
    b. a semicolon between the independent clauses
    c. commas around the inessential clause
    d. quotation marks around the word pads
    e. a comma before the infinitive

28. Thomas Doubting our fleet leader was incredulous however its true.
    a. commas around the appositive
    b. a semicolon between the independent clauses
    c. a comma after **however**
    d. an apostrophe in the contraction
    e. a comma after the dependent clause

29. In the spring of 88 the moondog teeth left marks like hs on the gate.
    a. an apostrophe before the contraction
    b. comma after the introductory prepositional phrases
    c. an apostrophe in the possessive noun
    d. italics on the letter as such
    e. an apostrophe in the plural letter as such

30. The ponderously burdened dunecrawler clanked across the crater.
    a. comma between adjectives preceding the subject
    b. a comma after the independent clause
    c. a semicolon between the independent clauses
    d. a comma before the prepositional phrases
    e. a comma before the participle phrase

31. I have thirty seven cloudgliders and George has one said Morton.
    a. a hyphen in the compound adjective
    b. a comma between the independent clauses
    c. quotation marks around Morton's words
    d. a comma inside the closing quotation marks
    e. a comma outside the closing quotation marks

32. The long dark night of June 23 1992 and the cold morning were scary.
    a. comma between adjectives preceding the noun
    b. a comma after the day
    c. a comma after the year
    d. a comma between the clauses
    e. a comma after **morning**

33. The heliologist moved forward and placed his instruments with care.
    a. a comma between the independent clauses
    b. an apostrophe in the direct object
    c. commas around the appositive
    d. a comma before the participle phrase
    e. a semicolon after the independent clause

34. The dune hermits greatest painting is The Distant 3 Suns.
    a. an apostrophe in the possessive noun
    b. a colon after the verb
    c. quotation marks around the title of the painting
    d. italics on the title of the painting
    e. italics on the number as such

35. The leader said I will instruct you the captain saluted and left.
    a. a comma after the first verb
    b. quotation marks around the leader's words
    c. a comma inside the quotation marks
    d. a semicolon inside the quotation marks
    e. a semicolon outside the quotation marks

36. The pro American tribes on Neptune form a three fourths majority.
    a. commas around the appositive
    b. a hyphen after the prefix
    c. a hyphen in the fraction
    d. an apostrophe in **fourths**
    e. a comma after the dependent clause

37. Well Hamlet the colony has revolted we should leave at once.
    a. a semicolon after the dependent clause
    b. a semicolon after the independent clause
    c. commas around the noun of direct address
    d. a comma after the interjection
    e. a comma before the prepositional phrase

38. Neptunes national anthem is Symphony Number Sebm in Beta Sharp.
    a. quotation marks around title (including the period)
    b. quotation marks around title (not including the period)
    c. a comma after the dependent clause
    d. an apostrophe in the possessive noun
    e. italics on the music composition title

39. The new commander taking Logans place has not been to Venus before.
    a. a comma after the dependent clause
    b. commas around the participle phrase
    c. commas around the gerund phrase
    d. an apostrophe in the possessive noun
    e. dashes around the abrupt break in thought

40. The landing of the sand patrol gave our team its first emergency.
    a. a comma after the gerund
    b. commas around the parenthetical remark
    c. commas around the appositive
    d. an apostrophe in the contraction
    e. a comma after the dependent clause

41. At 830 in the gray lunar dawn the glowing landers slowly descended.
   a. a colon in the time
   b. a semicolon in the time
   c. a comma between the clauses
   d. comma after the introductory prep. phrases
   e. a comma before the adverb

42. As Ed gaped the alien said Idjjwe smujmu simmywatt.
   a. a comma after the dependent clause
   b. a comma after the verb in the independent clause
   c. quotation marks around the alien statement
   d. italics on the alien statement
   e. period inside the closing quotation marks

43. Chapter five of Smiling Planet is titled Binary Dawn.
   a. commas around the appositive
   b. italics on the book title
   c. quotation marks around the chapter title
   d. italics on the chapter title
   e. an apostrophe in the possessive noun

44. The task of the gravity squad is to patrol to zone and to sector.
   a. a semicolon after the linking verb
   b. a colon after the linking verb
   c. a dash after the linking verb
   d. a comma after the first infinitive
   e. a comma after the second infinitive

45. Its better to have two thirds of a sandburger than a one fourth share.
   a. an apostrophe in the contraction
   b. a hyphen in the first fraction
   c. a hyphen in the second fraction
   d. commas around the prepositional phrase
   e. a comma before the dependent clause

46. New Herante Plutos oldest city is inhabited by Noncognus subzoicus.
   a. commas around the appositive
   b. a comma after the independent clause
   c. italics on the Latin species name
   d. an apostrophe in the possessive noun
   e. a comma after the dependent clause

47. The late 1990s were a time of well planned expeditions to the stars.
   a. a comma after the year
   b. an apostrophe in the year
   c. a hyphen in the compound adjective
   d. a comma before the final prepositional phrase
   e. a comma before the first prepositional phrase

48. The disastrous instructions to the lunar base were well intentioned.
   a. commas around the parenthetical remark
   b. commas around the appositive
   c. an apostrophe in **instructions**
   d. a comma after the subject
   e. a hyphen in the compound adjective

49. 35 and 66 are the numbers which its not safe to use Bill.
   a. quotation marks around the numbers
   b. italics on the numbers
   c. an apostrophe in the possessive pronoun
   d. an apostrophe in the contraction
   e. a comma before the noun of direct address

50. If you go to Mars please bring me a sandpainting.
   a. a semicolon between the clauses
   b. a comma after the dependent clause
   c. a comma after the independent clause
   d. quotation marks around the proper noun
   e. an apostrophe in the plural noun

1. In March we collapsed and the Star League launched its forces.
   a. a comma after the prepositional phrase
   b. a comma after the dependent clause
   c. a comma after the independent clause
   d. an apostrophe in the contraction
   e. commas before and after the appositive

2. In Chicago Illinois the meteors struck Johns house.
   a. a comma after the city
   b. a comma after the state appositive
   c. an apostrophe in the plural noun
   d. an apostrophe in the possessive noun
   e. a comma after the dependent clause

3. A very red star exploded as Roger the Martian visitor glanced upward.
   a. a comma between adjectives
   b. a comma after the dependent clause
   c. a comma after the independent clause
   d. commas around the appositive
   e. commas around the noun of direct address

4. Homer Johnsons book A Starship Returns is about a ship called Fractal.
   a. italics on the ship title
   b. an apostrophe in the possessive noun
   c. quotation marks around the book title
   d. italics on the book title
   e. commas around the appositive

5. The well timed attack and the cold conditions caused thirty two deaths.
   a. comma between adjectives that precede the noun.
   b. a hyphen in the compound adjective
   c. a comma after the dependent clause
   d. a hyphen in the compound number
   e. an apostrophe in the possessive noun

6. In a hostile tone of voice the Leader said Now its time to depart.
   a. a comma after the prepositional phrases
   b. an apostrophe in the contraction
   c. a comma before the direct quotation
   d. quotation marks around the quotation
   e. a period inside the closing quotation

7. When the poet wrote The Planets Ring he created a new poetic form.
   a. a comma after the independent clause
   b. an apostrophe in the possessive noun
   c. a comma after the dependent clause
   d. italics on the poem title
   e. quotation marks around the poem title

8. A two thirds majority wanted new space suits new food and new air.
   a. a hyphen in the compound adjective
   b. a colon at the beginning of the list
   c. a comma after the plural common noun
   d. a comma before the coordinating conj.
   e. a comma after the dependent clause

9. Stumbling clumsily forward the thin green Martian lost its balance.
   a. a comma after the prepositional phrase
   b. comma between adjectives preceding the n.
   c. a comma after the participle phrase
   d. a comma after the gerund phrase
   e. an apostrophe in the contraction

10. Frdgkie is the Martian word for sand it is a difficult noun to pronounce.
    a. quotation marks around the Martian noun
    b. italics on the Martian noun
    c. a comma after the independent clause
    d. a comma after the dependent clause
    e. a semicolon after independent clause

11. America the Beautiful is a sad song to hear when youre lost in space.
    a. italics on the song title
    b. quotation marks around the song title
    c. a comma after the dependent clause
    d. a comma after the independent clause
    e. an apostrophe in the contraction

12. Gee its tiring to visit six planets in a two week tour.
    a. a comma after the interjection
    b. an apostrophe in the possessive pronoun
    c. an apostrophe in the contraction
    d. a comma after the independent clauses
    e. a hyphen in the compound adjective

13. On the Saturn colony the incidence of vacuuphobia is up by two thirds.
    a. comma after the introductory phrase
    b. a hyphen in the fraction
    c. a comma after the dependent clause
    d. commas around the appositive
    e. commas around the parenthetical remark

14. On January 4 1996 Ralph our finest moonpilot got bewildered.
    a. a comma after the day
    b. a comma after the year
    c. a comma after the participle phrase
    d. commas around the appositive
    e. a comma after the dependent clause

15. Trapped in the gravitational field Royce peered through his porthole.
    a. a comma after the dependent clause
    b. comma after the introductory prepositional phrases
    c. a comma after the participle phrase
    d. commas around the appositive
    e. a semicolon between the clauses

16. In July Neptune lost its largest moon when a massive meteor struck.
    a. a comma after the prepositional phrase
    b. a comma after the month
    c. an apostrophe in the possessive pronoun
    d. an apostrophe in the contraction
    e. a comma between the clauses

17. Because the gamma ray storm was severe we remained at pad nine.
    a. a comma after the participle phrase
    b. a comma after the dependent clause
    c. a comma after the independent clause
    d. a semicolon between the clauses
    e. a comma after the prepositional phrase

18. The zero gravity soccer field is two miles long one wide and one high.
    a. a hyphen in the compound adjective
    b. a colon before the list
    c. a comma after the adjective *long*
    d. a comma after the adjective *wide*
    e. a comma between the clauses

19. Flying into the endzone was the astrohalfbacks greatest fantasy.
    a. a comma after the introductory participle phrase
    b. a comma after the dependent clause
    c. an apostrophe in the possessive noun
    d. commas around the appositive phrase
    e. commas around the parenthetical remark

20. Yes the Defense League lost twenty five fighters in the asteroid belt.
    a. a comma after the introductory adverb
    b. a comma after the interjection
    c. a comma after the dependent clause
    d. a hyphen in the compound adjective
    e. a comma before the prepositional phrase

21. The Mu Pride the best train on the planet can reach mach twenty one.
    a. quotation marks around the train title
    b. italics on the train title
    c. commas around the dependent clause
    d. commas around the appositive
    e. a hyphen in the compound number

22. Taken by surprise the azure craterbull glared at the cratologist.
    a. a comma after the dependent clause
    b. a comma after the gerund phrase
    c. a comma after the participle phrase
    d. commas around the appositive
    e. quotation marks around the subject

23. The microchip vendor who happens to have the letter r on his helmet is tall.
    a. a comma after the compound subject
    b. commas around the appositive
    c. commas around the nonessential clause
    d. a semicolon between the independent clauses
    e. italics on the letter as such

24. The Venus colony needs three things oxygen silicon and rubidium.
    a. a semicolon between the clauses
    b. a colon after the plural noun
    c. a comma after *oxygen*
    d. a comma before the coordinating conj.
    e. commas around the parenthetical remark

25. Did you read the article Blue Craters in this months Mars Magazine?
    a. quotation marks around the article title
    b. italics on the article title
    c. quotation marks around the magazine title
    d. italics on the magazine title
    e. an apostrophe in the possessive noun

26. On the Jupiter colony the black market in microchips is causing crime.
    a. comma after the introductory prep. phrase
    b. a comma after the dependent clause
    c. commas around the parenthetical remark
    d. a semicolon between the independent clauses
    e. a hyphen in the compound adjective

27. The bugs that ate the platinum landing pads are hard to exterminate.
    a. commas around the appositive
    b. a semicolon between the independent clauses
    c. commas around the inessential clause
    d. quotation marks around the word pads
    e. a comma before the infinitive

28. Thomas Doubting our fleet leader was incredulous however its true.
    a. commas around the appositive
    b. a semicolon between independent clauses
    c. a comma after *however*
    d. an apostrophe in the contraction
    e. a comma after the dependent clause

29. In the spring of 88 the moondog teeth left marks like hs on the gate.
    a. an apostrophe before the contraction
    b. comma after the introductory prep. phrases
    c. an apostrophe in the possessive noun
    d. italics on the letter as such
    e. an apostrophe in plural letter as such

30. The ponderously burdened dunecrawler clanked across the crater.
    a. comma between adjectives preceding the subject
    b. a comma after the independent clause
    c. a semicolon between the independent clauses
    d. a comma before the prepositional phrases
    e. a comma before the participle phrase

31. I have thirty seven cloudgliders and George has one said Morton.
    - **a. a hyphen in the compound adjective**
    - **b. a comma between the independent clauses**
    - **c. quotation marks around Morton's words**
    - **d. comma inside closing quotation marks**
    - e. a comma outside the closing quotation marks

32. The long dark night of June 23 1992 and the cold morning were scary.
    - **a. comma between adjectives preceding noun**
    - **b. a comma after the day**
    - **c. a comma after the year**
    - d. a comma between the clauses
    - e. a comma after *morning*

33. The heliologist moved forward and placed his instruments with care.
    - a. a comma between the independent clauses
    - b. an apostrophe in the direct object
    - c. commas around the appositive
    - d. a comma before the participle phrase
    - e. a semicolon after the independent clause

34. The dune hermits greatest painting is The Distant 3 Suns.
    - **a. an apostrophe in the possessive noun**
    - b. a colon after the verb
    - c. quotation marks around the title of the painting
    - **d. italics on the title of the painting**
    - e. italics on the number as such

35. The leader said I will instruct you the captain saluted and left.
    - **a. a comma after the first verb**
    - **b. quotation marks around the leader's words**
    - c. a comma inside the quotation marks
    - d. a semicolon inside the quotation marks
    - **e. semicolon outside the quotation marks**

36. The pro American tribes on Neptune form a three fourths majority.
    - a. commas around the appositive
    - **b. a hyphen after the prefix**
    - **c. a hyphen in the fraction**
    - d. an apostrophe in **fourths**
    - e. a comma after the dependent clause

37. Well Hamlet the colony has revolted we should leave at once.
    - a. a semicolon after the dependent clause
    - **b. a semicolon after the independent clause**
    - **c. commas around the noun of direct address**
    - **d. a comma after the interjection**
    - e. a comma before the prepositional phrase

38. Neptunes national anthem is Symphony Number Sebm in Beta Sharp.
    - a. quotation marks around title (including the period)
    - b. quotation marks around title (not including the period)
    - c. a comma after the dependent clause
    - **d. an apostrophe in the possessive noun**
    - **e. italics on the music composition title**

39. The new commander taking Logans place has not been to Venus before.
    - a. a comma after the dependent clause
    - b. commas around the participle phrase
    - c. commas around the gerund phrase
    - **d. an apostrophe in the possessive noun**
    - e. dashes around the abrupt break in thought

40. The landing of the sand patrol gave our team its first emergency.
    - a. a comma after the gerund
    - b. commas around the parenthetical remark
    - c. commas around the appositive
    - d. an apostrophe in the contraction
    - e. a comma after the dependent clause

41. At 830 in the gray lunar dawn the glowing landers slowly descended.
    a. **a colon in the time**
    b. a semicolon in the time
    c. a comma between the clauses
    d. **comma after introductory prep. phrases**
    e. a comma before the adverb

42. As Ed gaped the alien said Idjjwe smujmu simmywatt.
    a. **a comma after the dependent clause**
    b. **comma after the verb in independent clause**
    c. **quotation marks around the alien statement**
    d. **italics on the alien statement**
    e. **period inside closing quotation marks**

43. Chapter five of Smiling Planet is titled Binary Dawn.
    a. commas around the appositive
    b. **italics on the book title**
    c. **quotation marks around the chapter title**
    d. italics on the chapter title
    e. an apostrophe in the possessive noun

44. The task of the gravity squad is to patrol to zone and to sector.
    a. a semicolon after the linking verb
    b. a colon after the linking verb
    c. a dash after the linking verb
    d. **a comma after the first infinitive**
    e. **a comma after the second infinitive**

45. Its better to have two thirds of a sandburger than a one fourth share.
    a. **an apostrophe in the contraction**
    b. a hyphen in the first fraction
    c. **a hyphen in the second fraction**
    d. commas around prepositional phrase
    e. a comma before the dependent clause

46. New Herante Plutos oldest city is inhabited by Noncognus subzoicus.
    a. **commas around the appositive**
    b. a comma after the independent clause
    c. **italics on the Latin species name**
    d. **an apostrophe in the possessive noun**
    e. a comma after the dependent clause

47. The late 1990s were a time of well planned expeditions to the stars.
    a. a comma after the year
    b. an apostrophe in the year
    c. **a hyphen in the compound adjective**
    d. a comma before the final prepositional phrase
    e. a comma before the first prepositional phrase

48. The disastrous instructions to the lunar base were well intentioned.
    a. commas around the parenthetical remark
    b. commas around the appositive
    c. an apostrophe in *instructions*
    d. a comma after the subject
    e. a hyphen in the compound adjective

49. 35 and 66 are the numbers which its not safe to use Bill.
    a. quotation marks around the numbers
    b. **italics on the numbers**
    c. an apostrophe in the possessive pronoun
    d. **an apostrophe in the contraction**
    e. **comma before noun of direct address**

50. If you go to Mars please bring me a sandpainting.
    a. a semicolon between the clauses
    b. **a comma after the dependent clause**
    c. a comma after the independent clause
    d. quotation marks around the proper noun
    e. an apostrophe in the plural noun

Student Name:_____   Date:_____
Period:_____   Loop 1-5 P as *f* of G TEST

	A B C D E		A B C D E		A B C D E		A B C D E
1.	0 0 0 0 0	26.	0 0 0 0 0	51.	0 0 0 0 0	76.	0 0 0 0 0
2.	0 0 0 0 0	27.	0 0 0 0 0	52.	0 0 0 0 0	77.	0 0 0 0 0
3.	0 0 0 0 0	28.	0 0 0 0 0	53.	0 0 0 0 0	78.	0 0 0 0 0
4.	0 0 0 0 0	29.	0 0 0 0 0	54.	0 0 0 0 0	79.	0 0 0 0 0
5.	0 0 0 0 0	30.	0 0 0 0 0	55.	0 0 0 0 0	80.	0 0 0 0 0
6.	0 0 0 0 0	31.	0 0 0 0 0	56.	0 0 0 0 0	81.	0 0 0 0 0
7.	0 0 0 0 0	32.	0 0 0 0 0	57.	0 0 0 0 0	82.	0 0 0 0 0
8.	0 0 0 0 0	33.	0 0 0 0 0	58.	0 0 0 0 0	83.	0 0 0 0 0
9.	0 0 0 0 0	34.	0 0 0 0 0	59.	0 0 0 0 0	84.	0 0 0 0 0
10.	0 0 0 0 0	35.	0 0 0 0 0	60.	0 0 0 0 0	85.	0 0 0 0 0
11.	0 0 0 0 0	36.	0 0 0 0 0	61.	0 0 0 0 0	86.	0 0 0 0 0
12.	0 0 0 0 0	37.	0 0 0 0 0	62.	0 0 0 0 0	87.	0 0 0 0 0
13.	0 0 0 0 0	38.	0 0 0 0 0	63.	0 0 0 0 0	88.	0 0 0 0 0
14.	0 0 0 0 0	39.	0 0 0 0 0	64.	0 0 0 0 0	89.	0 0 0 0 0
15.	0 0 0 0 0	40.	0 0 0 0 0	65.	0 0 0 0 0	90.	0 0 0 0 0
16.	0 0 0 0 0	41.	0 0 0 0 0	66.	0 0 0 0 0	91.	0 0 0 0 0
17.	0 0 0 0 0	42.	0 0 0 0 0	67.	0 0 P as 0	92.	0 0 0 0 0
18.	0 0 0 0 0	43.	0 0 0 0 0	68.	0 0 0 0 0	93.	0 0 0 0 0
19.	0 0 0 0 0	44.	0 0 0 0 0	69.	0 0 0 0 0	94.	0 0 0 0 0
20.	0 0 0 0 0	45.	0 0 0 0 0	70.	0 0 0 0 0	95.	0 0 0 0 0
21.	0 0 0 0 0	46.	0 0 0 0 0	71.	0 0 0 0 0	96.	0 0 0 0 0
22.	0 0 0 0 0	47.	0 0 0 0 0	72.	0 0 0 0 0	97.	0 0 0 0 0
23.	0 0 0 0 0	48.	0 0 0 0 0	73.	0 0 0 0 0	98.	0 0 0 0 0
24.	0 0 0 0 0	49.	0 0 0 0 0	74.	0 0 0 0 0	99.	0 0 0 0 0
25.	0 0 0 0 0	50.	0 0 0 0 0	75.	0 0 0 0 0	100.	0 0 0 0 0

Student Name:_____   Date:_____
Period:_____   Loop 1-5 P as *f* of G TEST

	A B C D E		A B C D E		A B C D E		A B C D E
1.	0 0 + 0 0	26.	+ 0 0 0 0	51.	0 0 0 0 0	76.	0 0 0 0 0
2.	+ + 0 + 0	27.	0 0 0 0 0	52.	0 0 0 0 0	77.	0 0 0 0 0
3.	0 0 0 + 0	28.	+ + + + 0	53.	0 0 0 0 0	78.	0 0 0 0 0
4.	+ + 0 + +	29.	+ + 0 + +	54.	0 0 0 0 0	79.	0 0 0 0 0
5.	0 + 0 + 0	30.	0 0 0 0 0	55.	0 0 0 0 0	80.	0 0 0 0 0
6.	+ + + + +	31.	+ + + + 0	56.	0 0 0 0 0	81.	0 0 0 0 0
7.	0 + + + 0	32.	+ + + 0 0	57.	0 0 0 0 0	82.	0 0 0 0 0
8.	+ 0 + + 0	33.	0 0 0 0 0	58.	0 0 0 0 0	83.	0 0 0 0 0
9.	0 + + 0 0	34.	+ 0 0 + 0	59.	0 0 0 0 0	84.	0 0 0 0 0
10.	0 + 0 0 +	35.	+ + 0 0 +	60.	0 0 0 0 0	85.	0 0 0 0 0
11.	0 + 0 0 +	36.	0 + + 0 0	61.	0 0 0 0 0	86.	0 0 0 0 0
12.	+ 0 + 0 +	37.	0 + + + 0	62.	0 0 0 0 0	87.	0 0 0 0 0
13.	+ 0 0 0 0	38.	0 0 0 + +	63.	0 0 0 0 0	88.	0 0 0 0 0
14.	+ + 0 + 0	39.	0 0 0 + 0	64.	0 0 0 0 0	89.	0 0 0 0 0
15.	0 0 + 0 0	40.	0 0 0 0 0	65.	0 0 0 0 0	90.	0 0 0 0 0
16.	0 0 0 0 0	41.	+ 0 0 + 0	66.	0 0 0 0 0	91.	0 0 0 0 0
17.	0 + 0 0 0	42.	+ + + + +	67.	0 0 0 0 0	92.	0 0 0 0 0
18.	+ 0 + + 0	43.	0 + + 0 0	68.	0 0 0 0 0	93.	0 0 0 0 0
19.	0 0 + 0 0	44.	0 0 0 + +	69.	0 0 0 0 0	94.	0 0 0 0 0
20.	0 + 0 + 0	45.	+ 0 + 0 0	70.	0 0 0 0 0	95.	0 0 0 0 0
21.	0 + 0 + +	46.	+ 0 + + 0	71.	0 0 0 0 0	96.	0 0 0 0 0
22.	0 0 + 0 0	47.	0 0 + 0 0	72.	0 0 0 0 0	97.	0 0 0 0 0
23.	0 0 + 0 +	48.	0 0 0 0 0	73.	0 0 0 0 0	98.	0 0 0 0 0
24.	0 + + + 0	49.	0 + 0 + +	74.	0 0 0 0 0	99.	0 0 0 0 0
25.	+ 0 0 + +	50.	0 + 0 0 0	75.	0 0 0 0 0	100.	0 0 0 0 0

Cut a copy on dotted lines, then punch out +'s with a hole punch, tape back together on back, avoiding holes.

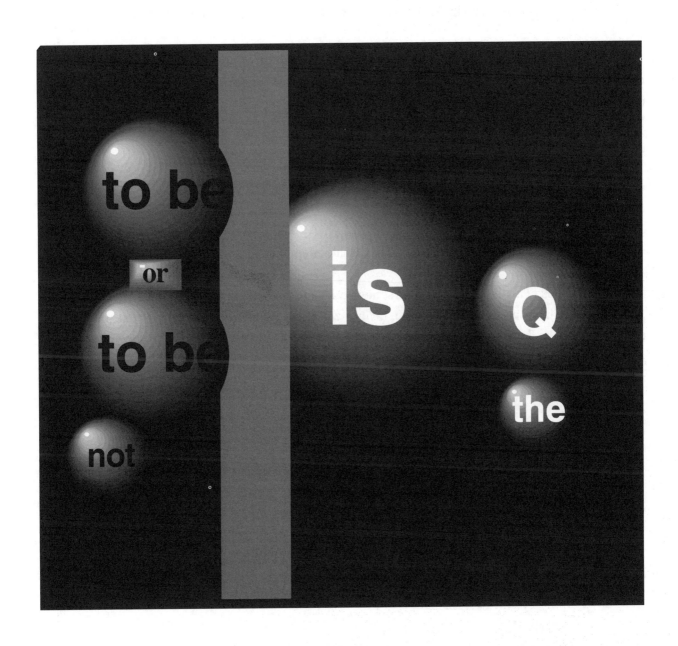

This is the desert where the elves decimated the trolls.

Parts of speech: *This* is a demonstrative pronoun; *is* is a verb; *the* is an adjective modifying the singular common noun *desert*; *where* is a subordinating conjunction; *the* is an adjective (definite article) modifying the plural common noun *elves*; *decimated* is a verb (past tense, transitive); *the* is an adjective modifying the plural common noun *trolls*.

Parts of the sentence: The sentence contains a subject/linking verb/subject complement structure in *This/is/desert*. It also contains a subject/action verb/direct object structure in *elves/decimated/trolls*.

Phrases: There are no prepositional, verbal, or appositive phrases.

Clauses: This is an ID complex sentence because it contains one independent clause, *This is the desert*, and one dependent clause, *where the elves decimated the trolls*. The clauses are connected by the relative adverb *where*, and the dependent clause is a relative dependent clause whose function is to modify the noun *desert*. In other words, the entire dependent clause functions as an adjective!

• • •

Where: Note that the word *where* is described both as a relative adverb and as a subordinating conjunction. The word serves a dual purpose; it joins the clauses, and it modifies the verb *decimated*.

ID: Remember the punctuation rule for this structure. Since the independent clause comes first, there is no comma.

This is the desert where the elves decimated the trolls.

Parts of Speech:	pron.	v.	adj.	n.	conj.	adj.	n.	v.	adj.	n.

Parts of Sentence:	subject	predicate	subject complement			subject	predicate		direct object

Phrases: no prepositional, appositive, or verbal phrases

Clauses: ---independent clause--- ----------------dependent clause--------------------
one independent clause, one dependent clause, ID complex declarative sentence

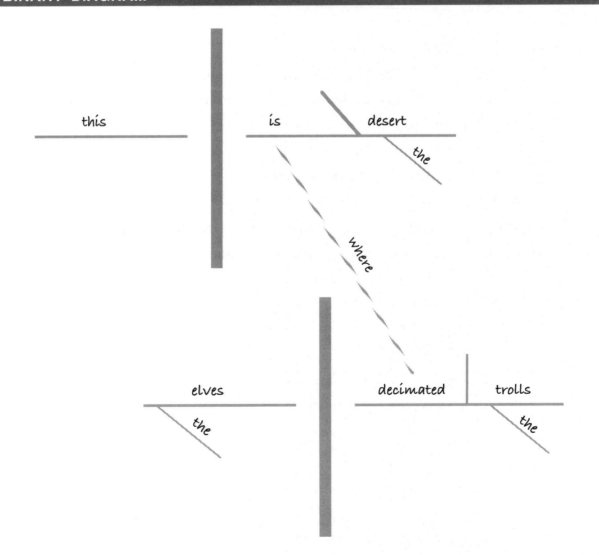

Questions for individual thought or small group discussion:

emotion: feelings

How could you use grammar and diction to make language cold, formal, and impersonal?

aesthetics: artistic qualities

What are some of the best adjectives a writer can use to describe olfactory or tactile sense impressions?

synthesis: making connections

Imagine a sentence with a common noun, an action verb, and twelve other words, all of them adjectives or adverbs. What, outside of language, does this remind you of?

analysis: breaking down into components

Make a long list of prepositions. Then sort the prepositions into different types, such as prepositions of time: before, after, etc. How many different types of prepositions can you find?

Use the grammar clues to solve this Mystery Sentence:

A sentence from a lullaby begins with a four-word dependent clause containing a subordinating conjunction, a definite article, a singular common noun, and an intransitive present tense action verb. This is followed by an independent clause containing a definite article, a singular common noun, and a future tense intransitive action verb.

When the wind blows, the cradle will rock.

From Mary Shelley's

Frankenstein

One secret which I alone possessed was the hope to which I had dedicated myself; and the moon gazed on my midnight labours, while, with unrelaxed and breathless eagerness, I pursued nature to her hiding-places. Who shall conceive the horrors of my secret toil, as I dabbled among the unhallowed damps of the grave, or tortured the living animal to animate the lifeless clay? My limbs now tremble, and my eyes swim with the remembrance; but then a resistless, and almost frantic, impulse, urged me forward; I seemed to have lost all soul or sensation but for this one pursuit.

Here is a striking passage from Mary Shelley's immortal monster novel, *Frankenstein*. She wrote the novel at the urging of her husband, the great British poet Percy Shelley, and their friend, the other great British poet George Gordon, Lord Byron. At first writing it as a short story, she later expanded it into a novel. When she began the work, she was nineteen years old. How is this passage different from one you would be likely to write? What do you notice about Shelley's use of sentence structure?

1. Write a sentence that contains six interjections in quotation marks, followed by a proper noun and an intransitive active voice verb.

2. Write a compound sentence with four nouns, all of them verbals; the sentence should contain no conjunction.

---

1. "Eek! Yikes! Ouch! Hey! Oof! Help!" Stubb exclaimed.

2. Thinking is trying to understand; it precedes knowing.

Loop Six Writing Lab:
Clause Structure

1. Write two separate sentences that are related in content.

2. Rewrite the sentences, combining them into an I,ccI compound sentence.

3. Rewrite the sentences again, combining them into a D,I complex sentence.

4. Rewrite the sentences again, combining them into an ID complex sentence.

5. Determine which of the variation you think is best, and write a paragraph explaining why.

"It yearns me not if men my garments wear."

-William Shakespeare

This sentence, from *Henry V*, IV. iii., expresses the king's priorities. He is not covetous for gold, or material possessions; rather, he is inspired by the idea that "we few, we happy few, we band of brothers" will achieve glory in battle.

Parts of speech: *It* is a a third person singular subject pronoun; *yearns* is a present tense active voice transitive action verb; *me* is a first person singular object pronoun; *not* is an adverb modifying the verb; *if* is a subordinating conjunction; *men* is a plural common noun; *my* is a first person singular possessive pronoun; *garments* is a plural common noun; and *wear* is present tense active voice transitive action verb. We do not normally use *years* transitively, as Shakespeare does here.

Parts of the sentence: *It* is the subject of the action verb predicate *yearns*, which has *me* as its direct object; *men* is the subject of the action verb predicate *wear*, which has *garments* as its direct object.

Phrases: There are no prepositional, appositive, or verbal phrases.

Clauses: This is an ID complex declarative sentence; the independent clause is *It yearns me not* and the dependent clause is *if men my garments wear*. The dependent clause is interesting for its word order, which would normally be "if men wear my garments."

FOUR-LEVEL ANALYSIS

	It	yearns	me	not	if	men	my	garments	wear.
Parts of Speech:	pron.	v.	pron.	adv.	conj.	n.	pron.	n.	v.
Parts of Sentence:	subj.	pred.	direct object			subj.		direct object	pred.

Phrases:	----no prepositional, appositive, or verbal phrases----

Clauses:	-------independent clause--------	---------------dependent clause----------------
	an ID complex declarative sentence	

Identify the **part of speech** in **bold** in each sentence below:

1. The **equivocating** politician praised both groups.   _____

2. A **superfluous** comment is a waste of time.   _____

3. The two nations formed a **bilateral** agreement.   _____

4. A **circumspect** reply is safer.   _____

5. A big job needs a **commensurate** reward.   _____

6. The creature cast a **malevolent** glare.   _____

7. She is a **neophyte** in the art world.   _____

8. The grouchy **misanthropist** wouldn't contribute.   _____

9. The **bellicose** tribe attacked without warning.   _____

10. They believe in an **anthropomorphic** god.   _____

Identify the **part of sentence** in *italics* in each sentence below:

11. The **captious** *remarks* were not sincere.   _____

12. Create a ***neologism***, like televoracious.   _____

13. The convict's muttered **malediction** was *inaudible*.   _____

14. Her **incredulous** expression showed her *feelings*.   _____

15. You can't keep *secrets* from an **omniscient** god.   _____

16. It was a *hobby* that became a **monomania**.   _____

17. You have a convincing but unfortunately **specious** *argument*.   _____

18. His speech **excoriated** the *opponent*.   _____

19. We saw an early ***prototype*** of the Mustang.   _____

20. It is a hostile, **xenophobic** *country*.   _____

For each sentence, identify the type of *phrase* in *italics* and its part of speech:

1. It can be difficult *to **mollify** someone's anger.*   _____

2. *Up the bank* splashed a water-logged **ichthyologist**.   _____

3. *Speaking seven languages,* she is a brilliant **polyglot**.   _____

4. Look *through the **diaphanous** draperies.*   _____

5. *The **somniferous** speaking* put him to sleep.   _____

6. He has a comfortable **sinecure** *in his uncle's firm.*   _____

7. *For modern critics,* Hamlet's famous **soliloquy** is the question.   _____

8. The **adherents** *of a militaristic foreign policy* want war.   _____

9. *To **abjure** one's former beliefs* is stressful.   _____

10. The **caustic** comments *about her clothes* hurt her.   _____

For each sentence, identify the **sentence structure**. Disregard bold type.

11. The idea was formed by a **confluence** of other ideas.   _____

12. He was **deposed** without violence; everyone approved.   _____

13. The offensive **egomaniac** praised himself as we expected.   _____

14. When it happened, it was **egregious** act of vandalism.   _____

15. Take an extra-strength **analgesic** for the headache, and sleep.   _____

16. Try to divine the future through superannuated **chiromancy**.   _____

17. The corrupt **oligarchy** kept control when the revolution failed.   _____

18. The bigot's **intractable** opinions were unchangeable.   _____

19. The **intransigent** true believers wouldn't budge; I know.   _____

20. When night fell, his **perfidious** cowardice made him infamous.   _____

Identify the **part of speech** in **bold** in each sentence below:

1.	The **equivocating** politician praised both groups.	adjective
2.	A **superfluous** comment is a waste of time.	adjective
3.	The two nations formed a **bilateral** agreement.	adjective
4.	A **circumspect** reply is safer.	adjective
5.	A big job needs a **commensurate** reward.	adjective
6.	The creature cast a **malevolent** glare.	adjective
7.	She is a **neophyte** in the art world.	noun
8.	The grouchy **misanthropist** wouldn't contribute.	noun
9.	The **bellicose** tribe attacked without warning.	adjective
10.	They believe in an **anthropomorphic** god.	adjective

Identify the *part of sentence* in *italics* in each sentence below:

11.	The **captious** *remarks* were not sincere.	subject
12.	Create a ***neologism***, like "televoracious."	direct object
13.	The convict's muttered **malediction** was *inaudible*.	subject complement
14.	Her **incredulous** expression showed her *feelings*.	direct object
15.	You can't keep *secrets* from an **omniscient** god.	direct object
16.	It was a *hobby* that became a **monomania**.	subject complement
17.	You have a convincing but unfortunately **specious** *argument*.	direct object
18.	His speech **excoriated** the *opponent*.	direct object
19.	We saw an early ***prototype*** of the Mustang.	direct object
20.	It is a hostile, **xenophobic** *country*.	subject complement

For each sentence, identify the type of *phrase* in *italics* and its part of speech:

1.	It can be difficult *to **mollify** someone's anger.*	infinitive, adverb
2.	*Up the bank* splashed a water-logged **ichthyologist**.	prepositional, adverb
3.	*Speaking seven languages,* she is a brilliant **polyglot**.	participle, adjective
4.	Look *through the **diaphanous** draperies.*	prepositional, adverb
5.	*The **somniferous** speaking* put him to sleep.	gerund, noun
6.	He has a comfortable **sinecure** *in his uncle's firm.*	prepositional, adverb
7.	*For modern critics,* Hamlet's famous **soliloquy** is the question.	prepositional, adverb
8.	The **adherents** *of a militaristic foreign policy* want war.	prepositional, adjective
9.	*To **abjure** one's former beliefs* is stressful.	infinitive, noun
10.	The **caustic** comments *about her clothes* hurt her.	prepositional, adjective

For each sentence, identify the **sentence structure**. Disregard bold type.

11.	The idea was formed by a **confluence** of other ideas.	simple
12.	He was **deposed** without violence; everyone approved.	compound
13.	The offensive **egomaniac** praised himself as we expected.	complex
14.	When it happened, it was **egregious** act of vandalism.	complex
15.	Take an extra-strength **analgesic** for the headache, and sleep.	compound
16.	Try to divine the future through superannuated **chiromancy**.	simple
17.	The corrupt **oligarchy** kept control when the revolution failed.	complex
18.	The bigot's **intractable** opinions were unchangeable.	simple
19.	The **intransigent** true believers wouldn't budge; I know.	compound
20.	When night fell, his **perfidious** cowardice made him infamous.	complex

For each of the following sentences, circle the letter of each answer that is true. The answer can be any combination, including all or none. This exercise will teach you the real process of punctuation as a function of grammar.

1. In the thriving Delaware colony the heavy market in iron tools was raising profits.
   a. comma after the introductory prepositional phrase
   b. a comma after the dependent clause
   c. commas around the parenthetical remark
   d. a semicolon between the independent clauses
   e. a hyphen in the compound adjective

2. The insects that ate the wooden braces are hard to eliminate.
   a. commas around the appositive
   b. a semicolon between the independent clauses
   c. commas around the nonessential clause
   d. quotation marks around the word **braces**
   e. a comma before the infinitive

3. Robert Dubious our new senator was opposed however its happening.
   a. commas around the appositive
   b. a semicolon between the independent clauses
   c. a comma after **however**
   d. an apostrophe in the contraction
   e. a comma after the dependent clause

4. In the winter of 76 the wolfs teeth left marks like letter vs on the windowsill.
   a. an apostrophe before the contraction
   b. comma after the introductory prepositional phrases
   c. an apostrophe in the possessive noun
   d. italics on the letter as such
   e. an apostrophe in the plural letter as such

5. The heavily loaded jeep careened across the plain.
   a. comma between adjectives preceding the subject
   b. a comma after the independent clause
   c. a semicolon between the independent clauses
   d. a comma before the prepositional phrases
   e. a comma before the participle phrase

Answer Key

1. In the thriving Delaware colony, the heavy market in iron tools was raising profits.
    a. comma after the introductory prep. phrase   d. a semicolon between the independent clauses
    b. a comma after the dependent clause   e. a hyphen in the compound adjective
    c. commas around the parenthetical remark

This introductory prepositional phrase is long enough to merit a comma; when these introductory phrases get wordy enough, we want to make sure they don't get mixed up with the subject of the sentence.

2. The insects that ate the wooden braces are hard to eliminate.
    a. commas around the appositive   d. quotation marks around the word **braces**
    b. a semicolon between the independent clauses   e. a comma before the infinitive
    c. commas around the nonessential clause

This sentence contains an adjective clause modifying the subject, but the question is, is the adjective clause essential or nonessential? We have to decide because if it is nonessential, we have to put commas around it. The best answer here is that the clause is essential; it tells which insects, and is not just an unnecessary interruption. Therefore, we do not need commas, because it is important and needs to be there.

3. Robert Dubious, our new senator, was opposed; however, it's happening.
    a. commas around the appositive   **d. an apostrophe in the contraction**
    b. a semicolon between the independent clauses   e. a comma after the dependent clause
    c. a comma after *however*

This illustrates the correct treatment of a compound sentence in which the second clause begins with the word however.

4. In the winter of '76, the wolf's teeth left marks like letter *v*'s on the windowsill.
    a. an apostrophe before the contraction   **d. italics on the letter as such**
    b. comma after the introductory prep. phrases   **e. apostrophe in the plural letter as such**
    c. an apostrophe in the possessive noun

Lots of action in this sentence. Remember that letters, numbers, and words as such are always in italics (or underlined). If you mean the word dog, *rather than the four-footed kind, you italicize* dog. *In this sentence, which is all in italics, I do just the reverse, and it means the same thing.*

5. The heavily loaded jeep careened across the plain.
    a. comma between adjectives preceding the subject   d. a comma before the prepositional phrases
    b. a comma after the independent clause   e. a comma before the participle phrase
    c. a semicolon between the independent clauses

No punctuation.

The meteor struck, and Leonidas smiled stoically.

Parts of speech: *The* is an adjective modifying the singular common noun *meteor*; *struck* is an action verb; *and* is a coordinating conjunction; *Leonidas* is a proper noun; *smiled* is a past tense intransitive action verb; and *stoically* is an adverb modifying the verb *smiled*.

Parts of the sentence: *meteor* is the subject of the verb *struck*, and *Leonidas* is the subject of the verb *smiled*. There are no subject complements, direct objects, or indirect objects in the sentence.

Phrases: There are no prepositional, infinitive, participle, gerund, or appositive phrases in the sentence.

Clauses: The sentence is a compound sentence because it contains two independent clauses; the first clause is *The meteor struck*, and the second clause is *Leonidas smiled stoically*. Either clause could be written as a sentence by itself. The two clauses are glued together by the coordinating conjunction *and*.

• • •

Punctuation: The comma before the *and* is necessary in this sentence. It is not always necessary to put a comma before every *and*, but it is necessary to put a comma before every coordinating conjunction *IF* the coordinating conjunction is used to join two independent clauses into a compound sentence. (Note on exceptions: *Extremely* short compound sentences sometimes dispense with the comma, and novelists might omit the comma for creative reasons, as to speed the flow of language, but for normal writing purposes, it is best to always include the comma.)

Leonidas: A famous name in history, Leonidas was the leader of the Spartans at the battle of Thermopylae. We have used his name to pay our respects.

The meteor struck, and Leonidas smiled stoically.

	The	meteor	struck,	and	Leonidas	smiled	stoically.
Parts of Speech:	adj.	n.	v.	conj.	n.	v.	adv.
Parts of Sentence:		subject	predicate		subject	predicate	
Phrases:			no prepositional, appositive, or verbal phrases				
Clauses:			two independent clauses, compound declarative sentence				

Here is the classic, balanced compound sentence, weighing evenly on both sides of the coordinating conjunction.

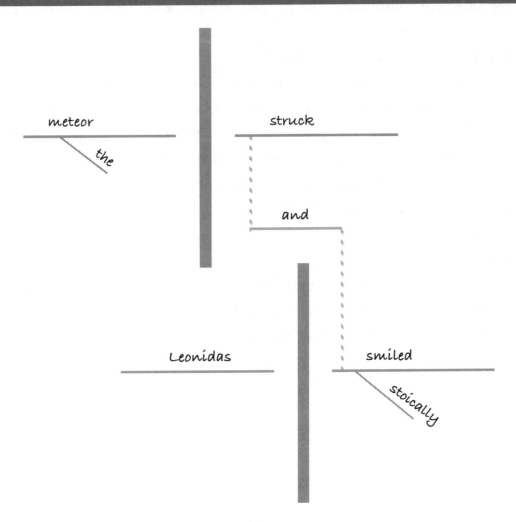

Questions for individual thought or small group discussion:

emotion: feelings

What nouns can you think of which are not the names of emotions but which are clear evidence of emotions, e.g., *grin*?

intuition: ideas from the blue

What is suggested to your mind by the following alliterated adjective and noun: *shadowy shape*? Take a minute to let an image develop in your mind, and then explain what it looks like. What does the adjective contribute to the image? What does the noun contribute?

divergence: thinking of alternatives

Apparently, modification is one of the most important functions of grammar. We have numerous ways to modify in grammar, including adjectives, adverbs, participles, prepositional phrases, and adjective clauses. What is it about our world and the way language relates to it that requires such a sophisticated modification system? Try to list as many interesting statements about this as you can.

analysis

We divide grammar into four levels: parts of speech, parts of sentence, phrases, and clauses. Is there a different way it could be divided, that would be useful? Explain.

Use the grammar clues to solve this Mystery Sentence:

A four-word simple declarative sentence is one of the most famous statements made by an American civil rights leader. The sentence begins with its subject, a first person singular personal pronoun. The next word is a present tense action verb, which happens to be a word which is often used as a helping verb in the perfect tenses. The sentence concludes with an indefinite article and a subject complement, a singular common noun.

I have a dream. (Martin Luther King)

From Kenneth Grahame's

The Wind in the Willows

The Mole was bewitched, entranced, fascinated. By the side of the river he trotted as one trots, when very small, by the side of a man who holds one spell-bound by exciting stories; and when tired at last, he sat on the bank, while the river still chattered on to him, a babbling procession of the best stories in the world, sent from the heart of the earth to be told at last to the insatiable sea.

One of the most profound, if metaphorical, descriptions of a river ever written, this passage from Kenneth Grahame's children's classic, *The Wind in the Willows*, enchants us with its poetry. Look at this passage long and carefully, and see what you can detect about Grahame's art as a writer. What do you notice about the diction? What are the sentence structures? Does he vary the sentence structures?

1.   Write a complex interrogative sentence that contains more adverbs than any other part of speech.

2.   Write a sentence that illustrates the difference between a direct object and a subject complement.

---

1. As the very curious albatross moved gradually away, did Flask slowly relax?

2. Queequeg is an engineer who hates engineers.

Loop Seven Writing Lab:
The Sentence and the Mind

1.   Write a one-page communication that contains no sentences.

2.   Read the page to someone, and find out if that person understands what you were trying to communicate.

3.   Talk in class about the question, not "why are sentences important to grammarians," but "Why are sentences important to the mind?"

"Now I must convince him and then I must kill him."

-Ernest Hemingway

This sentence from Ernest Hemingway's *The Old Man and the Sea* typifies Hemingway's style: short, ordinary words, and a running line that avoids typical clause punctuation in favor of a feeling of interior monologue. The old Man, Santiago, has realized that he must first dominate the fish's will, make the fish believe that he will be caught, and then he will be able to finish the fish.

Parts of speech: *Now* is an adverb modifying the verb; *I* is a first person singular subject pronoun; *must* is acting as an auxiliary verb; *convince* is a present tense active voice transitive action verb; *him* is a third person singular masculine gender object pronoun; *and* is a coordinating conjunction that joins two clauses together; *then* is an adverb modifying the verb; *I* is a singular subject pronoun; *must* is an auxiliary verb: *kill* is a present tense transitive action verb; and *him* is a third person subject pronoun.

Parts of the sentence: *I* is the subject of the verb/predicate *convince*, which has *him* as a direct object; the second *I* is the subject of the verb *kill* which has the second *him as* its direct object.

Phrases: There are no prepositional, appositive, or verbal phrases.

Clauses: This is a beautiful, clean, compound sentence. It illustrates why the compound structure exists, rather than there only being the simple option; these two ideas are related, and the second follows from the first. It is more true that they are connected actions, than it is true that they are independent actions. Hemingway flows them together by omitting the expected comma.

FOUR-LEVEL ANALYSIS

	Now	I	must	convince	him	and	then	I	must	kill	him.
Parts of Speech:	adv.	pron.	v.	v.	pron.	conj.	adv.	pron.	v.	v.	pron.
Parts of Sentence:		subject		predicate	direct object			subject	----pred.----		direct object
Phrases:	-----no prepositional, verbal, or appositive phrases-----										
Clauses:	-----------independent clause-----------						------independent clause-------				
	compound declarative sentence										

Identify the **part of speech** in **bold** in each sentence below:

1.   The **egocentric** snob didn't notice who he hurt. _____

2.   A paycheck is one of the **tangible** benefits of a job. _____

3.   The **demagogue** played on public prejudices. _____

4.   Don't **preclude** that option. _____

5.   British **cryptologists** cracked the German code. _____

6.   We deplore his narrow **ethnocentrism**. _____

7.   A humorless pedant is a poor **pedagogue**. _____

8.   Galileo was forced to **recant** his heliocentric statements. _____

9.   Permission to travel has been **revoked**. _____

10. The **pugnacious** bully got his comeuppance. _____

Identify the *part of sentence* in *italics* in each sentence below:

11. Her **incisive** *questions* cut deeply into the issue. _____

12. The German leader delivered a ***diatribe*** against France. _____

13. There is an inexplicable ***anomaly*** in the data. _____

14. Please **enumerate** your *reasons*. _____

15. You must *choose* among certain **circumscribed** alternatives. _____

16. We are *forced* **to intercede** on behalf of the orphan. _____

17. The **disputatious** reporter irritated the *official*. _____

18. The **loquacious** fellow wore their *ears* out. _____

19. We **abrogate** an *agreement* only out of dire necessity. _____

20.   A **prescient** *vision* came to him in a dream. _____

For each sentence, identify the type of *phrase* in *italics*:

1. It is time *to advocate* a new policy. _____

2. He was crushed by the **ponderous** burden *of the decision*. _____

3. *Living in fear*, the Gauls expected a brutal **retribution**. _____

4. The **android's** metallic eye glistened *from across the room*. _____

5. The crusade *against the infidels* was unsuccessful. _____

6. The **resurgence** *of patriotism* began slowly. _____

7. She, *a conventional person*, liked his **punctilious** formal conduct. _____

8. His **condescending** attitude was infuriating *to all of us*. _____

9. The two **collateral** issues could not be discussed *at one time*. _____

10. The past, *an eternal mystery*, is **irrevocable** and answers no call. _____

For each sentence, identify the **sentence structure**. Disregard bold type.

11. Please **elucidate** the matter for our less enlightened guest. _____

12. Franklin's witty **epigrams** amuse us; we still read them. _____

13. As time went on, his **eccentric** personality began to moderate. _____

14. It is wise to be **cognizant** of the laws regulating investments. _____

15. As I mentioned, the **stringent** regulations seemed severe. _____

16. The **anthropoid** apes have recognizable facial expressions. _____

17. Her **diffident** glance caught his eye when she looked up. _____

18. **Pandemonium** erupted on the playground; it was fun. _____

19. The diplomat's **urbane** manners set the tone since they left. _____

20. Because of his spirit, the **tractable** boy was a pleasure to know. _____

Identify the **part of speech** in **bold** in each sentence below:

1. The **egocentric** snob didn't notice who he hurt.   adjective

2. A paycheck is one of the **tangible** benefits of a job.   adjective

3. The **demagogue** played on public prejudices.   noun

4. Don't **preclude** that option.   verb

5. British **cryptologists** cracked the German code.   noun

6. We deplore his narrow **ethnocentrism**.   noun

7. A humorless pedant is a poor **pedagogue**.   noun

8. Galileo was forced **to recant** his heliocentric statements.   adverb

9. Permission to travel has been **revoked**.   verb

10. The **pugnacious** bully got his comeuppance.   adjective

Identify the *part of sentence* in *italics* in each sentence below:

11. Her **incisive** *questions* cut deeply into the issue.   subject

12. The German leader delivered a ***diatribe*** against France.   direct object

13. There is an inexplicable ***anomaly*** in the data.   subject complement

14. Please **enumerate** your *reasons*.   direct object

15. You must *choose* among certain **circumscribed** alternatives.   predicate

16. We are *forced* **to intercede** on behalf of the orphan.   predicate

17. The **disputatious** reporter irritated the *official*.   direct object

18. The **loquacious** fellow wore their *ears* out.   direct object

19. We **abrogate** an *agreement* only out of dire necessity.   direct object

20. A **prescient** *vision* came to him in a dream.   subject

For each sentence, identify the type of *italics phrase* and give its part of speech:

1.	It is time **to advocate** *a new policy.*	infinitive, adjective
2.	He was crushed by the **ponderous** burden *of the decision.*	prepositional, adjective
3.	*Living in fear*, the Gauls expected a brutal **retribution**.	participle, adjective
4.	The **android's** metallic eye glistened *from across the room.*	prepositional, adverb
5.	The crusade *against the **infidels*** was unsuccessful.	prepositional, adjective
6.	The **resurgence** *of patriotism* began slowly.	prepositional, adjective
7.	She, *a conventional person*, liked his **punctilious** formal conduct.	appositive, adjective
8.	His **condescending** attitude was infuriating *to all of us.*	prepositional, adverb
9.	The two **collateral** issues could not be discussed *at one time.*	prepositional, adverb
10.	The past, *an eternal mystery*, is **irrevocable** and answers no call.	appositive, adjective

For each sentence, identify the **sentence structure**. Disregard bold type.

11.	Please **elucidate** the matter for our less enlightened guest.	simple
12.	Franklin's witty **epigrams** amuse us; we still read them.	compound
13.	As time went on, his **eccentric** personality began to moderate.	complex
14.	It is wise to be **cognizant** of the laws regulating investments.	simple
15.	As I mentioned, the **stringent** regulations seemed severe.	complex
16.	The **anthropoid** apes have recognizable facial expressions.	simple
17.	Her **diffident** glance caught his eye when she looked up.	complex
18.	**Pandemonium** erupted on the playground; it was fun.	compound
19.	The diplomat's **urbane** manners set the tone since they left.	complex
20.	Because of his spirit, the **tractable** boy was a pleasure to know.	simple

For each of the following sentences, circle the letter of each answer that is true. The answer can be any combination, including all or none. This exercise will teach you the real process of punctuation as a function of grammar.

1. In April she returned and the organization recovered its profits.

    a. a comma after the prepositional phrase   d. an apostrophe in the contraction

    b. a comma after the dependent clause   e. commas before and after the appositive

    c. a comma after the independent clause

2. Near Boston Massachusetts the whales avoided Ahabs ship.

    a. a comma after the city   d. an apostrophe in the possessive noun

    b. a comma after the state appositive   e. a comma after the dependent clause

    c. an apostrophe in the plural noun

3. A better feeling arose when Stubb the experienced officer walked forward.

    a. a comma to separate the adjectives preceding the noun   d. commas around the appositive

    b. a comma before the dependent clause   e. commas around the noun of direct address

    c. a comma after the independent clause

4. Melvilles novel Moby Dick contains a ship named The Pequod.

    a. italics on the ship title   d. italics on the book title

    b. an apostrophe in the possessive noun   e. commas around the appositive

    c. quotation marks around the book title

5. The well intentioned remark and the reaction caused thirty five resignations.

    a. a comma between the modifiers that precede the noun.   d. a hyphen in the compound number

    b. a hyphen in the compound adjective preceding the noun.   e. an apostrophe in the possessive noun

    c. a comma after the dependent clause

For each of the following sentences, circle the letter of each answer that is true. The answer can be any combination, including all or none. This exercise will teach you the real process of punctuation as a function of grammar.

1. In April she returned, and the organization recovered its profits.
   a. a comma after the prepositional phrase
   b. a comma after the dependent clause
   c. a comma after the independent clause
   d. an apostrophe in the contraction
   e. commas before and after the appositive

   There is no contraction in the sentence; its is a possessive pronoun, which does not use an apostrophe since it is already possessive. No comma needed after the single, short prepositional phrase.

2. Near Boston, Massachusetts, the whales avoided Ahab's ship.
   a. a comma after the city
   b. a comma after the state appositive
   c. an apostrophe in the plural noun
   d. an apostrophe in the possessive noun
   e. a comma after the dependent clause

   The state appositive should be set off by commas before and after.

3. A better feeling arose when Stubb, the experienced officer, walked forward.
   a. a comma to separate the adjectives preceding the noun
   b. a comma before the dependent clause
   c. a comma after the independent clause
   d. commas around the appositive
   e. commas around the noun of direct address

   Appositives usually take two commas, since they typically interrupt sentences in order to define.

4. Melville's novel, *Moby Dick,* contains a ship named *The Pequod.*
   a. italics on the ship title
   b. an apostrophe in the possessive noun
   c. quotation marks around the book title
   d. italics on the book title
   e. commas around the appositive

   Novel titles and great vessel titles are in italics. If we did not put the two appositive commas in, some brief confusion might arise in the reading of the sentence.

5. The well intentioned remark and the reaction caused thirty five resignations.
   a. a comma between the modifiers that precede the noun.
   b. hyphen in compound adj. preceding noun.
   c. a comma after the dependent clause
   d. a hyphen in the compound number
   e. an apostrophe in the possessive noun

   The hyphen between well *and* intentioned *unites the two words into a single, modifying unity.*

Yesterday, Jupiter was full and unusually bright.

Parts of speech: *Yesterday* is an adverb modifying the past tense linking verb *was*; *Jupiter* is a singular proper noun; *full* is an adjective modifying *Jupiter*; *and* is a coordinating conjunction; *unusually* is an adverb modifying the adjective *bright*; *bright* is an adjective modifying the noun *Jupiter*.

Parts of the sentence: *Jupiter* is the subject, and *was* is the linking verb. There is a compound subject complement in the sentence, consisting of the two predicate adjectives, *full* and *bright*. Remember that subject complements go with linking verbs, whereas direct objects go with action verbs.

Phrases: There are no prepositional, verbal, or appositive phrases in the sentence.

Clauses: The sentence is a simple sentence since it contains only one clause. It is perhaps worth mentioning from time to time that in a simple sentence the entire sentence is the independent clause; all of the words are included in the clause.

• • •

Subject Complements: Here is a compound subject complement. It is a good time to remember the power of subject complements. First, subject complements are very cerebral; many of our strongest ideas, such as Shakespeare's statement that "Life is a walking shadow," involve subject complements. Why? Subject complements let us make equations, saying that A is B, and when A and B are not obviously the same thing at all, this involves a comparison—something that only a person can do. Life is not normally thought of as a shadow, let alone a walking one, and so when Shakespeare used a subject complement form to communicate this idea, he was making an exceptional leap of synthesis.

	Yesterday,	Jupiter	was	full	and	unusually	bright.
Parts of Speech:	adv.	n.	v.	adj.	conj.	adv.	adj.
Parts of Sentence:		subject	predicate	-----compound subject complement-----			
Phrases:	no prepositional, appositive, or verbal phrases						
Clauses:	one independent clause, simple declarative sentence						

This sentence beautifully illustrates the binary structure that is the core of every sentence. Every word in the sentence, except the subject noun, is part of the predicate. The subject stands alone, and everything else is about it.

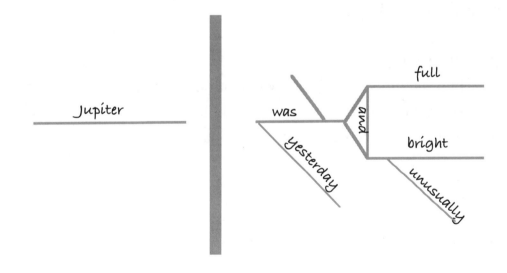

Questions for individual thought or small group discussion:

synthesis: making connections

Think about the word *modify*. We modify a car if we paint it red or alter its fenders. In what sense, if any, is it true to say that an adjective modifies a noun?

divergence: thinking of alternatives

How many interesting ways can of think of to organize sentences into a paragraph? Keep thinking until you create new ways that you have never heard of or read about before.

intuition: ideas from the blue

Use the following infinitive phrase as the subject of a scary sentence: To turn the key . . .

emotion: feelings

Think about how we use punctuation to communicate emotion. How would you punctuate shock, or thoughtfulness, or decisiveness? Could any emotion be punctuated in various ways?

Use the grammar clues to solve this Mystery Sentence:

One of the most famous sentences from the history of warfare in the United States is a simple declarative sentence which begins with a first person singular personal pronoun, then contains a verb phrase in which the verb, which is the first person singular present perfect tense of the verb *to begin*, is separated from its helping verb by two adverbs, then concludes with an infinitive.

I have not yet begun to fight. (John Paul Jones)

From Ernest Hemingway's

For Whom the Bell Tolls

The young man, whose name was Robert Jordan, was extremely hungry and he was worried. He was often hungry but he was not usually worried because he did not give any importance to what happened to himself and he knew from experience how simple it was to move behind the enemy lines in all this country. It was as simple to move behind them as it was to cross through them, if you had a good guide. It was only giving importance to what happened to you if you were caught that made it difficult; that and deciding whom to trust.

Ernest Hemingway's style has been the object of exceptional attention. Look at this passage carefully, and see if you can detect any characteristics that would differentiate Hemingway's writing from anyone else's. Does Hemingway follow the punctuation rules we do? How would you characterize his diction? What do you notice about his use of phrases? Are Hemingway's sentences as challenging to read as some we have seen?

1.   Write a compound declarative sentence that contains no conjunction but does contain an appositive phrase and a gerund.

2. Write a sentence that illustrates the use of quotation marks with other marks of punctuation.

---

1. Stubb, my friendly mentor, loves thinking.

2. "Ishmael," he crooned, "is that blubber on your nose?"

Loop Eight Writing Lab:
The Sentence and the Mind

1. Write a paragraph of five sentences or more in which every noun is modified by an adjective and every verb is modified by an adverb.

2. Convert every adjective into an adverb and every adverb into an adjective so that each sentence has at least two incorrect modifiers.

3. Discuss in class the question, "Why can't you make adverbs work as noun modifiers, and why can't you make adjectives work as verb modifiers?"

191

"It is so difficult to understand people who speak the truth."

-E. M. Forster

In his novel *A Room with a View*, E.M. Forster depicts levels of social sophistication that most of us have never thought about. Sometimes his subtle, suave wit reminds us, as in the sentence above, of Oscar Wilde. This sentence seems cynical, but the overall effect of the novel is positive.

Parts of speech: *It* is a third person singular subject pronoun; *is* is a present tense linking verb; *so* is an adverb that modifies the adjective *difficult*; *to understand* is an adverb; *people* is a common noun; *who* is a relative pronoun; *speak* is a present tense active voice transitive action verb; *the* is an adjective and definite article; and *truth* is a singular common noun.

Parts of the sentence: *It* is the subject of the linking verb *is* which links the subject to the subject complement (predicate adjective) *difficult*; *who* is the subject of the action verb predicate *speak* which transfers the action to its direct object *truth*.

Phrases: Interestingly, the subject complement *difficult* is modified by an infinitive phrase *to understand people* in which *people* serves as the object of the infinitive; *people* is in turn modified by an adjective clause. We therefore have a clause inside an infinitive phrase.

Clauses: This sentence has the feel of a simple sentence, because its dependent clause is buried within an infinitive phrase and obscured by its modification. Since it does not have one clause, however, it is best not to call it simple, but complex.

FOUR-LEVEL ANALYSIS

It is so difficult to understand people who speak the truth.

Parts of Speech:	pron.	v.	adv.	adj.	--------adv.-------	n.	pron.	v.	adj.	n.

Parts of Sentence: subj./pred. | subject complement | subj. | pred. | direct object

Phrases: ------infinitive phrase-------

Clauses: ------------------independent clause------------------ -------dependent clause-------
a complex declarative sentence

Identify the **part of speech** in **bold** in each sentence below:

1.   The quiet boy is an **introspective** loner.   _____

2.   We should not **intervene** in their dispute   _____

3.   Down's **syndrome** has well-known symptoms.   _____

4.   He resented his **subordinate** rank in the military.   _____

5.   A **dissonant** clamor arose in the streets.   _____

6.   The **belligerent** nations refused to negotiate.   _____

7.   It takes money to become a **credible** candidate.   _____

8.   "The shadow of **impending** doom" is a trite phrase.   _____

9.   Bach's **polyphonic** concertos are beautiful.   _____

10.   He wished to be completely **exculpated**.   _____

Identify the **part of sentence** in **bold** in each sentence below:

11.   "Rest room" is a **euphemism**.   _____

12.   Who was the anonymous **benefactor** to little Pip?   _____

13.   A Napoleon complex is a **form** of megalomania.   _____

14.   The oil magnates in Saudi Arabia control **billions**.   _____

15.   Her vivacious personality cheered **us** all.   _____

16.   The heliotropic vines clogged the **window**.   _____

17.   There is no **lack** of amour-propre in her!   _____

18.   The spry octagenarian won the **race**.   _____

19.   This **wine** is preferred by the cognoscenti.   _____

20.   He consumed a painful **surfeit** of food and drink.   _____

For each sentence, identify the type of *phrase* in *italics* and give its part of speech:

1. He will quickly **delineate** all *of the options.* _____

2. *To complicate matters,* the planet moves in a **retrograde** motion. _____

3. Some people feel a black **melancholy** *on rainy days.* _____

4. *Intracranial meditating* will not exorcise her demons. _____

5. You need **cardiovascular** exercise *to lose weight properly.* _____

6. The flash was an **epiphany**, *a sudden appearing of insight.* _____

7. The blue planet, *a gas giant*, reached **perihelion**. _____

8. Americans possess an **inherent** right *to free speech.* _____

9. Is the national government a **plutocracy**, *sagging under elitism?* _____

10. Money, *the **sine qua non** for acceptance*, was scarce. _____

For each sentence, identify the **sentence structure**. Disregard bold type.

11. I said that the right/wrong **dichotomy** seemed simplistic. _____

12. The fascist dictator was a **pathological** liar; he was evil. _____

13. When we looked, we found a **cryptic** inscription in the stone. _____

14. He drew an **isosceles** trapezoid on the board, and they understood. _____

15. The team's careful search did not locate the **pathogen**. _____

16. As we listened, his **vociferous** protests could be heard for blocks. _____

17. Please take steps **to rectify** the situation and to make it right. _____

18. His **sanctimonious** lectures were hypocritical, but no one noticed. _____

19. The **tortuous** mountain highway wound steeply up as we drove. _____

20. The insect's **metamorphosis** was miraculous; it was wonderful. _____

Identify the **part of speech** in **bold** in each sentence below:

1.	The quiet boy is an **introspective** loner.	adjective
2.	We should not **intervene** in their dispute	verb
3.	Down's **syndrome** has well-known symptoms.	noun
4.	He resented his **subordinate** rank in the military.	adjective
5.	A **dissonant** clamor arose in the streets.	adjective
6.	The **belligerent** nations refused to negotiate.	adjective
7.	It takes money to become a **credible** candidate.	adjective
8.	"The shadow of **impending** doom" is a trite phrase.	adjective
9.	Bach's **polyphonic** concertos are beautiful.	adjective
10.	He wished to be completely **exculpated**.	adjective

Identify the **part of sentence** in **bold** in each sentence below:

11.	"Rest room" is a **euphemism**.	subject complement
12.	Who was the anonymous **benefactor** to little Pip?	subject complement
13.	A Napoleon complex is a **form** of megalomania.	subject complement
14.	The oil magnates in Saudi Arabia control **billions**.	direct object
15.	Her vivacious personality cheered **us** all.	direct object
16.	The heliotropic vines clogged the **window**.	direct object
17.	There is no **lack** of amour-propre in her!	subject complement
18.	The spry octagenarian won the **race**.	direct object
19.	This **wine** is preferred by the cognoscenti.	subject
20.	He consumed a painful **surfeit** of food and drink.	direct object

288

For each sentence, identify the type of *phrase* in *italics* and give its part of speech:

1.	He will quickly **delineate** all *of the options.*	prepositional, adverb
2.	*To complicate matters,* the planet moves in a **retrograde** motion.	infinitive, adverb
3.	Some people feel a black **melancholy** *on rainy days.*	prepositional, adverb
4.	*Intracranial meditating* will not exorcise her demons.	gerund, noun
5.	You need **cardiovascular** exercise *to lose weight properly.*	infinitive, adverb
6.	The flash was an **epiphany**, *a sudden appearing of insight.*	appositive, adjective
7.	The blue planet, *a gas giant*, reached **perihelion**.	appositive, adjective
8.	Americans possess an **inherent** right *to free speech.*	prepositional, adjective
9.	Is the national government a **plutocracy**, *sagging under elitism*?	participle, adjective
10.	Money, *the **sine qua non** for acceptance*, was scarce.	appositive, adjective

For each sentence, identify the **sentence structure**. Disregard bold type.

11.	I said that the right/wrong **dichotomy** seemed simplistic.	complex
12.	The fascist dictator was a **pathological** liar; he was evil.	compound
13.	When we looked, we found a **cryptic** inscription in the stone.	complex
14.	He drew an **isosceles** trapezoid on the board, and they understood.	compound
15.	The team's careful search did not locate the **pathogen**.	simple
16.	As we listened, his **vociferous** protests could be heard for blocks.	complex
17.	Please take steps **to rectify** the situation and to make it right.	simple
18.	His **sanctimonious** lectures were hypocritical, but no one noticed.	compound
19.	The **tortuous** mountain highway wound steeply up as we drove.	complex
20.	The insect's **metamorphosis** was miraculous; it was wonderful.	compound

For each of the following sentences, circle the letter of each answer that is true. The answer can be any combination, including all or none. This exercise will teach you the real process of punctuation as a function of grammar.

1. With a rising sense of apprehension my colleague thought Now its time.

    a. a comma after the prepositional phrases

    b. an apostrophe in the contraction

    c. a comma before the direct quotation

    d. quotation marks around the direct quotation

    e. a period inside the closing quotation marks

2. When the poet wrote Silver Mune he recalled Jupiter's ancient epic.

    a. a comma after the independent clause

    b. an apostrophe in the possessive noun

    c. a comma after the dependent clause

    d. italics on the poem title

    e. quotation marks around the poem title

3. A one third minority chose batteries cables and connectors.

    a. a hyphen in the compound adjective

    b. a colon at the beginning of the list

    c. a comma after the plural common noun

    d. a comma before the coordinating conjunction

    e. a comma after the dependent clause

4. Pausing suddenly the venerable grizzled sailor realized its identity.

    a. a comma after the prepositional phrase

    b. a comma between the adjectives preceding the noun

    c. a comma after the participle phrase

    d. a comma after the gerund phrase

    e. an apostrophe in the contraction

5. Pensar is the Spanish verb for think it is a common verb.

    a. quotation marks around the Spanish verb

    b. italics on the Spanish verb

    c. a comma after the independent clause

    d. a comma after the dependent clause

    e. a semicolon after the independent clause

For each of the following sentences, circle the letter of each answer that is true. The answer can be any combination, including all or none. This exercise will teach you the real process of punctuation as a function of grammar.

1. With a rising sense of apprehension, my colleague thought, "Now it's time."
   a. a comma after the prepositional phrases   **d. quotation marks around quotation**
   b. an apostrophe in the contraction   **e. period inside closing quotation marks**
   c. a comma before the direct quotation

   We put a comma after multiple introductory prepositional phrases.

2. When the poet wrote "Silver Mune," he recalled Jupiter's ancient epic.
   a. a comma after the independent clause   d. italics on the poem title
   b. an apostrophe in the possessive noun   **e. quotation marks around the poem title**
   c. a comma after the dependent clause

   The title of a poem or chapter is in quotation marks; the title of an entire book is in italics.

3. A one-third minority chose batteries, cables, and connectors.
   a. a hyphen in the compound adjective   d. a comma before the coordinating conjunction
   b. a colon at the beginning of the list   e. a comma after the dependent clause
   c. a comma after the plural common noun

   We will insist on using comma before the last item in a list, rather than omitting the final comma, as some manuals advise.

4. Pausing suddenly, the venerable, grizzled sailor realized its identity.
   a. a comma after the prepositional phrase   d. a comma after the gerund phrase
   b. comma between adjectives preceding noun   e. an apostrophe in the contraction
   c. a comma after the participle phrase

   We separate a list of adjectives preceding a noun, except for the definite or indefinite article. In other words, we would NOT write, "It was the, perspicacious man who called."

5. *Pensar* is the Spanish verb for think; it is a common verb.
   a. quotation marks around the Spanish verb   d. a comma after the dependent clause
   b. italics on the Spanish verb   **e. semicolon after independent clause**
   c. a comma after the independent clause

   We put all foreign language words in italics. This is a compound sentence with an I;I structure.

Attacking and withdrawing are unpleasant alternatives.

Parts of speech: *Attacking* is a noun (a gerund); *and* is a conjunction (a coordinating conjunction); *withdrawing* is a noun (also a gerund); *are* is a present tense linking verb; *unpleasant* is an adjective modifying the plural common noun *alternatives*.

Parts of the sentence: The sentence has a compound subject composed of two nouns joined by a coordinating conjunction: *Attacking and withdrawing*. The verb *are* is a linking verb which links the compound subject to the subject complement *alternatives*; *alternatives* is a subject complement because it renames the subject—it completes the subject. The point of a sentence containing a subject complement is to tell what the subject is, not what the subject does. It is a question of identity.

Phrases: There are no prepositional, gerund, infinitive, participle, or appositive phrases. There are two individual gerunds, *Attacking* and *withdrawing*, but neither gerund has complements or modifiers attached to it. A gerund, as this sentence shows, is a noun that ends in -ing. One way to know that the word is a gerund and not a verb is to understand that -ing verbs must have helping verbs with them: ***have been*** *attacking*, ***will be*** *withdrawing*, etc.

Clauses: The sentence contains only one clause, so it is a simple sentence. The subject/predicate set is *Attacking-withdrawing/are*.

	Attacking	and	withdrawing	are	unpleasant	alternatives.
Parts of Speech:	n.	conj.	n.	v.	adj.	n.
Parts of Sentence:	----------compound subject----------			predicate		subject complement
Phrases:	no prepositional or appositive phrases; compound gerund as subject					
Clauses:	one independent clause, simple declarative sentence					

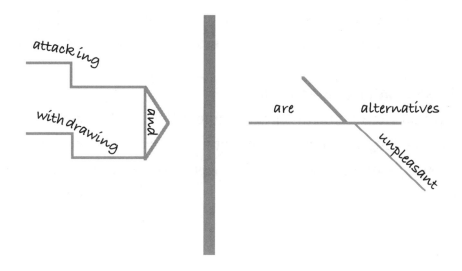

Questions for individual thought or small group discussion:

analysis: breaking down into components

   We call *to be*, *to do*, *to dance*, etc., infinitives. The word *infinitive* contains the ancient pieces *in*, meaning without, and *fin*, meaning limit. In what sense are infinitives without limit?   What limit are they without?

evaluation: judging value with criteria

   In a compound sentence, two or more independent clauses (ideas) are shown to be related, and the compound structure implies that each idea is of equal value.   In a complex sentence, the idea in the subordinate clause is understood to be of a lower (sub) order (ord) of importance than the idea in the independent clause, though the ideas are still related. With this in mind, which is better:

   Clarity, which is the essence of communication, is important.

   Clarity is important; it is the essence of communication.

synthesis: making comparisons

   If you were going to represent five different elements of grammar with living things, such as saying that a conjunction is like a jungle vine that connects things together, what would your five combinations be? Explain.

Use the grammar clues to solve this Mystery Sentence:

A sentence from a fairy tale begins with a proper noun of direct address, used twice, followed by an imperative independent clause containing an understood subject, a present tense transitive verb, an adverb, a second person singular possessive pronoun, and a singular common noun as a direct object. All words are one-syllable words except for the noun of direct address, which contains three syllables.

Rapunzel, Rapunzel, let down your hair.

From Marjorie Kinnan Rawlings's

The Yearling

A clear space opened at the creek's bank. Jody saw a vast black shapeless form break through. Penny Halted and lifted his gun. On the instant, a small brown missile hurled itself at the shaggy head. Old Julia had caught up with her enemy. She leaped and retreated, and in the moment of retreat, was at him again. Rip darted in beside her. Slewfoot wheeled and slashed at him. Julia flashed at his flank. Penny held his fire. He could not shoot, for the dogs.

This passage, from Marjorie Kinnan Rawlings's *The Yearling*, describes how Jody, his father, and their dogs fight with Old Slewfoot, the bear in the Florida swamp. What characterizes the sentences in this passage? Why?

1. Write a complex sentence that contains a gerund, a participle, and an infinitive, but has no prepositions.

2. Write a compound sentence with two semicolons and a comma.

---

1. Since thinking is learned behavior, it is easy to acquire.
2. Ahab sailed north; the wind came up; a silver moon shone, and the sails filled.

Loop Nine Writing Lab
Appositive Phrases

1. Write a paragraph about a famous individual, in which you mention various other famous individuals, and be sure to insert a brief appositive phrase after the first mention of each individual's name, so that the reader will know who each person is. It would be good if you also mention various objects and places that need clarification with appositives. Use as many appositives as you can to clarify everything for the reader.

2. Rewrite the paragraph so that it contains all of the same information, including all of the information that was in the appositives, except this time, do not use appositives. Do it some other way.

3. Compare the two versions of the sentences.

4. Write a statement that explains the use and benefit of appositives.

"I contracted for it; I earned it; it was paid to me."

- Frederick Douglass

Although Frederick Douglass worked to earn money, his slave owner took the money away; it was one of the great indignities that Douglass resented and that motivated him to seize his own freedom. His *Narrative* is among the greatest works of American literature.

Parts of speech: *I* is a first person singular subject pronoun; *contracted* is a singular past tense intransitive action verb; *for* is a preposition relating its object, the pronoun *it*, to another word in the sentence, in this case the verb; *I* is a singular subject pronoun; *earned* is a past tense transitive action verb; *it* is a third person singular object pronoun; the third *it* is a third person singular subject pronoun; *was paid* is a passive voice past tense action verb; *to* is a preposition; *me* is a first person singular object pronoun. This sentence puts *it* through all its paces; we see *it* as the object of preposition, as the direct object, and as the subject of a verb!

Parts of the sentence: *I* is the subject of the verb *contracted*; *I* is the subject of the verb *earned*, and *it* is the direct object of *earned*; *it* is the subject of the passive voice action verb *was paid*.

Phrases: Two prepositional phrases: *for it* modifies contracted, *to me* modifies *was paid*.

Clauses: This compound declarative sentence contains three clauses in only eleven words, and uses semicolons to make a chain of I;I structures. The first clause is *I contracted for it*; the second clause is *I earned it*; and the third clause is *it was paid to me*.

FOUR-LEVEL ANALYSIS

	I	contracted	for	it;	I	earned	it;	it	was	paid	to	me.
Parts of Speech:	pron.	v.	prep.	pron.	pron.	v.	pron.	pron.	v.	v.	prep.	pron.
Parts of Sentence:	subj.	pred.			subj.	pred.	direct object	subj.	----pred---			
Phrases:			-prep. phrase-							-prep. phrase-		
Clauses:	---------indep. clause----------				----indep. clause-----			---------indep. clause-------				

an I;I;I compound declarative sentence

Identify the **part of speech** in **bold** in each sentence below:

1. His **chronic** illness dragged on for years.   _____

2. His colorful **hyperbole** livened his conversation.   _____

3. Dr. King's **sonorous** voice echoed over the crowd.   _____

4. Her **germane** comments really hit the mark.   _____

5. His **convivial** friends loved to celebrate.   _____

6. His **cognomen** is "Huckleberry."   _____

7. The **anarchist** passed out leaflets to passersby.   _____

8. Your **animadversions** on his behavior are superfluous.   _____

9. The deliberate snub was a low, **pusillanimous** act.   _____

10. The mayor ducked a question with a clever **subterfuge**.   _____

Identify the *part of sentence* in *italics* in each sentence below.

11. Her **saturnine** personality won *her* few friends.   _____

12. *They* were forcefully **expatriated** from the fatherland.   _____

13. Flagpole sitting is a highly **sedentary** *occupation*.   _____

14. Ishmael was a popular *fellow* of appealing **bonhomie**.   _____

15. The company will make a **bona fide** *offer*.   _____

16. The wealthy **bon vivant** lived the good *life*.   _____

17. The **mutable** *laws* of high fashion can't be predicted.   _____

18. It is *unnecessary* to **impute** evil motives to opponents.   _____

19. It can be *dangerous* to disrupt the **status quo**.   _____

20. The incident offers an instructive *paradigm* for future guidance.   _____

For each sentence, identify the type of *phrase* in *italics*:

1. The debate created a **schism** *in the Democratic Party*. _____

2. His **bootless** effort *to win acceptance* was pathetic. _____

3. *Seized with enthusiasm*, the media created the champ's **apotheosis**. _____

4. The rumblings were the **precursor** of what was *soon to come*. _____

5. Dyslexics sometimes **transpose** letters *in a word*. _____

6. The Prime Minister, *a veteran*, endured her opponent's **invective**. _____

7. The origin of atoms, *a **cosmological** question*, is unknown. _____

8. His **effusion** *of officious greetings* made us wince. _____

9. It was bittersweet *to present a **posthumous** award*. _____

10. Mole loved the **euphony** *of the wind in the willows*. _____

For each sentence, identify the **sentence structure**. Disregard bold type.

11. The **refractory** child broke and rebroke the rules. _____

12. We need fresh ideas; we do not need hollow **platitudes**. _____

13. He began to feel **acrophobia**, but he didn't have xenophobia. _____

14. When they first arrive, some visitors feel **agoraphobia**. _____

15. Notice the fable's eerie **verisimilitude** if you can. _____

16. We even loved his many **idiosyncrasies**. _____

17. The government chose to regard the act as **casus belli**. _____

18. The nation survived a peaceful **interregnum**, but it didn't last. _____

19. As you will see, it was an unintentional **infraction** of the rules. _____

20. He will receive a **condign** punishment for his offense. _____

Identify the **part of speech** in bold in each sentence below:

1.	His **chronic** illness dragged on for years.	adjective
2.	His colorful **hyperbole** livened his conversation.	noun
3.	Dr. King's **sonorous** voice echoed over the crowd.	adjective
4.	Her **germane** comments really hit the mark.	adjective
5.	His **convivial** friends loved to celebrate.	adjective
6.	His **cognomen** is "Huckleberry."	noun
7.	The **anarchist** passed out leaflets to passersby.	noun
8.	Your **animadversions** on his behavior are superfluous.	noun
9.	The deliberate snub was a low, **pusillanimous** act.	adjective
10.	The mayor ducked a question with a clever **subterfuge**.	noun

Identify the *part of sentence* in *italics* in each sentence below.

11.	Her **saturnine** personality won *her* few friends.	indirect object
12.	*They* were forcefully **expatriated** from the fatherland.	subject
13.	Flagpole sitting is a highly **sedentary** *occupation*.	subject complement
14.	Ishmael was a popular *fellow* of appealing **bonhomie**.	subject complement
15.	The company will make a **bona fide** *offer*.	direct object
16.	The wealthy **bon vivant** lived the good *life*.	direct object
17.	The **mutable** *laws* of high fashion can't be predicted.	subject
18.	It is *unnecessary* to **impute** evil motives to opponents.	subject complement
19.	It can be *dangerous* to disrupt the **status quo**.	subject complement
20.	The incident offers an instructive ***paradigm*** for future guidance.	direct object

For each sentence, identify the type of *phrase* in *italics*:

1.	The debate created a **schism** *in the Democratic Party*.	prepositional, adverb
2.	His **bootless** effort *to win acceptance* was pathetic.	infinitive, adjective
3.	*Seized with enthusiasm*, the media created the champ's **apotheosis**.	participle, adjective
4.	The rumblings were the **precursor** of what was *soon to come*.	infinitive, adjective
5.	Dyslexics sometimes **transpose** letters *in a word*.	prepositional, adjective
6.	The Prime Minister, *a veteran*, endured her opponent's **invective**.	appositive, adjective
7.	The origin of atoms, *a cosmological question*, is unknown.	appositive, adjective
8.	His **effusion** *of officious greetings* made us wince.	prepositional, adjective
9.	It was bittersweet *to present a posthumous award*.	infinitive, adverb
10.	Mole loved the **euphony** *of the wind in the willows*.	prepositional, adjective

For each sentence, identify the **sentence structure**. Disregard bold type.

11.	The **refractory** child broke and rebroke the rules.	simple
12.	We need fresh ideas; we do not need hollow **platitudes**.	compound
13.	He began to feel **acrophobia**, but he didn't have xenophobia.	compound
14.	When they first arrive, some visitors feel **agoraphobia**.	complex
15.	Notice the fable's eerie **verisimilitude** if you can.	complex
16.	We even loved his many **idiosyncrasies**.	simple
17.	The government chose to regard the act as **casus belli**.	simple
18.	The nation survived a peaceful **interregnum**, but it didn't last.	compound
19.	As you will see, it was an unintentional **infraction** of the rules.	complex
20.	He will receive a **condign** punishment for his offense.	simple

For each of the following sentences, circle the letter of each answer that is true. The answer can be any combination, including all or none. This exercise will teach you the real process of punctuation as a function of grammar.

1. Hail Marching Legions is the song to sing if its a new invasion.

    a. italics on the song title

    b. quotation marks around the song title

    c. a comma before the dependent clause

    d. a comma before the independent clause

    e. an apostrophe in the contraction

2. Yes its mandatory to include three objects in a two dimensional plane.

    a. a comma after the interjection

    b. an apostrophe in the possessive pronoun

    c. an apostrophe in the contraction

    d. a comma after the independent clause

    e. a hyphen in the compound adjective

3. In the Great Dismal Swamp the outbreak of malaria is up by one third.

    a. a comma after the introductory prepositional phrase

    b. a hyphen in the fraction

    c. a comma after the dependent clause

    d. commas around the appositive

    e. commas around the parenthetical remark

4. On September 11 2009 Smithers our ablest engineer designed the new bridge.

    a. a comma after the day

    b. a comma after the year appositive

    c. a comma after the participle phrase

    d. commas around the appositive

    e. a comma after the dependent clause

5. Caught in the blue tube Tashtego reached for the harpoon.

    a. a comma after the dependent clause

    b. a comma after the introductory prepositional phrases

    c. a comma after the participle phrase

    d. commas around the appositive

    e. a semicolon between the clauses

For each of the following sentences, circle the letter of each answer that is true. The answer can be any combination, including all or none. This exercise will teach you the real process of punctuation as a function of grammar.

1. "Hail Marching Legions" is the song to sing if it's a new invasion.
   a. italics on the song title
   b. quotation marks around the song title
   c. a comma before the dependent clause
   d. a comma before the independent clause
   e. an apostrophe in the contraction

   It's *is the contraction of* it *and* is, *and therefore needs an apostrophe.*

2. Yes, it's mandatory to include three objects in a two-dimensional plane.
   a. a comma after the interjection
   b. an apostrophe in the possessive pronoun
   c. an apostrophe in the contraction
   d. a comma after the independent clause
   e. hyphen in the compound adjective

   We do put a comma after an introductory interjection.

3. In the Great Dismal Swamp, the outbreak of malaria is up by one third.
   a. a comma after the introductory prepositional phrase
   b. a hyphen in the fraction
   c. a comma after the dependent clause
   d. commas around the appositive
   e. commas around the parenthetical remark

   Even though this is only a single introductory prepositional phrase, we will put a comma because it is a longer phrase. If the fraction preceded a noun, we would use a hyphen, but in this case, one *is just an adjective that modifies its noun* third, *so no hyphen is needed.*

4. On September 11, 2009, Smithers, our ablest engineer, designed the new bridge.
   a. a comma after the day
   b. a comma after the year appositive
   c. a comma after the participle phrase
   d. commas around the appositive
   e. a comma after the dependent clause

   We might first read this as though Smithers *were a noun of direct address, but since no answer mentions that, it is a best guess to think that* our ablest engineer *is an appositive defining* Smithers.

5. Caught in the blue tube, Tashtego reached for the harpoon.
   a. a comma after the dependent clause
   b. a comma after the introductory prepositional phrases
   c. a comma after the participle phrase
   d. commas around the appositive
   e. a semicolon between the clauses

   We use commas after introductory participle phrases.

As the doomed mansion burned, she tried desperately to escape.

Parts of speech: *As* is a subordinating conjunction; *the* and *doomed* are adjectives modifying the singular common noun *mansion*; *burned* is an action verb; *she* is a third person singular pronoun (We don't know the antecedent.); *tried* is a past tense transitive action verb; *desperately* is an adverb modifying the verb *tried*; *to escape* is an infinitive verbal noun.

Parts of the sentence: *mansion* is the subject of the verb *burned*, and the pronoun *she* is the subject of the verb *tried*; *to escape* is the direct object of *she/tried*. Neither clause contains a subject complement or an indirect object.

Phrases: Neither clause contains a prepositional phrase. There are also no participle phrases, gerund phrases, or infinitive phrases. We do see a single participle (verb form used as adjective), *doomed*, though it has no complements or modifiers to form a phrase. We also see an infinitive, *to escape*, which also lacks the required complements and modifiers to make a phrase. So in this sentence the infinitive is simply the direct object of the second clause, and not an infinitive phrase.

Clauses: This complex sentence contains two clauses. The first clause, *As the doomed mansion burned*, is a dependent clause, because it makes no sense by itself. This clause clearly needs (depends on) an independent clause to complete its meaning. This dependent clause begins with a subordinating conjunction, *As*, which is enough to make the clause dependent (It subordinates the clause). Notice that if you remove the subordinating conjunction and let the clause read *The doomed mansion burned*, the clause makes sense and is then an independent clause.

The second clause in the sentence, *she tried desperately to escape*, is an independent clause. The subject is *she*, and the verb--or simple predicate—is *tried*. Since the independent clause comes last, we put a comma between the clauses.

• • •

Escape? Yes, the heroine did escape! We're thinking here of images from *Gone with the Wind*, which later inspired countless novels and films.

As the doomed mansion burned, she tried desperately to escape.

Parts of Speech:	conj.	adj.	adj.	n.	v.	pron.	v.	adv.	n.

Parts of Sentence:	subject	predicate	subject	predicate		direct object

Phrases: no prepositional or appositive phrases; an infinitive as direct object

Clauses: one independent clause, simple declarative sentence

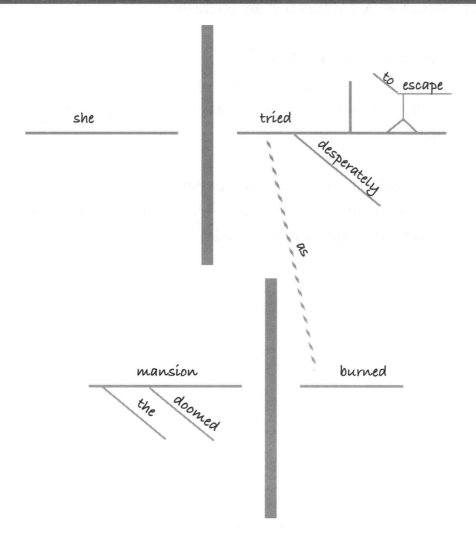

Questions for individual thought or small group discussion:

synthesis: making connections

What grammatical structure do you think most resembles an algebraic equation?

divergence: thinking of alternatives

How many true statements can you make about indirect objects? Think about this question until the obvious answers are exhausted, and you produce some answers that are interesting.

intuition: ideas from the blue

In a dream you hear a series of sharp imperative sentences, followed by a subject pronoun. What are the words, and what is happening?

analysis: breaking ideas into components

There are eight kinds of words, but how many groups do these eight kinds make? Explain your analysis.

Use the grammar clues to solve this Mystery Sentence:

A famous sentence by Franklin Roosevelt begins with a definite article and an adjective both modifying a singular common noun which is the subject of the clause. This subject is then modified by an interrupting adjective clause containing a first person plural subject pronoun, a present tense action verb, and an infinitive used as an adverb. The main clause then concludes with a present tense linking verb a singular common noun, and a reflexive pronoun.

The only thing we have to fear is fear itself.

From George Eliot's

Silas Marner

Even people whose lives have been made various by learning, sometimes find it hard to keep a fast hold on their habitual views of life, on their faith in the invisible—nay, on the sense that their past joys and sorrows are a real experience, when they are suddenly transported to a new land, where the beings around them know nothing of their history, and share none of their ideas—where their mother earth shows another lap, and human life has other forms than those on which their souls have been nourished.

George Eliot's real name was Mary Ann Evans, but in her time, brilliant women found it difficult to be published, and so Evans took *George Eliot* as her *nom de plume*. How many sentences are there in this passage from the beginning of the second chapter of George Eliot's classic novel? What is the subject/predicate set of the main clause? What are the advantages of the style Eliot uses in this passage?

From Edgar Allan Poe's

The Tell-tale Heart

But even yet I refrained and kept still. I scarcely breathed. I held the lantern motionless. I tried how steadily I could maintain the ray upon the eye. Meantime the hellish tattoo of the heart increased. It grew quicker and quicker, and louder and louder every instant. The old man's terror *must* have been extreme!

Study this passage from Edgar Allan Poe's classic short story carefully, and see if you can explain how the sentence structures change with the content. Can you see why what you are describing could dictate the way you make your sentences? Should Poe have shortened this? What words should he have removed?

1. Write a sentence that has a gerund as a subject, a gerund as a direct object, and a gerund as a subject complement.

2. Write a sentence of ten or more words that has an unmodified common noun as a subject, and that has only one clause.

---

1. Surviving gave Ishmael feeling, and feeling is living.

2. Queequeg immediately hurled the long, steel harpoon into the blue foam.

Loop Ten Writing Lab
Modification

1. Write a descriptive paragraph about a unique scene; it could be a scene at the ocean, in the mountains, or in a storm—something vivid and unusual.

2. Revise the paragraph, removing all adjectives and adverbs, and replacing the nouns they modified with more specific nouns if you wish. Try to get the same effect and detail without using any modifiers.

3. Compare the two versions of the paragraph.

4. Write a statement explaining what you learned about the effect of modification.

"Either that wallpaper goes, or I do."

Oscar Wilde

There are times when it is best to think before issuing an ultimatum, as in the case of the last words that Oscar Wilde ever spoke, "Either that wallpaper goes, or I do." Analyze the grammar of Wilde's fatal epigram.

Parts of speech: *Either/or* is a correlative conjunction used to join two clauses together; *that* is a demonstrative adjective modifying the singular common noun *wallpaper*; *goes* is a present tense action verb; *I* is a singular first person personal pronoun; and *do* is a present tense action verb. Both *goes* and *do* are intransitive.

Parts of the sentence: The subject/predicate set of the first clause is *wallpaper/goes*, and the subject/predicate set of the second clause is *I/do*. Since there are no linking verbs, there are no subject complements, and a glance shows there are no direct objects, either. If there are no direct objects, there can be no indirect objects.

Phrases: The sentence contains no prepositional, verbal, or appositive phrases.

Clauses: The sentence is a compound declarative sentence in which the clause *that wallpaper goes* is joined to the clause *I do* by the correlative conjunction *Either/or*.

FOUR-LEVEL ANALYSIS

	Either	**that**	**wallpaper**	**goes,**	**or**	**I**	**do.**
Parts of Speech:	conj.	adj.	n.	v.	conj.	pron.	v.
Parts of Sentence:			subject	predicate		subj.	pred.
Phrases:	no prepositional, appositive, or verbal phrases						
Clauses:	two independent clauses, compound declarative sentence						

These were the last words of Oscar Wilde!

Identify the **part of speech** in **bold** in each sentence below:

1.   They had a private **colloquy** in the corner.   _____

2.   Is the fetus mature enough to be **viable**?   _____

3.   Here is a brief **synopsis** of the course.   _____

4.   The argonauts longed to stand on **terra firma** at last.   _____

5.   We cannot **sanction** the use of our name.   _____

6.   The editor was an unapologetic **Russophobe**.   _____

7.   The doctor presented a **prognosis** of the disease.   _____

8.   We purchased a large **polychrome** sculpture.   _____

9.   Her deeds of **philanthropy** were legendary.   _____

10. Everyone admired the **perspicacity** of her mind.   _____

Identify the *part of sentence* in *italics* in each sentence below:

11. The text showed the ***mobocracy*** of the revolution.   _____

12. The Soviet **gerontocracy** is losing *control*.   _____

13. His **magniloquent** oratory was *impressive*.   _____

14. The police tried *to arrest a **kleptomaniac***.   _____

15. Her ***joie de vivre*** was inspiring.   _____

16. The *school* must act **in loco parentis**.   _____

17. The thinker was *reluctant* to deal with **mundane** matters.   _____

18. He gave a refreshing, **unequivocal** *answer*.   _____

19. The icy ***nihilism*** of his mind could be unnerving.   _____

20. He paid *one* of them an **invidious** compliment.   _____

For each sentence, identify the type of *phrase* in *italics* and give its part of speech:

1.   *To increase accuracy*, science uses a process of **induction**.   _____

2.   *Governed by fear*, the Iranian **hagiocracy** banned swimsuits.   _____

3.   The pedant confined himself *to a scholarly Latin diction*.   _____

4.   Johnson, *the disconsolate widower*, missed his wife.   _____

5.   *His disingenuous offering* of assistance fooled the ingenue.   _____

6.   The **fractious** mob clamored *to avenge the outrage*.   _____

7.   The mendicant, *a plaza regular*, wore a **nondescript** garment.   _____

8.   The **prolific** writer wrote seven books *in two years*.   _____

9.   We read the novel, *a chronicle of the brave knight-errant*.   _____

10. *Crushed into stone*, coal is the remains of a **primeval** forest.   _____

For each sentence, identify the **sentence structure**. Disregard bold type.

11. The speech was a **panegyric** on her talent; it was effective.   _____

12. Your task is to read Dante's **magnum opus**, the *Divina Comedia*.   _____

13. He loved grandfather's **antediluvian** ideas, and he took his advice.   _____

14. We need to process a customer's request **expeditiously**.   _____

15. The **decadent** century saw little greatness in art as we have seen.   _____

16. His arrogant, **supercilious** manner offended everyone.   _____

17. It is true; her **inexorable** fate followed her everywhere.   _____

18. When dawn broke, they greeted an **emissary** from the Queen.   _____

19. The **improvident** spendthrift went broke, but he recovered.   _____

20. As I said, the **moribund** corporation fired half its work force.   _____

Identify the **part of speech** in **bold** in each sentence below:

1.	They had a private **colloquy** in the corner.	noun
2.	**Is** the fetus mature enough to be **viable**?	adjective
3.	Here is a brief **synopsis** of the course.	noun
4.	The argonauts longed to stand on **terra firma** at last.	noun
5.	We cannot **sanction** the use of our name.	verb
6.	The editor was an unapologetic **Russophobe**.	noun
7.	The doctor presented a **prognosis** of the disease.	noun
8.	We purchased a large **polychrome** sculpture.	adjective
9.	Her deeds of **philanthropy** were legendary.	noun
10.	Everyone admired the **perspicacity** of her mind.	noun

Identify the *part of sentence* in *italics* in each sentence below:

11.	The text showed the ***mobocracy*** of the revolution.	direct object
12.	The Soviet **gerontocracy** is losing *control*.	direct object
13.	His **magniloquent** oratory was *impressive*.	subject complement
14.	The police tried *to arrest a **kleptomaniac***.	direct object
15.	Her ***joie de vivre*** was inspiring.	subject
16.	The *school* must act **in loco parentis**.	noun
17.	The thinker was *reluctant* to deal with **mundane** matters.	subject complement
18.	He gave a refreshing, **unequivocal** *answer*.	direct object
19.	The icy ***nihilism*** of his mind could be unnerving.	subject
20.	He paid *one* of them an **invidious** compliment.	indirect object

For each sentence, identify the type of *phrase* in *italics*:

1. *To increase accuracy*, science uses a process of **induction**.   infinitive, adverb

2. *Governed by fear*, the Iranian **hagiocracy** banned swimsuits.   participle, adjective

3. The pedant confined himself *to a scholarly Latin diction*.   prepositional, adverb

4. Johnson, *the **disconsolate** widower*, missed his wife.   appositive, adjective

5. *His **disingenuous** offering* of assistance fooled the ingenue.   gerund, noun

6. The **fractious** mob clamored *to avenge the outrage*.   infinitive, adverb

7. The mendicant, *a plaza regular*, wore a **nondescript** garment.   appositive, adjective

8. The **prolific** writer wrote seven books *in two years*.   prepositional, adverb

9. We read the novel, *a **chronicle** of the brave knight-errant*.   appositive, adjective

10. *Crushed into stone*, coal is the remains of a **primeval** forest.   participle, adjective

For each sentence, identify the **sentence structure**. Disregard bold type.

11. The speech was a **panegyric** on her talent; it was effective.   compound

12. Your task is to read Dante's **magnum opus**, the *Divina Comedia*.   simple

13. He loved grandfather's **antediluvian** ideas, and he took his advice.   compound

14. We need to process a customer's request **expeditiously**.   simple

15. The **decadent** century saw little greatness in art as we have seen.   complex

16. His arrogant, **supercilious** manner offended everyone.   simple

17. It is true; her **inexorable** fate followed her everywhere.   compound

18. When dawn broke, they greeted an **emissary** from the Queen.   complex

19. The **improvident** spendthrift went broke, but he recovered.   compound

20. As I said, the **moribund** corporation fired half its work force.   complex

For each of the following sentences, circle the letter of each answer that is true. The answer can be any combination, including all or none. This exercise will teach you the real process of punctuation as a function of grammar.

1. In May the ship reached its darkest moment when a tsunami struck.
   a. a comma after the prepositional phrase
   b. a comma after the month
   c. an apostrophe in the possessive pronoun
   d. an apostrophe in the contraction
   e. a comma between the clauses

2. As the heat wave abated Queequeg leered at the shipmate.
   a. a comma after the participle phrase
   b. a comma after the dependent clause
   c. a comma after the independent clause
   d. a semicolon between the clauses
   e. a comma after the prepositional phrase

3. The double braced hull is tight caulked and dry.
   a. a hyphen in the compound adjective
   b. a colon before the list
   c. a comma after the adjective **tight**
   d. a list comma after the adjective **caulked**
   e. a comma between the clauses

4. Swimming among the whales was the expatriots deepest desire.
   a. a comma after the introductory participle phrase
   b. a comma after the dependent clause
   c. an apostrophe in the possessive noun
   d. commas around the appositive phrase
   e. commas around the parenthetical remark

5. Yeah the expedition found twenty five whales beyond the outer reef.
   a. a comma after the introductory adverb
   b. a comma after the interjection
   c. a comma after the dependent clause
   d. a hyphen in the compound adjective
   e. a comma before the prepositional phrase

For each of the following sentences, circle the letter of each answer that is true. The answer can be any combination, including all or none. This exercise will teach you the real process of punctuation as a function of grammar.

1. In May the ship reached its darkest moment when a tsunami struck.
    a. a comma after the prepositional phrase
    b. a comma after the month
    c. an apostrophe in the possessive pronoun
    d. an apostrophe in the contraction
    e. a comma between the clauses

    No punctuation. When a complex sentence begins with the independent clause, that is when we do not put a comma. The rules are D,I and ID.

2. As the heat wave abated, Queequeg leered at the shipmate.
    a. a comma after the participle phrase
    b. a comma after the dependent clause
    c. a comma after the independent clause
    d. a semicolon between the clauses
    e. a comma after the prepositional phrase

    This is a D,I complex sentence.

3. The double-braced hull is tight, caulked, and dry.
    a. a hyphen in the compound adjective
    b. a colon before the list
    c. a comma after the adjective **tight**
    d. a list comma after the adjective **caulked**
    e. a comma between the clauses

    Here is another list.

4. Swimming among the whales was the expatriots deepest desire.
    a. a comma after the introductory participle phrase
    b. a comma after the dependent clause
    c. an apostrophe in the possessive noun
    d. commas around the appositive phrase
    e. commas around the parenthetical remark

    The gerund phrase Swimming among the whales *is a noun and the subject of the sentence; therefore we should not put a comma after it—that would split the subject off from its verb!*

5. Yeah, the expedition found twenty-five whales beyond the outer reef.
    a. a comma after the introductory adverb
    b. a comma after the interjection
    c. a comma after the dependent clause
    d. a hyphen in the compound adjective
    e. a comma before the prepositional phrase

    We put a comma after an introductory interjection; interjections, after all, have no grammatical function, and are logically separate from the other words. The comma shows this separateness.

Grammar Review Test

Preparation Notes

In addition to questions on all of the Four-Level Analysis sentences from the beginnings of the loops, the Grammar Review Test contains a section of questions on clause punctuation. Students will be presented with sentences they have never seen before, and they will be expected to identify the clause structure, determine what punctuation is needed, and show where the punctuation should go. A thorough review of the notes on clause punctuation and identification is in order.

Students should be reminded that on a given question, more than one answer may be true; they should pick the *best*, most complete, answer.

The meteor struck, and Leonidas smiled stoically.

1. The word **meteor** is
    a. a noun
    b. a pronoun
    c. an adjective
    d. an interjection

2. The word **Leonidas**
    a. a noun
    b. a plural noun
    c. a common, plural noun
    d. a proper, singular noun

3. The word **stoically** is
    a. an adjective
    b. an adverb
    c. a preposition
    d. a verb

4. The verbs are in
    a. present tense
    b. past tense
    c. a preposition
    d. a verb

5. The sentence is
    a. simple
    b. compound
    c. complex
    d. compound-complex

6. The word **smiled** is
    a. a linking verb
    b. an action verb
    c. neither
    d. both

7. The word **smiled** is
    a. transitive
    b. intransitive
    c. both
    d. none of the above

8. The sentence contains
    a. one preposition
    b. two prepositions
    c. three prepositions
    d. no preposition

9. The sentence contains
    a. a direct object
    b. a subject complement
    c. an indirect object
    d. none of the above

10. The sentence contains
    a. one clause
    b. two independent clauses
    c. one dependent clause
    d. no dependent clause

11. The sentence purpose is
    a. declarative
    b. interrogative
    c. imperative
    d. exclamatory

12. **The meteor struck** is
    a. the subject
    b. a gerund phrase
    c. a dependent clause
    d. an independent clause

13. The word **and** is
    a. a subordinating conjunction
    b. a coordinating conjunction
    c. a correlative conjunction
    d. a conjunctive adverb

14. The sentence contains
    a. one infinitive
    b. one gerund
    c. one participle
    d. no verbal

15. The sentence contains
    a. one prepositional phrase
    b. two prepositional phrases
    c. three prepositional phrases
    d. no prepositional phrase

16. The sentence contains
    a. a compound subject
    b. a compound predicate
    c. a compound direct object
    d. none of the above

Attacking and withdrawing are unpleasant alternatives.

17. The word **Attacking** is
    a. a noun
    b. a verb
    c. an adverb
    d. an adjective

18. The word **and** is
    a. a noun
    b. an interjection
    c. a preposition
    d. a conjunction

19. The word **unpleasant** is
    a. a noun
    b. an adjective
    c. an adverb
    d. a common noun

20. The word **alternatives** is
    a. a noun
    b. a common noun
    c. a singular common noun
    d. a plural common noun

21. The word **are** is
    a. a verb
    b. a present tense verb
    c. a present tense linking verb
    d. an action verb

22. The sentence contains
    a. one adjective
    b. two adjectives
    c. three adjectives
    d. four adjectives

23. The sentence contains
    a. one adverb
    b. two adverbs
    c. three adverbs
    d. no adverb

24. The sentence purpose is
    a. declarative
    b. interrogative
    c. imperative
    d. exclamatory

25. The sentence contains
    a. one dependent clause
    b. two dependent clauses
    c. three dependent clauses
    d. none of the above

26. The sentence contains
    a. one gerund
    b. no gerund
    c. one infinitive
    d. two gerunds

27. The sentence structure is
    a. simple
    b. compound
    c. complex
    d. compound-complex

28. The sentence contains a
    a. compound subject
    b. compound predicate
    c. compound direct object
    d. compound subject complement

29. The word **alternatives** is
    a. a direct object
    b. an indirect object
    c. a subject complement
    d. none of the above

30. The conjunction is
    a. coordinating
    b. subordinating
    c. correlative
    d. none of the above

31. The word **withdrawing** is
    a. a linking verb
    b. an action verb
    c. a transitive verb
    d. not a verb

32. The sentence contains
    a. one clause
    b. two clauses
    c. one clause and one phrase
    d. two clauses and one phrase

Suddenly, the massive hatch slammed down.

33. The word **Suddenly** is an
    a. adjective
    b. adverb
    c. interjection
    d. conjunction

34. The word **hatch** is
    a. a noun
    b. a pronoun
    c. a verb
    d. an adverb

35. The word **down** is
    a. a preposition
    b. an adverb
    c. an adjective
    d. a verb

36. The word **massive** is
    a. a verb
    b. an adverb
    c. a noun
    d. an adjective

37. The verb is in the
    a. present tense
    b. future tense
    c. past tense
    d. past perfect tense

38. The sentence contains
    a. one preposition
    b. two prepositions
    c. three prepositions
    d. none of the above

39. The sentence contains
    a. no direct object
    b. no indirect object
    c. no subject complement
    d. all of the above

40. The sentence contains
    a. one independent clause
    b. one dependent clause
    c. two independent clauses
    d. one independent, one dependent

41. The verb is
    a. action
    b. linking
    c. action, past tense
    d. action present tense

42. The verb is
    a. transitive
    b. intransitive
    c. linking
    d. none of the above

43. The sentence purpose is
    a. declarative
    b. imperative
    c. exclamatory
    d. interrogative

44. The sentence structure is
    a. simple
    b. compound
    c. complex
    d. compound-complex

45. The sentence contains
    a. no adverb
    b. one adverb
    c. two adverbs
    d. three adverbs

46. The sentence contains
    a. a proper, singular noun
    b. a common, plural noun
    c. a common, singular noun
    d. a proper, plural noun

47. The sentence contains
    a. one infinitive
    b. one participle
    c. one gerund
    d. none of the above

48. The sentence contains
    a. a compound subject
    b. a compound predicate
    c. a compound direct object
    d. none of the above

As the doomed mansion burned, she tried desperately to escape.

49. The word **doomed** is
    a. an adjective
    b. an adverb
    c. an interjection
    d. a preposition

50. The word **she** is
    a. a noun
    b. a pronoun
    c. a verb
    d. an adverb

51. The word **As** is
    a. an adjective
    b. an adverb
    c. a preposition
    d. a conjunction

52. The word **desperately** is
    a. an adjective
    b. an adverb
    c. a verb
    d. an interjection

53. The term **to escape**
    a. is a noun
    b. is an adverb
    c. is an adjective
    d. is a pronoun

54. The sentence contains
    a. one direct object
    b. one indirect object
    c. one subject complement
    d. no direct object

55. The verb **tried** is
    a. transitive, present tense
    b. intransitive, past tense
    c. intransitive, past tense
    d. intransitive, present tense

56. The sentence contains
    a. one gerund
    b. one participle
    c. two infinitives
    d. no verbal

57. The sentence contains
    a. a coordinating conjunction
    b. a subordinating conjunction
    c. a correlative conjunction
    d. none of the above

58. The word **mansion** is
    a. proper, plural
    b. proper, singular
    c. common, plural
    d. common, singular

59. The sentence purpose is
    a. declarative
    b. imperative
    c. exclamatory
    d. interrogative

60. The sentence contains
    a. one dependent clause
    b. two dependent clauses
    c. one clause
    d. two independent clauses

61. The sentence structure is
    a. simple
    b. compound
    c. complex
    d. compound-complex

62. The antecedent of **she** is
    a. mansion
    b. doomed
    c. burned
    d. unknown

63. The word **burned** is
    a. action, transitive
    b. action, intransitive
    c. linking
    d. linking, past tense

64. The sentence contains
    a. one adjective
    b. two adjectives
    c. three adjectives
    d. no adjective

Yesterday, Jupiter was full and unusually bright.

65. The word **bright** is
    a. a noun
    b. an adjective
    c. an adverb
    d. an interjection

66. The word **Jupiter** is
    a. a noun
    b. a pronoun
    c. a proper noun
    d. a proper, singular noun

67. The word **Yesterday** is
    a. a noun
    b. an adjective
    c. an adverb
    d. an interjection

68. The word **full** is
    a. an adjective
    b. an adverb
    c. a noun
    d. a preposition

69. The word **unusually** is
    a. an adjective
    b. an adverb
    c. a conjunction
    d. an interjection

70. The sentence contains a
    a. compound subject
    b. compound direct object
    c. compound predicate
    d. compound subject complement

71. The sentence contains
    a. a transitive verb
    b. an intransitive verb
    c. a linking verb
    d. none of the above

72. The sentence contains
    a. a gerund
    b. an infinitive
    c. a participle
    d. no verbal

73. The word **unusually** modifies
    a. full
    b. Jupiter
    c. was
    d. bright

74. The word **bright** modifies
    a. Jupiter
    b. was
    c. unusually
    d. full

75. The sentence structure is
    a. simple
    b. compound
    c. complex
    d. compound-complex

76. The sentence purpose is
    a. declarative
    b. imperative
    c. interrogative
    d. exclamatory

77. The sentence contains
    a. one clause
    b. one dependent clause
    c. two clauses
    d. two independent clauses

78. The sentence contains
    a. one phrase
    b. two phrases
    c. three phrases
    d. no phrases

79. The word **Yesterday** modifies
    a. Jupiter
    b. was
    c. full
    d. bright

80. The sentence contains
    a. one preposition
    b. two prepositions
    c. three prepositions
    d. no prepositions

Clause Punctuation: For each sentence, decide what the clause structure is, what punctuation is necessary (if any), and what word (if any) the clause punctuation should follow. Consider only clause punctuation.

When the androids arrive we will be in big trouble.
    81. Structure: a) simple b) compound c) ID complex d) DI complex
    82. Punctuation: a) semicolon b) comma c) no punctuation needed
    83. Location after: a) androids b) arrive c) we d) none

The raiders were captured the mothership landed.
    84. Structure: a) simple b) compound c) ID complex d) DI complex
    85. Punctuation: a) semicolon b) comma c) no punctuation needed
    86. Location after: a) raiders b) captured c) mothership d) none

Dominic was nebulous and the princess gradually lost hope.
    87. Structure: a) simple b) compound c) ID complex d) DI complex
    88. Punctuation: a) semicolon b) comma c) no punctuation needed
    89. Location after: a) Dominic b) nebulous c) princess d) none

In the spring eight Moondogs escaped into the Sea of Craters.
    90. Structure: a) simple b) compound c) ID complex d) DI complex
    91. Punctuation: a) semicolon b) comma c) no punctuation needed
    92. Location after: a) spring b) Moondogs c) escaped d) none

Ichthyosaurs have jaws but Jovian arthropods have mandibles.
    93. Structure: a) simple b) compound c) ID complex d) DI complex
    94. Punctuation: a) semicolon b) comma c) no punctuation needed
    95. Location after: a) Ichthyosaurs b) jaws c) but d) none

When the dome blew it scattered tulip seeds over the landscape.
    96. Structure: a) simple b) compound c) ID complex d) DI complex
    97. Punctuation: a) semicolon b) comma c) no punctuation needed
    98. Location after: a) dome b) blew c) seeds d) none

In Titan's green twilight the attack sails came silently closer.
    99. Structure: a) simple b) compound c) ID complex d) DI complex
    100. Punctuation: a) semicolon b) comma c) no punctuation needed

The meteor struck, and Leonidas smiled stoically.

1. The word **meteor** is
   a. a noun
   b. a pronoun
   c. an adjective
   d. an interjection

2. The word **Leonidas**
   a. a noun
   b. a plural noun
   c. a common, plural noun
   d. a proper, singular noun

3. The word **stoically** is
   a. an adjective
   b. an adverb
   c. a preposition
   d. a verb

4. The verbs are in
   a. present tense
   b. past tense
   c. a preposition
   d. a verb

5. The sentence is
   a. simple
   b. compound
   c. complex
   d. compound-complex

6. The word **smiled** is
   a. a linking verb
   b. an action verb
   c. neither
   d. both

7. The word **smiled** is
   a. transitive
   b. intransitive
   c. both
   d. none of the above

8. The sentence contains
   a. one preposition
   b. two prepositions
   c. three prepositions
   d. no preposition

9. The sentence contains
   a. a direct object
   b. a subject complement
   c. an indirect object
   d. none of the above

10. The sentence contains
    a. one clause
    b. two independent clauses
    c. one dependent clause
    d. no dependent clause

11. The sentence purpose is
    a. declarative
    b. interrogative
    c. imperative
    d. exclamatory

12. **The meteor struck** is
    a. the subject
    b. a gerund phrase
    c. a dependent clause
    d. an independent clause

13. The word **and** is
    a. a subordinating conjunction
    b. a coordinating conjunction
    c. a correlative conjunction
    d. a conjunctive adverb

14. The sentence contains
    a. one infinitive
    b. one gerund
    c. one participle
    d. no verbal

15. The sentence contains
    a. one prepositional phrase
    b. two prepositional phrases
    c. three prepositional phrases
    d. no prepositional phrase

16. The sentence contains
    a. a compound subject
    b. a compound predicate
    c. a compound direct object
    d. none of the above

Attacking and withdrawing are unpleasant alternatives.

17. The word **Attacking** is
     a. a noun
     b. a verb
     c. an adverb
     d. an adjective

18. The word **and** is
     a. a noun
     b. an interjection
     c. a preposition
     d. a conjunction

19. The word **unpleasant** is
     a. a noun
     b. an adjective
     c. an adverb
     d. a common noun

20. The word **alternatives** is
     a. a noun
     b. a common noun
     c. a singular common noun
     d. a plural common noun

21. The word **are** is
     a. a verb
     b. a present tense verb
     c. a present tense linking verb
     d. an action verb

22. The sentence contains
     a. one adjective
     b. two adjectives
     c. three adjectives
     d. four adjectives

23. The sentence contains
     a. one adverb
     b. two adverbs
     c. three adverbs
     d. no adverb

24. The sentence purpose is
     a. declarative
     b. interrogative
     c. imperative
     d. exclamatory

25. The sentence contains
     a. one dependent clause
     b. two dependent clauses
     c. three dependent clauses
     d. none of the above

26. The sentence contains
     a. one gerund
     b. no gerund
     c. one infinitive
     d. two gerunds

27. The sentence structure is
     a. simple
     b. compound
     c. complex
     d. compound-complex

28. The sentence contains a
     a. compound subject
     b. compound predicate
     c. compound direct object
     d. compound subject complement

29. The word **alternatives** is
     a. a direct object
     b. an indirect object
     c. a subject complement
     d. none of the above

30. The conjunction is
     a. coordinating
     b. subordinating
     c. correlative
     d. none of the above

31. The word **withdrawing** is
     a. a linking verb
     b. an action verb
     c. a transitive verb
     d. not a verb

32. The sentence contains
     a. one clause
     b. two clauses
     c. one clause and one phrase
     d. two clauses and one phrase

Suddenly, the massive hatch slammed down.

33. The word **Suddenly** is an
    a. adjective
    b. adverb
    c. interjection
    d. conjunction

34. The word **hatch** is
    a. a noun
    b. a pronoun
    c. a verb
    d. an adverb

35. The word **down** is
    a. a preposition
    b. an adverb
    c. an adjective
    d. a verb

36. The word **massive** is
    a. a verb
    b. an adverb
    c. a noun
    d. an adjective

37. The verb is in the
    a. present tense
    b. future tense
    c. past tense
    d. past perfect tense

38. The sentence contains
    a. one preposition
    b. two prepositions
    c. three prepositions
    d. none of the above

39. The sentence contains
    a. no direct object
    b. no indirect object
    c. no subject complement
    d. all of the above

40. The sentence contains
    a. one independent clause
    b. one dependent clause
    c. two independent clauses
    d. one independent, one dependent

41. The verb is
    a. action
    b. linking
    c. action, past tense
    d. action present tense

42. The verb is
    a. transitive
    b. intransitive
    c. linking
    d. none of the above

43. The sentence purpose is
    a. declarative
    b. imperative
    c. exclamatory
    d. interrogative

44. The sentence structure is
    a. simple
    b. compound
    c. complex
    d. compound-complex

45. The sentence contains
    a. no adverb
    b. one adverb
    c. two adverbs
    d. three adverbs

46. The sentence contains
    a. a proper, singular noun
    b. a common, plural noun
    c. a common, singular noun
    d. a proper, plural noun

47. The sentence contains
    a. one infinitive
    b. one participle
    c. one gerund
    d. none of the above

48. The sentence contains
    a. a compound subject
    b. a compound predicate
    c. a compound direct object
    d. none of the above

As the doomed mansion burned, she tried desperately to escape.

49. The word **doomed** is
    a. an adjective
    b. an adverb
    c. an interjection
    d. a preposition

50. The word **she** is
    a. a noun
    b. a pronoun
    c. a verb
    d. an adverb

51. The word **As** is
    a. an adjective
    b. an adverb
    c. a preposition
    d. a conjunction

52. The word **desperately** is
    a. an adjective
    b. an adverb
    c. a verb
    d. an interjection

53. The term **to escape**
    a. is a noun
    b. is an adverb
    c. is an adjective
    d. is a pronoun

54. The sentence contains
    a. one direct object
    b. one indirect object
    c. one subject complement
    d. no direct object

55. The verb **tried** is
    a. transitive, present tense
    b. intransitive, past tense
    c. intransitive, past tense
    d. intransitive, present tense

56. The sentence contains
    a. one gerund
    b. one participle
    c. two infinitives
    d. no verbal

57. The sentence contains
    a. a coordinating conjunction
    b. a subordinating conjunction
    c. a correlative conjunction
    d. none of the above

58. The word **mansion** is
    a. proper, plural
    b. proper, singular
    c. common, plural
    d. common, singular

59. The sentence purpose is
    a. declarative
    b. imperative
    c. exclamatory
    d. interrogative

60. The sentence contains
    a. one dependent clause
    b. two dependent clauses
    c. one clause
    d. two independent clauses

61. The sentence structure is
    a. simple
    b. compound
    c. complex
    d. compound-complex

62. The antecedent of **she** is
    a. mansion
    b. doomed
    c. burned
    d. unknown

63. The word **burned** is
    a. action, transitive
    b. action, intransitive
    c. linking
    d. linking, past tense

64. The sentence contains
    a. one adjective
    b. two adjectives
    c. three adjectives
    d. no adjective

Yesterday, Jupiter was full and unusually bright.

65. The word **bright** is
    a. a noun
    b. an adjective
    c. an adverb
    d. an interjection

66. The word **Jupiter** is
    a. a noun
    b. a pronoun
    c. a proper noun
    d. a proper, singular noun

67. The word **Yesterday** is
    a. a noun
    b. an adjective
    c. an adverb
    d. an interjection

68. The word **full** is
    a. an adjective
    b. an adverb
    c. a noun
    d. a preposition

69. The word **unusually** is
    a. an adjective
    b. an adverb
    c. a conjunction
    d. an interjection

70. The sentence contains a
    a. compound subject
    b. compound direct object
    c. compound predicate
    d. compound subject complement

71. The sentence contains
    a. a transitive verb
    b. an intransitive verb
    c. a linking verb
    d. none of the above

72. The sentence contains
    a. a gerund
    b. an infinitive
    c. a participle
    d. no verbal

73. The word **unusually** modifies
    a. full
    b. Jupiter
    c. was
    d. bright

74. The word **bright** modifies
    a. Jupiter
    b. was
    c. unusually
    d. full

75. The sentence structure is
    a. simple
    b. compound
    c. complex
    d. compound-complex

76. The sentence purpose is
    a. declarative
    b. imperative
    c. interrogative
    d. exclamatory

77. The sentence contains
    a. one clause
    b. one dependent clause
    c. two clauses
    d. two independent clauses

78. The sentence contains
    a. one phrase
    b. two phrases
    c. three phrases
    d. no phrases

79. The word **Yesterday** modifies
    a. Jupiter
    b. was
    c. full
    d. bright

80. The sentence contains
    a. one preposition
    b. two prepositions
    c. three prepositions
    d. no prepositions

Clause Punctuation: For each sentence, decide what the clause structure is, what punctuation is necessary (if any), and what word (if any) the clause punctuation should follow. Consider only clause punctuation.

When the androids arrive we will be in big trouble.
    81. Structure: a) simple b) compound c) ID complex **d) DI complex**
    82. Punctuation: a) semicolon **b) comma** c) no punctuation needed
    83. Location after: a) androids **b) arrive** c) we d) none

The raiders were captured the mothership landed.
    84. Structure: a) simple **b) compound** c) ID complex d) DI complex
    85. Punctuation: **a) semicolon** b) comma c) no punctuation needed
    86. Location after: a) raiders **b) captured** c) mothership d) none

Dominic was nebulous and the princess gradually lost hope.
    87. Structure: a) simple **b) compound** c) ID complex d) DI complex
    88. Punctuation: a) semicolon **b) comma** c) no punctuation needed
    89. Location after: a) Dominic **b) nebulous** c) princess d) none

In the spring eight Moondogs escaped into the Sea of Craters.
    90. Structure: **a) simple** b) compound c) ID complex d) DI complex
    91. Punctuation: a) semicolon b) comma **c) no punctuation needed**
    92. Location after: a) spring b) Moondogs c) escaped **d) none**

Ichthyosaurs have jaws but Jovian arthropods have mandibles.
    93. Structure: a) simple **b) compound** c) ID complex d) DI complex
    94. Punctuation: a) semicolon **b) comma** c) no punctuation needed
    95. Location after: a) Ichthyosaurs **b) jaws** c) but d) none

When the dome blew it scattered tulip seeds over the landscape.
    96. Structure: a) simple b) compound c) ID complex **d) DI complex**
    97. Punctuation: a) semicolon **b) comma** c) no punctuation needed
    98. Location after: a) dome **b) blew** c) seeds d) none

In Titan's green twilight the attack sails came silently closer.
    99. Structure: **a) simple** b) compound c) ID complex d) DI complex
    100. Punctuation: a) semicolon b) comma **c) no punctuation needed**

Student Name:_____   Date:_____
Period:_____   Grammar Review Test

	A B C D		A B C D		A B C D		A B C D
1.	O O O O	26.	O O O O	51.	O O O O	76.	O O O O
2.	O O O O	27.	O O O O	52.	O O O O	77.	O O O O
3.	O O O O	28.	O O O O	53.	O O O O	78.	O O O O
4.	O O O O	29.	O O O O	54.	O O O O	79.	O O O O
5.	O O O O	30.	O O O O	55.	O O O O	80.	O O O O
6.	O O O O	31.	O O O O	56.	O O O O	81.	O O O O
7.	O O O O	32.	O O O O	57.	O O O O	82.	O O O O
8.	O O O O	33.	O O O O	58.	O O O O	83.	O O O O
9.	O O O O	34.	O O O O	59.	O O O O	84.	O O O O
10.	O O O O	35.	O O O O	60.	O O O O	85.	O O O O
11.	O O O O	36.	O O O O	61.	O O O O	86.	O O O O
12.	O O O O	37.	O O O O	62.	O O O O	87.	O O O O
13.	O O O O	38.	O O O O	63.	O O O O	88.	O O O O
14.	O O O O	39.	O O O O	64.	O O O O	89.	O O O O
15.	O O O O	40.	O O O O	65.	O O O O	90.	O O O O
16.	O O O O	41.	O O O O	66.	O O O O	91.	O O O O
17.	O O O O	42.	O O O O	67.	O O O O	92.	O O O O
18.	O O O O	43.	O O O O	68.	O O O O	93.	O O O O
19.	O O O O	44.	O O O O	69.	O O O O	94.	O O O O
20.	O O O O	45.	O O O O	70.	O O O O	95.	O O O O
21.	O O O O	46.	O O O O	71.	O O O O	96.	O O O O
22.	O O O O	47.	O O O O	72.	O O O O	97.	O O O O
23.	O O O O	48.	O O O O	73.	O O O O	98.	O O O O
24.	O O O O	49.	O O O O	74.	O O O O	99.	O O O O
25.	O O O O	50.	O O O O	75.	O O O O	100.	O O O O

	A	B	C	D			A	B	C	D			A	B	C	D			A	B	C	D
1.	+	0	0	0		26.	0	0	0	+		51.	0	0	0	+		76.	+	0	0	0
2.	0	0	0	+		27.	+	0	0	0		52.	0	+	0	0		77.	+	0	0	0
3.	0	+	0	0		28.	+	0	0	0		53.	+	0	0	0		78.	0	0	0	+
4.	0	+	0	0		29.	0	0	+	0		54.	+	0	0	0		79.	0	+	0	0
5.	0	+	0	0		30.	+	0	0	0		55.	0	0	+	0		80.	0	0	0	+
6.	0	+	0	0		31.	0	0	0	+		56.	0	+	0	0		81.	0	0	0	+
7.	0	+	0	0		32.	+	0	0	0		57.	0	+	0	0		82.	0	+	0	0
8.	0	0	0	+		33.	0	+	0	0		58.	0	0	0	+		83.	0	+	0	0
9.	0	0	0	+		34.	+	0	0	0		59.	+	0	0	0		84.	0	+	0	0
10.	0	0	0	+		35.	0	+	0	0		60.	+	0	0	0		85.	+	0	0	0
11.	+	0	0	0		36.	0	0	0	+		61.	0	0	+	0		86.	0	+	0	0
12.	0	0	0	+		37.	0	0	+	0		62.	0	0	0	+		87.	0	+	0	0
13.	0	+	0	0		38.	0	0	0	+		63.	0	+	0	0		88.	0	+	0	0
14.	0	0	0	+		39.	0	0	0	+		64.	0	+	0	0		89.	0	+	0	0
15.	0	0	0	+		40.	+	0	0	0		65.	0	+	0	0		90.	+	0	0	0
16.	0	0	0	+		41.	0	0	+	0		66.	0	0	0	+		91.	0	0	+	0
17.	+	0	0	0		42.	0	+	0	0		67.	0	0	+	0		92.	0	0	0	+
18.	0	0	0	+		43.	+	0	0	0		68.	+	0	0	0		93.	0	+	0	0
19.	0	+	0	0		44.	+	0	0	0		69.	0	+	0	0		94.	0	+	0	0
20.	0	0	0	+		45.	0	0	+	0		70.	0	0	0	+		95.	0	+	0	0
21.	0	0	+	0		46.	0	0	+	0		71.	0	0	+	0		96.	0	0	0	+
22.	+	0	0	0		47.	0	0	0	+		72.	0	0	0	+		97.	0	+	0	0
23.	0	0	0	+		48.	0	0	0	+		73.	0	0	0	+		98.	0	+	0	0
24.	+	0	0	0		49.	+	0	0	0		74.	+	0	0	0		99.	+	0	0	0
25.	0	0	0	+		50.	0	+	0	0		75.	+	0	0	0		100.	0	0	+	0

Cut on the dotted lines, punch out the +'s, and tape the key back together on the back.

Punctuating Grammar

P as ʃ of G

Loops Six-Ten

Instructions for the **Punctuating Grammar Test**:

This test is designed to test your understanding of punctuation as a means of displaying the grammatical structure of a sentence. We group words together to form grammatical "objects" such as subjects, predicates, phrases, and clauses, and we group these objects to form communicable ideas which we call *sentences*. When we speak, we separate the grammatical objects with pauses and intonations, but when we are writing, we need a visible way to show where one grammatical object ends and the next begins. We call this visible way of displaying the grammar of a sentence *punctuation*.

There are fifty questions in this test, and each question is worth two points, for a total of one hundred points.

In this test, each question has five possible choices, A through E. *The correct answer to the question can be any combination of choices, including all and none. In order to get the two points of credit for the question, you must get the entire correct combination. There is no partial credit.*

The reason there is no partial credit is that though the content of these sentences is imaginative and unusual, the grammar of the sentences is not. The grammar is quite elementary and ordinary, and it is reasonable to expect that any good student with an understanding of elementary grammar would be able to understand and punctuate the sentences.

The choices offered are not necessarily accurate descriptions of the sentence in the question. If a choice is "a comma after the dependent clause," that does not mean that the sentence contains a dependent clause. You have to know whether there is one or not, just as if you were composing the sentence yourself.

A final point: In some sentences, it is possible that there is a mark of punctuation present for two good reasons. For example, in the sentence, *Oh, Hamlet, we all have epiphanies*, the first comma must be present both to separate the interjection and also to enclose the noun of direct address. In such a case, you should mark *both* of those reasons. This does not mean that you think there should be two commas in a row; it simply indicates that you are aware of both purposes for punctuating.

1. In July I decided and the Corporation deleted its losses.
   a. a comma after the prepositional phrase
   b. a comma after the dependent clause
   c. a comma after the independent clause
   d. an apostrophe in the contraction
   e. commas before and after the appositive

2. Below Omaha Nebraska the critters excavated Toms capsule.
   a. a comma after the city
   b. a comma after the state
   c. an apostrophe in the plural noun
   d. an apostrophe in the possessive noun
   e. a comma after the dependent clause

3. A new mood developed when Bose the stellar navigator edged forward.
   a. a comma to separate the adjectives preceding the noun
   b. a comma after the dependent clause
   c. a comma after the independent clause
   d. commas around the appositive
   e. commas around the noun of direct address

4. Lincolns novel The Mending is about a stellar dirigible called Hamlet.
   a. italics on the ship title
   b. an apostrophe in the possessive noun
   c. quotation marks around the book title
   d. italics on the book title
   e. commas around the appositive

5. The well placed charge and the mutiny caused twenty one defections.
   a. a comma between the adjectives that precede the noun.
   b. a hyphen in the compound adjective preceding the noun.
   c. a comma after the dependent clause
   d. a hyphen in the compound number
   e. an apostrophe in the possessive noun

6. With a new sense of confidence my pal thought Now its over.
   a. a comma after the prepositional phrases
   b. an apostrophe in the contraction
   c. a comma before the direct quotation
   d. quotation marks around the direct quotation
   e. a period inside the closing quotation marks

7. As the poet wrote Spectrum he remembered Irelands ancient meter.
   a. a comma after the independent clause
   b. an apostrophe in the possessive noun
   c. a comma after the dependent clause
   d. italics on the poem title
   e. quotation marks around the poem title

8. A one fourth minority wanted freezebites vacpacs and labsters.
   a. a hyphen in the compound adjective
   b. a colon at the beginning of the list
   c. a comma after the plural common noun
   d. a comma before the coordinating conjunction
   e. a comma after the dependent clause

9. Halting abruptly the old gray Martian discovered its identity.
   a. a comma after the prepositional phrase
   b. a comma between the adjectives preceding the noun
   c. a comma after the participle phrase
   d. a comma after the gerund phrase
   e. an apostrophe in the contraction

10. Howwul is the Martian word for think it is a neologism.
    a. quotation marks around the Martian noun
    b. italics on the Martian noun
    c. a comma after the independent clause
    d. a comma after the dependent clause
    e. a semicolon after the independent clause

11. The Ginsberg Shuffle is the song to sing if its a timetank leak.
    a. italics on the song title
    b. quotation marks around the song title
    c. a comma after the dependent clause
    d. a comma after the independent clause
    e. an apostrophe in the contraction

12. No its improper to enter six planets in a two planet race.
    a. a comma after the interjection
    b. an apostrophe in the possessive pronoun
    c. an apostrophe in the contraction
    d. a comma after the independent clauses
    e. a hyphen in the compound adjective

13. In the Jovian swamp the outbreak of ring fever is up by one fourth.
    a. a comma after the introductory prepositional phrase
    b. a hyphen in the fraction
    c. a comma after the dependent clause
    d. commas around the appositive
    e. commas around the parenthetical remark

14. On May 18 2021 Billy our youngest architect drew the new plan.
    a. a comma after the day
    b. a comma after the year
    c. a comma after the participle phrase
    d. commas around the appositive
    e. a comma after the dependent clause

15. Stranded in the laser tunnel Rasha reached for the key.
    a. a comma after the dependent clause
    b. a comma after the introductory prepositional phrases
    c. a comma after the participle phrase
    d. commas around the appositive
    e. a semicolon between the clauses

16. In December Mare Saudia lost its new colony when a dome collapsed.
    a. a comma after the prepositional phrase
    b. a comma after the month
    c. an apostrophe in the possessive pronoun
    d. an apostrophe in the contraction
    e. a comma between the clauses

17. As the magnetic surge subsided she glanced at the perimeter.
    a. a comma after the participle phrase
    b. a comma after the dependent clause
    c. a comma after the independent clause
    d. a semicolon between the clauses
    e. a comma after the prepositional phrase

18. The double vectored screen is a kilo long a kilo wide and a kilo high.
    a. a hyphen in the compound adjective
    b. a colon before the list
    c. a comma after the adjective **long**
    d. a comma after the adjective **wide**
    e. a comma between the clauses

19. Being among the icebirds was the exobiologists happiest dream.
    a. a comma after the introductory participle phrase
    b. a comma after the dependent clause
    c. an apostrophe in the possessive noun
    d. commas around the appositive phrase
    e. commas around the parenthetical remark

20. Well the expedition found seventy two ruins on the outer moon.
    a. a comma after the introductory adverb
    b. a comma after the interjection
    c. a comma after the dependent clause
    d. a hyphen in the compound adjective
    e. a comma before the prepositional phrase

21. The Spirit of Saint Francis the last ship on Mars is thirty one meters.
    a. quotation marks around the ship title
    b. italics on the ship title
    c. commas around the dependent clause
    d. commas around the appositive
    e. a hyphen in the compound number

22. Shocked into awareness the chemist gazed through the porthole.
    a. a comma after the dependent clause
    b. a comma after the gerund phrase
    c. a comma after the participle phrase
    d. commas around the appositive
    e. quotation marks around the subject

23. The Letter Y which is a dna boutique is near Olympus Mons.
    a. a comma after the compound subject
    b. commas around the appositive
    c. commas around the nonessential clause
    d. a semicolon between the independent clauses
    e. italics on the letter as such

24. The Hong Kong Express visits three moons Io Phobos and Demos.
    a. a semicolon between the clauses
    b. a colon after the plural noun
    c. a comma after **Io**
    d. a comma before the coordinating conjunction
    e. italics on the vessel of transport

25. Did you view the story Black Whole in last months Cosmo magazine?
    a. quotation marks around the article title
    b. italics on the article title
    c. quotation marks around the magazine title
    d. italics on the magazine title
    e. an apostrophe in the possessive noun

26. On planet Mare Britannia the flights of starlings are causing concern.
    a. a comma after the introductory prepositional phrase
    b. a comma after the dependent clause
    c. commas around the parenthetical remark
    d. a semicolon between the independent clauses
    e. a hyphen in the compound adjective

27. The robots that led the trek are expected to signal.
    a. commas around the appositive
    b. a semicolon between the independent clauses
    c. commas around the inessential clause
    d. quotation marks around the word **signal**
    e. a comma before the infinitive

28. Winston our vacuum specialist was optimistic however its too late.
    a. commas around the appositive
    b. a semicolon between the independent clauses
    c. a comma after **however**
    d. an apostrophe in the contraction
    e. a comma after the dependent clause

29. In the fall of 43 the corps found the hidden ys and zs on the bone.
    a. an apostrophe before the contraction
    b. a comma after the introductory prepositional phrases
    c. an apostrophe in the possessive noun
    d. italics on the letters as such
    e. an apostrophe in the plural letters as such

30. A dark brown crustacean clattered over the crater.
    a. a comma between the adjectives preceding the subject
    b. a comma after the independent clause
    c. a semicolon between the independent clauses
    d. a comma before the prepositional phrases
    e. a comma before the participle phrase

31. We sent fifty two colonists and they sent one said Edsel.
    a. a hyphen in the compound adjective
    b. a comma between the independent clauses
    c. quotation marks around Edsel's words
    d. a comma inside the closing quotation marks
    e. a comma outside the closing quotation marks

32. The thin green dawn of April 4 2006 and the early wind were cold.
    a. a comma between the adjectives preceding the noun
    b. a comma after the day
    c. a comma after the year
    d. a comma between the clauses
    e. a comma after *wind*

33. The meteorologist stepped forward and fixed her gaze on the vortex.
    a. a comma between the independent clauses
    b. an apostrophe in the direct object
    c. commas around the appositive
    d. a comma before the participle phrase
    e. a semicolon after the independent clause

34. The sculptors largest sculpture is called Year 2 Day.
    a. an apostrophe in the possessive noun
    b. a colon after the verb
    c. quotation marks around the title of the sculpture
    d. italics on the title of the sculpture
    e. italics on the numeral

35. The leader said Fire one the gunner blinked and froze.
    a. a comma after the first verb
    b. quotation marks around the leader's words
    c. a comma inside the quotation marks
    d. a semicolon inside the quotation marks
    e. a semicolon outside the quotation marks

36. The post British colonies on Phobos form a two thirds majority.
    a. commas around the appositive
    b. a hyphen after the prefix
    c. a hyphen in the fraction
    d. an apostrophe in **thirds**
    e. a comma after the dependent clause

37. Oh John the waters are rising we should move to the beach.
    a. a semicolon after the dependent clause
    b. a semicolon after the independent clause
    c. commas around the noun of direct address
    d. a comma after the interjection
    e. a comma before the prepositional phrase

38. Santianas classic masterpiece is The Translunar Symphony.
    a. quotation marks around the title (including the period)
    b. quotation marks around the title (not including the period)
    c. a comma after the dependent clause
    d. an apostrophe in the possessive noun
    e. italics on the music composition title

39. The young dietician joining Smiths flight has not left earth yet.
    a. a comma after the dependent clause
    b. commas around the participle phrase
    c. commas around the gerund phrase
    d. an apostrophe in the possessive noun
    e. dashes around the abrupt break in thought

40. Descending into the shadow gave our radar its first echoblips.
    a. a comma after the gerund
    b. commas around the parenthetical remark
    c. commas around the appositive
    d. an apostrophe in the contraction
    e. a comma after the dependent clause

41. At 715 in the morning we silently slipped away.
   a. a colon in the time
   b. a semicolon in the time
   c. a comma between the clauses
   d. a comma after the introductory prep. phrases
   e. a comma before the adverb

42. When we arrived the Jovian cried Jaabsan woznee akkkh.
   a. a comma after the dependent clause
   b. a comma after the verb in the independent clause
   c. quotation marks around the Jovian statement
   d. italics on the Jovian statement
   e. period inside the closing quotation marks

43. Chapter one of the Delinopedia is called I Lie Queue.
   a. quotation marks around the book title
   b. italics on the book title
   c. quotation marks around the chapter title
   d. italics on the chapter title
   e. an apostrophe in the possessive noun

44. The job of the zapreader is to speed to skim and to censor.
   a. a semicolon after the linking verb
   b. a colon after the linking verb
   c. a dash after the linking verb
   d. a comma after the first infinitive
   e. a comma after the second infinitive

45. Its easier to lose one fifth of an empire than a one half share.
   a. an apostrophe in the contraction
   b. a hyphen in the first fraction
   c. a hyphen in the second fraction
   d. commas around the prepositional phrase
   e. a comma before the dependent clause

46. Makloohinburg Mercurys safest city is defended by Homo pensivus.
   a. commas around the appositive
   b. a comma after the independent clause
   c. italics on the Latin species name
   d. an apostrophe in the possessive noun
   e. a comma after the dependent clause

47. The early 2020s were an age of well documented studies of the fauna.
   a. a comma after the year
   b. an apostrophe in the year
   c. a hyphen in the compound adjective
   d. a comma before the final prepositional phrase
   e. a comma before the first prepositional phrase

48. The pneumatic shocks at the launching pad were under inflated.
   a. commas around the parenthetical remark
   b. commas around the appositive
   c. an apostrophe in *shocks*
   d. a comma after the subject
   e. a hyphen in the compound adjective

49. The numbers 17 and 23 are the codes which its important to use Ophelia.
   a. quotation marks around the numbers
   b. italics on the numbers
   c. an apostrophe in the possessive pronoun
   d. an apostrophe in the contraction
   e. a comma before the noun of direct address

50. As we explore Titania point the torches forward.
   a. a semicolon between the clauses
   b. a comma after the dependent clause
   c. a comma after the independent clause
   d. quotation marks around the proper noun
   e. an apostrophe in the plural noun

1. In July I decided, and the Corporation deleted its losses.
    - a. a comma after the prepositional phrase
    - b. a comma after the dependent clause
    - **c. a comma after the independent clause**
    - d. an apostrophe in the contraction
    - e. commas before and after the appositive

2. Below Omaha, Nebraska, the critters excavated Tom's capsule.
    - **a. a comma after the city**
    - **b. a comma after the state**
    - c. an apostrophe in the plural noun
    - **d. an apostrophe in the possessive noun**
    - e. a comma after the dependent clause

3. A new mood developed when Bose, the stellar navigator, edged forward.
    - a. comma to separate adjectives preceding noun
    - b. a comma after the dependent clause
    - c. a comma after the independent clause
    - **d. commas around the appositive**
    - e. commas around the noun of direct address

4. Lincoln's novel, *The Mending*, is about a stellar dirigible called *Hamlet.*
    - **a. italics on the ship title**
    - **b. apostrophe in the possessive noun**
    - c. quotation marks around the book title
    - **d. italics on the book title**
    - **e. commas around the appositive**

5. The well-placed charge and the mutiny caused twenty-one defections.
    - a. comma between adjectives that precede noun.
    - **b. hyphen in the compound adjective.**
    - c. a comma after the dependent clause
    - **d. a hyphen in the compound number**
    - e. an apostrophe in the possessive noun

6. With a new sense of confidence, my pal thought, "Now it's over."
    - **a. comma after prepositional phrases**
    - **b. an apostrophe in the contraction**
    - **c. a comma before the direct quotation**
    - **d. quotation marks around the direct quotation**
    - **e. a period inside the closing quotation marks**

7. As the poet wrote "Spectrum," he remembered Ireland's ancient meter.
    - a. a comma after the independent clause
    - **b. apostrophe in possessive noun**
    - **c. a comma after the dependent clause**
    - d. italics on the poem title
    - **e. quotation marks around the poem title**

8. A one-fourth minority wanted freezebites, vacpacs, and labsters.
    - **a. a hyphen in the compound adjective**
    - b. a colon at the beginning of the list
    - **c. a comma after the plural common noun**
    - **d. comma before coordinating conjunction**
    - e. a comma after the dependent clause

9. Halting abruptly, the old, gray Martian discovered its identity.
    - a. a comma after the prepositional phrase
    - **b. comma between adjectives**
    - **c. a comma after the participle phrase**
    - d. a comma after the gerund phrase
    - e. an apostrophe in the contraction

10. *Howwul* is the Martian word for think; it is a neologism.
    - a. quotation marks around Martian noun
    - **b. italics on the Martian noun**
    - c. a comma after the independent clause
    - d. a comma after the dependent clause
    - **e. semicolon after the independent clause**

11. "The Ginsberg Shuffle" is the song to sing if it's a timetank leak.
    a. italics on the song title
    b. quotation marks around song title
    c. a comma after the dependent clause
    d. a comma after the independent clause
    e. an apostrophe in the contraction

12. No, it's improper to enter six planets in a two-planet race.
    a. comma after introductory interj
    b. an apostrophe in the possessive pronoun
    c. an apostrophe in the contraction
    d. a comma after the independent clauses
    e. a hyphen in the compound adjective

13. In the Jovian swamp, the outbreak of ring fever is up by one fourth.
    a. comma after intro prep phrase
    b. a hyphen in the fraction
    c. a comma after the dependent clause
    d. commas around the appositive
    e. commas around the parenthetical remark

14. On May 18, 2021, Billy, our youngest architect, drew the new plan.
    a. a comma after the day
    b. a comma after the year
    c. a comma after the participle phrase
    d. commas around the appositive
    e. a comma after the dependent clause

15. Trapped in the laser tunnel, Rasha reached for the key.
    a. a comma after the dependent clause
    b. comma after the intro prep phrases
    c. a comma after the participle phrase
    d. commas around the appositive
    e. a semicolon between the clauses

16. In December Mare Saudia lost its new colony when a dome collapsed.
    a. a comma after the prepositional phrase
    b. a comma after the month
    c. an apostrophe in the possessive pronoun
    d. an apostrophe in the contraction
    e. a comma between the clauses

17. As the magnetic surge subsided, she glanced at the perimeter.
    a. a comma after the participle phrase
    b. a comma after the dependent clause
    c. a comma after the independent clause
    d. a semicolon between the clauses
    e. a comma after the prepositional phrase

18. The double-vectored screen is a kilo long, a kilo wide, and a kilo high.
    a. a hyphen in the compound adjective
    b. a colon before the list
    c. a comma after the adjective *long*
    d. a comma after the adjective *wide*
    e. a comma between the clauses

19. Being among the icebirds was the exobiologist's happiest dream.
    a. comma after the intro participle phrase
    b. a comma after the dependent clause
    c. an apostrophe in the possessive noun
    d. commas around the appositive phrase
    e. commas around the parenthetical remark

20. Well, the expedition found seventy-two ruins on the outer moon.
    a. a comma after the introductory adverb
    b. a comma after the interjection
    c. a comma after the dependent clause
    d. a hyphen in the compound adjective
    e. a comma before the prepositional phrase

21. *The Spirit of Saint Francis*, the last ship on Mars, is thirty-one meters.
    a. quotation marks around the ship title
    b. italics on the ship title
    c. commas around the dependent clause
    d. commas around the appositive
    e. a hyphen in the compound number

22. Shocked into awareness, the chemist gazed through the porthole.
    a. a comma after the dependent clause
    b. a comma after the gerund phrase
    c. a comma after the participle phrase
    d. commas around the appositive
    e. quotation marks around the subject

23. The Letter *Y*, which is a dna boutique, is near Olympus Mons.
    a. a comma after the compound subject
    b. commas around the appositive
    c. commas around nonessential clause
    d. a semicolon between the independent clauses
    e. italics on the letter as such

24. *The Hong Kong Express* visits three moons: Io, Phobos, and Demos.
    a. a semicolon between the clauses
    b. a colon after the plural noun
    c. a comma after *Io*
    d. a comma before the coordinating conj.
    e. italics on the vessel of transport

25. Did you view the story "Black Whole" in last month's *Cosmo* magazine?
    a. quotation marks around article title
    b. italics on the article title
    c. quotation marks around the magazine title
    d. italics on the magazine title
    e. an apostrophe in the possessive noun

26. On planet Mare Britannia, the flights of starlings are causing concern.
    a. comma after intro prep phrase
    b. a comma after the dependent clause
    c. commas around the parenthetical remark
    d. a semicolon between the independent clauses
    e. a hyphen in the compound adjective

27. The robots that led the trek are expected to signal.
    a. commas around the appositive
    b. a semicolon between the independent clauses
    c. commas around the inessential clause
    d. quotation marks around the word **signal**
    e. a comma before the infinitive

28. Winston, our vacuum specialist, was optimistic; however, it's too late.
    a. commas around the appositive
    b. semicolon between indep clauses
    c. a comma after *however*
    d. an apostrophe in the contraction
    e. a comma after the dependent clause

29. In the fall of '43, the corps found the hidden *y*'s and *z*'s on the bone.
    a. an apostrophe before the contraction
    b. comma after intro prep phrases
    c. an apostrophe in the possessive noun
    d. italics on the letters as such
    e. an apostrophe in the plural letters as such

30. A dark brown crustacean clattered over the crater.
    a. comma between adjectives preceding subject
    b. a comma after the independent clause
    c. a semicolon between the independent clauses
    d. a comma before the prepositional phrases
    e. a comma before the participle phrase